Telling tales

Manchester University Press

Telling tales

Work, narrative and identity in a market age

Angela Lait

Manchester University Press
Manchester and New York

distributed in the United States exclusively
by Palgrave Macmillan

Copyright © Angela Lait 2012

The right of Angela Lait to be identified as the author of this work has been asserted by her in accordance with the Copyright, Designs and Patents Act 1988.

Published by Manchester University Press
Oxford Road, Manchester M13 9NR, UK
and Room 400, 175 Fifth Avenue, New York, NY 10010, USA
www.manchesteruniversitypress.co.uk

Distributed in the United States exclusively by
Palgrave Macmillan, 175 Fifth Avenue, New York,
NY 10010, USA

Distributed in Canada exclusively by
UBC Press, University of British Columbia, 2029 West Mall,
Vancouver, BC, Canada V6T 1Z2

British Library Cataloguing-in-Publication Data
A catalogue record for this book is available from the British Library

Library of Congress Cataloging-in-Publication Data applied for

ISBN 978 0 7190 8522 2 hardback

First published 2012

The publisher has no responsibility for the persistence or accuracy of URLs for any external or third-party internet websites referred to in this book, and does not guarantee that any content on such websites is, or will remain, accurate or appropriate.

Typeset
by 4word Ltd, Bristol
Printed in Great Britain
by CPI Antony Rowe Ltd, Chippenham, Wiltshire

To Claire and Richard

Contents

List of illustrations		*page* ix
Preface		x
Acknowledgements		xiii

Introduction		1
1	**Business**	10
	I: Taking charge: management and self-management in a flexible culture	
	II: Manuals of becoming: self-help for the failing	
2	**Identity**	48
	Sink or swim: the dilemma of the failing middle-class professional	
3	**Trauma**	80
	Ian McEwan's *Saturday*: a tale of the vulnerable professional	
4	**Escape**	118
	Heaven, heroes and horticulture: the search for solace and meaning	
5	**Recovery**	145
	Narratives of becoming: slow working towards a better life-story	
6	**Autobiography**	174
	Writing the self	
	Conclusion	198
	The meaning and value of self-mastery	

Appendix 1 216
Defra Departmental Report covers
Appendix 2 218
Table showing the positive and negative meanings
of descriptors commonly associated with 'fast' and
'slow' conditions

Bibliography 220
Index 234

Illustrations

1 Departmental Report cover 2002   216
2 Departmental Report cover 2003   217
3 Departmental Report cover 2004   217

Images licensed under the Open Government Licence

Preface

What follows is a story about what it means to work in the twenty-first century in a market age heavily reliant on corporate communications for its version of reality. It seems pertinent, therefore, that I begin by telling *my* story of what sparked an interest in how language is used in the workplace, the impact on employees' well-being and the wider implications that has for culture and society. It starts from when I met Andy (not his real name), a lifelong civil servant expecting to stay in post until retirement. Andy was one of a number of capable, talented, knowledgeable and willing employees I'd noticed getting increasingly stressed and imagining various ways to escape what they had begun to feel was entrapment. When Andy announced he was leaving to care for an elderly female relative, I didn't know what to make of this untypical male narrative. Now I realise this was part of Andy's story – the story he was telling about himself, because even though it showed him as less than macho, it was how he could not only explain himself to me, but more importantly, how he could acceptably explain himself to himself. It was more palatable to say that he was becoming a carer than to admit he was failing to 'make it' in a workplace whose conditions had recently altered so radically that the demands placed upon him were beyond further forbearance.

What has become apparent since then is that Andy's story was not an untruth or self-delusion. He *was* a carer. That's why he, and tens of thousands like him, like me, had entered the public sector – to serve others, on a lower than private sector salary because the satisfaction from giving true service compensated for the lower income and because his job said something about him, something he was proud for others to see, and something by which he was willing to define himself. As philosopher Kim Atkins says (quoting Ricouer), where we are caught up with multiple people and events, 'the question arises concerning the "actual stories the subject can take up and hold as constitutive of his personal identity" ' (2004: 341–366). Andy was opting for a story of caring over one of workplace 'success' because he was finding the newly imposed demands of an economically driven work culture fundamentally at odds with the values, conditions and experience that could lead to his satisfaction and happiness in labour, which a requirement to stay employed was only making more painful.

After Andy left I found myself, like other unhappy staff, also becoming frustrated and heading for the anti-depressants. I'd trained for many years to become proficient in my chosen profession and had worked for one of the UK's top magazine publishers, which was known for its high production values. Seeing every new issue, I'd feel really good about what my efforts had helped to produce. Basically, back then, I was satisfied with my production and with time well spent.

Working in a government department from 2001 was different. It was impossible to do a good job because a good job was not required. A quick job was. An eleventh-hour request would come for something to be published; the copy was shoddy, my professional judgement would want it rewritten or edited, but time-pressure meant it would have to go as it was. The designers, similarly pressed to meet the Department's deadline, would slap it on the page with ragged baselines, orphans, widows, all the elements I'd been trained to spot and eliminate to recognise the finished article as a professional job. Proofing time was minimal so typos were many. There was no time either to commission appropriate photographs, write good headlines or add meaningful captions so that skim-readers would at least catch the publication's salient message – no willingness, therefore, to acknowledge my professional competence. There were too few staff to cope in the reduced time available for job completion and the finished product would arrive with numerous mistakes (some, admittedly, the ordinary reader may miss) and be unfit to include in my portfolio for prospective future employers. At the magazine I'd be thrilled to see my byline on an article or my name as editor on the contents page. In this new working environment I found myself wondering, 'What does this "production" of mine say about me, about my abilities, about my standards, about my professionalism?' I did not like the answer.

At times the under-resourcing became too acute to ignore. When the Department hired temporary agency staff who, with good organisational ability but no professional knowledge and less personal investment in the outcome, quite happily processed (rather than professionally produced) the work, they appeared efficient and acquiescent, and I started to look obstructive and uncooperative by insisting on proper time for completing jobs to my standards and satisfaction. It became obvious that my professional ability and judgement weren't wanted or valued by anyone other than myself, so I wasn't making a difference to anything except my own steadily deteriorating mental health. What really irritated were messages from internal communications channels telling me I was 'empowered' to accomplish what needed to be done in the course of my work. If I was so empowered, why was I suffering the classic symptoms of stress and depression, i.e. feeling I was lacking control and achievement and without the power to do anything about it? If I was empowered, then I was only empowered to be the sort of person who could happily turn out imperfect or unprofessional work.

About this time, though I had a punishing commute to and from Whitehall, I took up watercolour painting. Working from various instruction manuals, and practising over time, I began to feel rather pleased with the results. The high level of concentration required provided a two-fold benefit – it improved my technique and blocked thoughts of my work dissatisfaction. I engaged in several other creative activities also – garden design and planting, cake icing and decorating – all of which gave me intense satisfaction. I did not seem to be alone either. A mass of TV programmes, magazines and books on cookery and gardening were obviously servicing a need in the market for such material and I began to think about what the significance of that was. In particular, I felt that my work dissatisfaction and the uptake of my new hobbies were not merely coincidental, so I asked myself a simple question: 'What is it that I am getting from these creative "labours" that I am not getting at work?' It seemed such an important question for my well-being that I spent three years trying to answer that question and this book is the result of that exploration.

Acknowledgements

There are many who have contributed to the completion of this study, either directly or indirectly, whom I would like to thank.

Firstly, I am grateful to my PhD supervisors at the University of Manchester, Michael Sanders and Peter Knight, for their encouragement, guidance and help throughout the period of study that led to this publication.

Thanks are also due to Richard Sennett whose book *The Corrosion of Character* launched this project and whose encouraging comments on my work helped me to believe my ideas are worth pursuing.

I also acknowledge many individuals known to me personally – family, friends, other academics and professionals, particularly Erica Anderson, John Hards, John Payne, Georgia Morgan, Lucy Vignoles, and David and Janet Wood – whose support and interest during the writing of this project is much appreciated.

Not to be forgotten are all those at Manchester University Press who were involved in managing this production or gave helpful suggestions on its content.

Most of all I thank my daughter Claire and her husband Richard, for their unstinting love and laughter when I needed it most. To them both I dedicate this work.

Introduction

Fast time and workplace identity

Narrative in the workplace

The global financial crisis of the early twenty-first century focused attention on the processes that sustain the excesses of corporate capitalism. While academics for 40 years have debated the social effects of the new economy, only impending recession prompted widely asked questions about the longer-term costs of a financial market whose deregulated systems have allowed capital accumulation that is not tied to a base of real (i.e. concrete and realisable) value and is accrued as a result of quick-win, short-term decision making. The flexibility typical of financial markets has also come to characterise much of our existence over the last two decades both through the work conditions experienced in private corporations and industries, and more recently the public sector, and through the attendant timeframes and social values within which we attempt to form and secure our identity. However, the fast turnover rates sustaining corporate capitalism through innovation and information exchange rest on instability, frequent structural changes and relocations (office moves, staffing reorganisation and downsizing layoffs), hot-desking, limited-term project-working and staff mobility. This book argues that this structural instability and the accelerated pace of life driven by the conditions for 'flexible accumulation' (Harvey, 1991: 107, 145–147) makes meaningful existence and fulfilment in work ever more difficult.

In Western economies, work is a significant measure of identity and personal value, so the removal of many of the certainties and stabilities of employment has great impact on the individual. In fragmented and flexible conditions, Sennett (1998) argues, it is impossible to narrate oneself through a coherent and progressively developing career, while an increasing workload, caused by cost-efficiency measures, adds discomfort to an already challenging disorientation. What seems surprising is that the alienation once associated with the manual labour of older manufacturing industries is today being experienced by employees much further up the management chain in contemporary knowledge and service economies. The history of work conditions is illuminating. Marx, de Tocqueville, Veblen and Ruskin, to name a few, noted how automation and mechanisation generated particular problems for the human worker when technological advance changed temporality by revolutionary rather than evolutionary degree. Moreover, technology holds contradictory promise: for the employer the prospect of increasing production, for the worker the possibility of shorter working hours. The tension is that if either side presses its advantage, the other is (painfully) compromised. Such is the contested terrain of the workplace.

Certainly, early technological developments prompting Frederick Taylor's time and motion experiments gave advantage to production but at a cost of human stress and political unrest. The retreat from this excessive control came when Elton Mayo's Hawthorne Effect found that a human worker needs to be valued for very particular types of contribution (not just output) to secure well-being. Key among these is the need for the opportunity to talk or express oneself, to make sense of experience, to give it shape and meaning by narration and communication – a point centrally important to the argument presented in this book. Later organisation theorists, Abraham Maslow and Frederick Herzberg, extended the human needs model into the now-familiar forms of human resource management that attempt to factor these needs into nurturing personnel policies, though these are ultimately self-serving insofar as they are produced in the expectation of obtaining, in return, the worker's total body *and* soul commitment.

Despite HR intentions, technological advance impacting management practices and organisational structures is again compromising basic human needs. The means by which one can adapt to a new business (or world) order, particularly where that model itself requires constant and repeated adaptation, is problematic if little account is taken of the slower psychological and neurological processes involved in 'changing our minds'. Notwithstanding the management rhetoric of self-empowerment, (which accompanies and is promoted as a benefit of today's non-hierarchical corporate organisation), the flattened structure supposedly replacing the Weberian model is largely theoretical (though the networking *modus operandi* is evident enough). In fact recently, in the public sector, the audit culture's bureaucratic requirement to measure and survey the worker's every move is a form of top-down power so strong that self-authority within the workplace is mostly absent. The employee managed in this way has little or no autonomy, but has a lot of responsibility. Where decision-making and risk-taking are devolved downward (in line with the corporate empowerment story) but authority, power and appropriate resources are not, far from feeling newly empowered, employees feel powerless and stressed. Middle-class professionals – especially those in public service who by rank, education and past experience are acculturated to notions of freedom, self-definition and work satisfaction – embrace the empowerment claim. However, when the gap between rhetoric and experience is exposed, the resulting cognitive dissonance requires that either the belief in autonomy or the circumstances producing the contradiction is altered.

The argument of this book focuses on that uncomfortable dissonance as a driver for sufferers to evaluate, re-imagine and narrate anew both themselves and the circumstances of their existence, to challenge the vast corporate communication machine peddling its official story with a story of their own making. It is approached from my perspective as a UK Government civil servant and trained journalist employed in a specialist communications role and also as a literary critic believing that stories are the cognitive instruments through which we understand ourselves and our world, and that such stories encode strong ideological messages so we must attend to the language through which they are told. This is particularly so as contemporary vocabulary is dominated by a powerful market rhetoric so embedded in Anglo-American culture that we are in danger of failing to see the full effect it is having on individuals, on society and on the world.

The literary angle

Issues of identity, subjectivity and storytelling are burgeoning subjects of discussion explored under the rubric of Organisational Studies within schools of sociology and management. In particular, management research has paid attention to narrative and storytelling as both the medium through which organisational reality is comprehended (Czarniawska, 1997; Gabriel, 2000) and the key determinant of workplace subjectivity and identity (Willmott, 1997; Oswick *et al.*, 2000; Humphreys, 2002; Collinson, 2003; De Cock and Land, 2005; Musson and Duberley, 2006). Campbell Jones (2007), concerned at the lack of literary theory and analytical expertise in this exercise, believes his management colleagues hold:

> the assumption that literature is more 'accessible' than other forms of writing... [and] treat literary writing as if it were relatively transparent... [when] rather than instructing us in a new easiness [literature] might present a way of confronting the difficulties and impossibilities of interpretation and action.

This study addresses that lack through a broader and deeper literary analysis of an organisation's own productions, as well as connected forms of supportive self-help writing and creative fictional and autobiographical literature. By opening these texts to fuller disclosure of their less obvious discursive connections, the findings are contextualised within a wider cultural framework and show how the flexible behaviours required for working in the new economy impact the human agent and why alternative activities such as gardening, cookery and writing prove redemptive.

The texts under scrutiny all appeared during a period already identified specifically with new economy conditions – the end of the twentieth and beginning of the twenty-first century. The last decade of the twentieth century is seen as something of a watershed. Eriksen (2001) quotes Eric J Hobsbawm's claim that the twentieth century ran from 1914 to 1991 and considers the twenty-first century began at that point (8). The starting point for this study is 1989, when Peter Mayle published *A Year in Provence*, which led to growing production and interest in autobiographical travel literature. A coincidental rising interest in gardening and cookery is evident with the advent of the BBC's *Good Food* and *Gardeners' World* magazines and exhibitions (launched between 1989 and 1992). More recently, celebrity chefs Hugh Fearnley-Whittingstall, Jamie Oliver *et al.* have used food and horticulture to make political comment. On the business side, the same period saw an increase in programmes of corporate restructuring and branding supported by internal and external communications (particularly in public service institutions) that through publications and verbal briefings were designed to get key audiences 'on message'. What follows is an account of the role played by literature (in its broadest textual sense) in human subjectivity and identity-formation over that period of organisational change, increasing corporate communication and rising interest in creative activities.

The account tells how social and organisational structures and processes changed towards the end of the twentieth century, making it more difficult to construct identity with any coherence. It is the story of how the deluge of messaging we receive through multiple information channels delivers to us both subtle and insistent normative codes about the possibilities and pitfalls of choosing who we wish to be. It is a story intimately linked with the technological developments that have increased the pace of living and altered our working practices not least by increasing the space and time overlap between public (work) and private (home) spheres. It is a story about the pursuit of creative labour as a response to the stressful conditions, unsatisfying work and compromised home life sustaining postmodern living. It explains why the time-regulated growing and subsequent preparation, cooking, eating and sharing of food with others is a natural response to the loss of work satisfaction in accelerated time and is a call to reinstate the reflective time and the fulfilment found in the creative productivity, self-nurturing, giving and social connection that is proving impossible to maintain under the current ideological and economic hegemony. Ultimately, it tells of the human need to be employed usefully and satisfactorily in work co-identical with our ethical self and how the formal capture of the autobiographic self-making and self-telling process proves how we must negotiate the terms of that existence in the course of creating, writing, owning and living the stories of who we are.

This literary approach to business literature is validated by Amernic and Craig (2006), who call for urgent close analysis of corporate outpourings by persons competent in textual analysis, and by Boje (2001), who argues that 'corporate writing has been imitated and celebrated by academic writers without much critical reflection on the kinds of issues it raises' (507). Sweezy considers a study of work conditions is best undertaken by those with 'direct experience', otherwise it is all too easy to swallow the myths capitalism want kept current (Braverman,1998: xxv–xxvi), and Braverman calls for attention to these matters by 'active and interested parties', not sociological theorists with questionnaires (1998: 21). My qualification as an 'interested party' comes from experience in a cutting-edge technologically advanced creative industry of the early 1990s, and as a civil servant in central government ministries, their regional offices and regulatory bodies when it became evident that business processes were eroding the control, creativity and pride once achieved through work. In addition, my academic training in literature has given me an acute appreciation of the power of language to encode ideology and the skills (and thirst) to identify its hidden messages, while my professional training alerts me to the application and usefulness of those techniques in modern corporate communication.

Overview

Chapter 1 considers the importation of market values to the public sector and their import for the attitudes and behaviours of its middle-class professional employees. By analysing the presentation of corporate image and character in publications from the Department for Environment, Food and Rural Affairs, it is possible to see how the organisation struggles to reconcile the flexibility and responsiveness characteristic of modern business with the unity and stability needed for a coherent image, and to consider the implications for well-being and identity of employees acculturated to these necessary principles of flexibility and responsiveness. Next, an examination of business survivor manuals addressing the needs of employees failing to cope with time-pressure and the required transformation into perfect new economy workers discovers their use of appealing narrative principles – linear structure, heroic character and the metaphor of nurturing – to reinforce preferred identity models.

Chapter 2 covers the theoretical foundations on which assumptions about the subjectivity and identity of the professional middle class have been made, including the ideological pressures and contradictions that explain the roots of identity destabilisation and why the group under scrutiny seek solace in the form that they do.

Chapter 3 uses Ian McEwan's novel *Saturday* to show how story is used to make sense of experience and how coherent identity is constructed by the suppression of contradiction. Henry Perowne struggles with the emotional impact of post-9/11 insecurity on an identity chiefly influenced by clinical rationality, while the novel's subtext reveals how the audit culture's bureaucratic requirements are eroding that professional identity further. In considering both the nature of fulfilling work and Perowne's withdrawal to the domestic arena, we are able to discover the factors involved in re-establishing his well-being.

Chapter 4 investigates satisfying work more fully through analysis of popular practical instruction books on cookery and horticulture, including an account of recovering mental health by working on an allotment, showing how particular narrative forms countering the new economy ideals are based on values and time sequences linked to our well-being as biological creatures. The chapter concludes by considering how alternative values are commodified by marketing the concept of nostalgia through media-manufactured heroes who function in a culture bereft of religion and its icons to make it appear that heaven on earth is possible.

Chapter 5 discusses the role of 'escape' literature in recovering from the effects of work alienation. It considers how organic activities involving slow time, such as horticulture, cookery and the craft of writing about them, give a strong cultural message concerning the current organisation of time, work satisfaction and relationships. In particular, it deals with how the human feels attuned to balance, continuity and interconnectedness through the cyclical patterns and regulated rhythms of slower evolutionary change evident in natural systems. Its conclusion affirms how in ethical and mindful living, and in creative production, we achieve the purpose and meaning essential to well-being and good mental health that ultimately proceeds from a more anchored and stable (but nevertheless developing) self.

Chapter 6 looks at the nature of the autobiographic text, drawing on the form's history and contemporary manifestation in migrant travelogues to understand its particular appeal at this time of structural instability and biographical uncertainty. This section examines the implications of employing ordered narrative as a means to capture an active and developing character as part of a self-controlled process of autonomous identity-making, not least because the craft of constructing an autobiography is so clearly related to creating a personal identity.

The Conclusion summarises the argument of this study and considers what are the longer-term implications for a society whose working life is organised for flexible efficiency and whose personalities are schooled in the art of working competitively against their fellows rather than with them.

The story is told from the viewpoint of the public sector middle-class professional, because by doing so it is clearer to see identity insecurities as related to the introduction of a discourse supporting the flexible, immediate and responsive conditions of work in the post-Fordist organisation. Evidence of middle-class destabilisation, intensified by other social and political factors affecting the group, allows the modelling of that identity insecurity to an outcome involving activities that feature heavily in autobiographic travelogues. However, the story makes no claim that the work circumstances under discussion are limited in effect only to middle-class professionals in the public sector or that responding to this problem in various degrees involving food and horticulture or writing are the only or inevitable outcomes. The findings will resonate with a much wider section of working men and women who feel their personal value systems are being overruled by market-generated ones and feel a need to handle that psychologically and practically. Also more generally applicable is the claim that autonomous identity is intimately and ethically tied to the language and forms through which that selfhood is expressed, that a requirement for any dramatic adaptation of identity cannot be instantaneous and requires the will of the individual, and that targeted self-development requires time for patience, diligence and reflection.

I am aware that the theory presented, concentrating at species level on recognised human impulses, needs and desires that affect us all regardless of cultural specificity, risks charges of ignoring issues of gender, nationality, race, creed and so on that are so integral to experience. However, while I accept that no one lives separated from social conditions, the study's validity rests in acknowledging the individual as one who, in being a *particular* product of (partly quantifiable and mostly unquantifiable) genetic coding and social influence together with personal and collective experience, is neither entirely coincidental with, nor entirely independent of, any 'other', and is therefore *both* individual and social, unique *and* partaking of all others. The focus of this study on the middle-class professional in public service is thought to be sufficiently specific and, moreover, this group's particular relationship to hegemony and its historic links with liberal ideology makes it a logical beginning from which to form valid (and, hopefully, interesting) connections that are more widely applicable, leaving others to discover what such connections might mean for various particular group identities.

Finally, a study so necessarily broad-ranging and interdisciplinary means the potential range of material is too vast to cover fully each of the disciplines my subject encompasses. However, that broadness has allowed the tracing of specific and intriguing connections between paid work, other activities and character that would not be possible if more narrowly conceived. Therefore, scholars of any one of those disciplines will almost certainly find texts of their particular interest overlooked or issues covered in insufficient depth. My starting and finishing points are resolutely literary and I accept that it is possible, indeed desirable, for others with different expertise to take any of the issues raised as a departure point to delve more deeply.

1
Business

1: Taking charge: management and self-management in a flexible culture

Introduction

In the late twentieth century, under the impetus and direction of US-style neoliberal politics and economics, managerial practices affecting workplace conditions and worker experience transferred to other Western-style economies, including the UK under Margaret Thatcher. However, it was the Blair/Clinton alignment that saw New Labour's agenda guided and implemented by specific communications strategies and tactics based on US ideological methods and messages impact fully on British politics. Thomas Frank (2000) traces the US influence into the very heart of government:

> In Britain, [...] the 'New Economy' was embraced in the late nineties as the miracle-worker that would snap the country out of its long decline [...] At the London think tank Demos, the thought of Gilder, Tom Peters, and Kevin Kelly, was spun into the finest gold of 'New Labour' industrial policy. Charles Leadbetter [...] [made] a mystic link between entrepreneurship and national identity [...] Demos held seminars at Downing Street, Mulgan [Demos director] became a member of Blair's 'policy unit,' and Leadbetter [a journalist] [...] was once rumoured to be the prime minister's very favorite political thinker.
> (Thomas Frank, 2000: 347–348)

Business texts produced under this new economy thinking carry strong ideological meaning and implications, not only for workers. Amernic and Craig (2006) believe they form part of 'a global genre of

CEO-speak [and though] culturally specific to the US and Canada [...] reflect attitudes and behaviours in other countries as well'. These are public narratives intending 'to persuade and influence behaviour [using] the language of business, accounting and the market' (138) and they mark the inter-penetration of US and UK business culture, including a rise in working hours that puts the UK much closer to the US than to its European neighbours (Cowling, 2005: 2).

This chapter discusses how such persuasive and pervasive market influence interpellates the subject, through various forms of corporate communication, including organisational structure, practices and languages, to become a new kind of worker, a new kind of citizen. It argues that the public sector alliance with market principles fundamentally alters the culture and diminishes the rewards of proper service on which, in large part, the identity of public servants rests. As valued standards of professionalism give way under both the administrative load of an audit culture and the requirements for lean staffing and speed on which efficiency relies, the pressure is intensified by an IT revolution that supports quick and responsive working, for, as Thomas Hylland Eriksen (2001) informs:

> when there is only a little email and few calls, such technologies are doubtless liberating. When the number of incoming messages exceeds a certain threshold, the functioning of the very same technologies flips into its opposite. They begin to imprison the users, fill the gaps and kill those empty slow periods that are so important for creativity and directionless thinking.
> (Thomas Hylland Eriksen, 2001: 143)

Under such circumstances calls for employees to be creative and claims that they are being empowered to manage their own outputs and personal development are nonsense because the rising volume and frequency of influential corporate messaging promoting flexible and responsive behaviour set strict terms within which workers must operate and non-compliance is penalised. In fact, the parameters of personal growth are so heavily circumscribed and encoded in organisational discourse that the freedom to self-develop according to traditional notions of liberal individualism is not possible.[1] When the contradiction between management rhetoric and personal experience is clearly exposed, middle-class public servants acculturated to value independence and autonomy are pitched into dissonance and struggle to reconcile (or make the transition between) a selfhood based on the time-hungry, qualitative values of proper professional service with one reaching for the time-tight, quantitative values associated with the delivery of output-based objectives. In effect, the official narratives of modern business promoting the instantaneous adoption of speed and flexibility required for increased rates of turnover and profit make psychologically stressful demands on certain individuals whose identity is invested in values of professionalism and service and in behaviours and attitudes directly contradicting those required of employees urged to deliver expediently and efficiently, values that indicate organisational stories and personal characters with other, more coherent and stable formal properties.

This chapter examines the visual and verbal techniques of organisational messaging whose purpose is to encourage the behaviours and attitudes essential to the growth and survival of the so-called 'new economy', contextualising this acculturation process in the public sector by analysing a government department's publications. These official scripts confirm how the discursively encoded management practices of the modern workplace leave power relations unchanged from traditional ones but exercise control in more covert ways. Analysis of communications from the UK government's Department for Environment, Food and Rural Affairs (Defra) discloses the uneasy marriage between business and public service as apparently sensible messages struggle to contain the structural instabilities and fragmentation of the flexible organisation that, for all its diversification, still attempts to present itself as a structurally coherent, stable and unified entity for inward investment and public confidence.

Managing the message

Today, a corporate priority is to use communications to maintain and manage relationships with various parties (stakeholders) that have an interest in its business. Key internal and external audiences are given an authorised version of the corporate story through verbal, written and visual communication including the bureaucratic, language-dependent processes of accounting, recording and reporting, and flows of management information. Importantly, these communications are part of the same story about the organisation, about creating and presenting a sense of its self in which all its parts, including employees, contribute to coherent and coordinated vision of its image and character.[2]

The 1990s surge in corporate branding attempted to engage *all* partners in a single, unified vision of the organisation whose clarity of purpose would at once convince shareholders of its worth as an investment vehicle (or citizens of its joined-up approach to government) and give employees a sense of belonging to a dynamic and identifiable organisation. 'Key messages' coordinate disparate parts of information activity and find their apogee in the mission statement or company slogan, which functions to focus corporate effort on the achievement of its business aims and objectives, while the brand logo, a visual cipher for the company's character, encapsulates its essence and philosophy in image form. For success, all aspects of communication – designs, images, colours, statements, expressed behaviours and attitudes through external and internal channels – must work in support of the company's ethos, character and image which are controlled and defended by brand managers.

Employees, being both receivers and disseminators of the corporate message, cross the unseen boundary between internal and external, negotiating the difference between objective image and subjective experience, perhaps several times each day. In upholding its status and market position, the company must ensure these mouthpieces do not function to undercut, subvert, confuse or mis-communicate its messages. Avoiding contradiction is essential as the dissonance resulting from any recognised gap between the organisation's presentational rhetoric and the reality of stakeholder experience may give rise to falling sales, dissent or counter-narratives. Resistors or whistle-blowers are marginalised, silenced or expelled in an effort to preserve the consistency, the inviolability of the corporate presence. Its voice dominates by swiftly countering, with forceful rebuttals and cries of misinterpretation and misrepresentation, any commentators not reflecting what the organisation wants reported about itself in public.[3] While external effort is gauged by brand recognition and sales success, internal buy-in is judged by the absence of dissent or resistance. Employees are often compelled contractually, morally or by economic necessity to tow (or toe) the company line. The metaphor of towing the line, or toeing the line, referring once to a physical yoking of a laden canal vessel, or the confining within a parliamentary line of demarcation, takes on new meaning in modern business where a 'line' is the common term for an agreed and consistent message prepared as a protection strategy by company press officers anticipating hostile enquiry from journalists. Disaffected employees are potentially powerful detractors of the company image,[4] so the organisation's strategic aim is to limit dissent by controlling the words, behaviours and attitudes through which its image is both constructed and reflected. Influencing attitude and behaviour in the various social and public arenas is key to corporate reputation management. So while the staff handbook, HR practice and bureaucratic process function to induce conformity internally, corporations increasingly seek opportunities to make persuasive address also to an external audience and the careful creation of organisational narratives aims to attain public acceptance and to achieve consistency between the two. A key move in the public arena came 'in the middle of the nineteenth century' when the corporation became 'a legally designated "person" designed to valorize self-interest and invalidate moral concern' (Bakan, 2004: 28). Thus the corporate 'personality' exercised its voice in 1908 when the US telephone giant AT&T launched the first PR campaign, which 'imbued the company with human values in an effort to overcome people's suspicions of it as a soulless and inhuman entity' (17).

The public language of the market

Still today, to present itself in more appealing and responsible terms, business deploys what Thomas Frank (2000) calls 'people-friendly styles' to explain itself differently to a wider public (39). It does so through outpourings in the form of annual reports, prospectuses, shareholders' letters, press releases, interviews and public speeches – using language designed to be socially, politically and ideologically influential. This corporate literature, say Amernic and Craig (2006) should be attended to as forming 'a significant part of the ideological paraphernalia of society' (6) particularly as:

> the words and language of CEOs are chosen carefully, with strategic purposes in mind. They are neither passive nor neutral implements for communication. And they are not chosen in a perfunctory way to report some objective reality. Rather the words

and language are powerful and seductive rhetorical implements for fashioning outlook and opinion.

(Amernic and Craig (2006: 4)

If 'sharing a language... provides the subtlest and most powerful of all tools for controlling the behaviour of... other persons' (4 quoting CW Morris), then corporate-speak's synthesised monoglossia effects a wholesale interpellation of workers through both personnel processes and publicly-directed corporate promotion.

It is Frank's argument (2000) that modern communication and knowledge transfer technologies provide ways of disseminating 'the word' so comprehensively that nations (or even the world) appear united by the dominant rhetoric of a 'democracy of the competitive marketplace' in which individuals vote by exercising choice to buy (48). In reality this freedom to act is susceptible to advertising bent on manipulating desire, opinion and behaviour. Corporations also spend vast sums spreading the new economy faith (3–4), convincing 'of technological and economic "change" so massive, so earth-shaking and so all-enriching that there is no way to understand it rationally; inducing an awestruck reverence for "the market" and its triumph' (56) using spiritual language, religious trope and all the mythological power left without signification when formal religion is jettisoned. The new faith forestalls question and hampers the growth of political consciousness by encouraging followers to surrender to a powerful and complex world beyond their understanding and to 'embrace the laissez-faire way as we would a religion' (59). Internally, communications specialists sell a corporate version of reality also by hawking concepts of vision, progress, autonomy and self-realisation, seasoned with a dash of change, flexibility and immediacy, and served with a dressing of empowerment and potential, all aimed at moulding the attitudes and behaviours of the ideal workforce to the requirements of this awesome, dynamic market. Those not happy to worship at the market altar face difficulty and a search elsewhere for spiritual fulfilment.

All change – promoting transformation

Developments in Defra's communications activity between 2002 and 2004 show how insistently the market terminology of 'CEO-speak' is used in messaging designed to transform the department into a 'responsive service provider' (Defra, 2003: 103) and to play its key part in moulding worker identity. It is by analysing the structural and visual elements, and a seemingly benign alteration in the frequency of certain words in its communications, that the less benevolent consequences of the encoded ideological shift become apparent: first, the amplification of the transformation message is achieved in covert ways that preclude true employee empowerment; second, the narrative coherence required by any (human or organisational) entity for unity and long-term stability is disrupted by structural fragmentation; third, a hollow rhetoric of care is exposed through the evident incompatibility between achieving lean efficiency and securing employees' well-being.

Defra's adoption of this customer-focused people-friendliness and increased market acuity is evident in publications between May 2002 (its first Departmental Report following its formation in June 2001) and 2004 in which a number of significant changes of style and content identify a fundamental shift in the department's guiding principles as it embraces the market's terminology and its culture of flexibility, change and superficial transformation. Four elements of the reports – cover design, typography, written content and ministerial photo – show that shift resulting also in fragmentation, confusion, loss of authority and decreasing focus on staff.

Visual clues for the departmental transformation are found in the Minister's photographs of the 2002–4 reports. In the first portrait (2002: 2) the Minister is photographed from a low-angled camera so the viewer looks slightly up at the subject. She appears against a backdrop of historic architecture with a forward-facing gaze conveying directness, authority, stability and gravitas. In the next (2003: 6), she is placed against a studio background, with no contextual clues, looking at the level camera but with shoulders and head inclined to give a softer, more indirect demeanour. The third (2004: 9) is a radical shift: still the plain studio backdrop but her hair has been coloured, cut and reshaped, her shoulders placed one forward of the other (a less confrontational pose) and crucially the camera angle is higher, diminishing the Minister, so the viewer gazes downwards as on a child whose eyes are, of necessity, tilted slightly upwards in the pose of vulnerability made famous by the late Princess of Wales. Such visual clues are both powerful and assimilated easily and quickly as a move towards approachability.

The responsive shape-shifting required in these photographs is also evident in a radically changing cover design between 2002 and 2004 (see Appendix 1). The 2002 cover uses a single large photo with the capitalised acronym DEFRA and the Department name placed centrally in a lower bar. In 2003 the cover image segments into three areas with the website address appearing in a band above the picture and the new lowercase logo placed in the right-hand corner of a lower panel. By 2004 the central area is divided into nine separate images, each depicting an aspect of the department's work, while the upper and lower bands carry the title and the logo. This inclusive diversity is the publications' equivalent of the eclecticism and multidimensionality that David Harvey (1999) notes is central to postmodern structural aesthetics (66–98). However, the price paid for such breadth of vision is a loss of focal precision, clearly seen in the way Defra's statement of business interests dissolves into nonsense and confusion.

In its 2002 report, Defra claims that it 'deals with the essentials of life – food, air, land, water and communities' (Defra, 2002: 5). A booklet entitled *Working for the Essentials of Life* (Defra, undated(a)), published the same year, sees a significant alteration as 'communities' is replaced by 'people' (2). This encodes a significant semantic shift between conceptions of the population as a collective (communities – reflecting the necessary support for well-being) or as an aggregation (people) that evidently is dissolvable into individuals. The confusion of what is required to sustain life (air, land, water and communities) with the actual life forms (people) escalates in the 2003 mutation, which redefines the 'essentials of life' as 'food, air, land, water, people, animals and plants' (Defra, 2003: 8), grouping people with two more life forms, some of which are also edible. Thus the linguistic bid to be inclusive, to represent equally each unit of the business (as the 2004 multi-image cover photo does) *and* to package the organisation's diversity as a sound bite for presentational purpose results in a loss of coherence and meaning.

This rebranding of the department and its publications was part of the Blairite modernising agenda that also changed the capitalised acronym 'DEFRA' (in 2002) to approachable, lowercase 'defra', by which the dominant presence is deliberately diminished.[5] A supporting typographical move was made by exchanging the authoritarian serif font, Times New Roman, used by Defra's forerunner, the Ministry for Agriculture, Fisheries and Food (MAFF) (1997), for sans serif Arial or Helvetica (commonly used in children's books for ease of recognition and as the ubiquitous signifier of 'relaxed' style). However, this effort by government to enter the public consciousness as subdominant, unthreatening and friendly sits uneasily alongside the authority and influence necessary for governing. It is unsurprising, therefore, to find that the power operates as keenly as ever, but is applied in new ways. Since Edward Bernays declared business could profit from the predictability of managed public behaviour, methods of psychological manipulation have developed greatly and in subtle ways that escape detection. Changing the capitalised DEFRA to defra and positioning it on the lower right-hand corner on the cover is not the literal and symbolic decentring it at first appears. In left-to-right reading cultures the prime position for assimilation (as advertising charges inform us) is where the reader places a finger to turn the page. Thus the new friendly logo appears less dominant yet has replaced its obvious impressive power with a far cannier, but equally affecting, one (see also Bakan, 2004: 57). Superficially, the logo font change, in which dominance is dropped in favour of friendliness, parallels the Minister's photographic transformation. So it is doubly interesting that when corporate language is examined (below), the development is in the opposite direction towards an increasingly hardened discourse of efficiency and uncompromising management practice copied from the boardroom robustness of the private sector.

Corporate business and the public sector

The signalling of a cultural shift towards the performance-driven, cost-effective market dynamism of corporate business has implications for the character and identity of public sector workforces and marks the end of public sector employment as a positive choice made to avoid the worst excesses of corporate business. For example, in Chapter 3 of the 2002 report the eight-page, present-time account of 'What we do' has 16 instances of the word 'customer' and three of 'change' while in 2003 in its equivalent, but more forward-looking, 21-page Chapter 4 'Building our capacity to deliver', this rises to 51 mentions of 'customer' and 32 of 'change'. The ten-fold increase of 'change' and the tripling of the word count – 2,720 to 8,930 – is testimony to the discursive thrust the new direction is given while, in an uncanny reversal of those figures, what it means in practice for employees is a reduction from '8,000 people in the core department when Defra was formed in 2001, to around 3,200 in 2008' (Defra, undated(a): 8).[6] Similarly, 27 uses of the word 'new' confirms the aim is for 'innovation and change to increase the Department's effectiveness' (Defra, 2003: 83). Driving for a 'leaner more effective Department' (undated(a): 86) carries the implicit claim that leaner is more effective, while diminishing Treasury handouts confirm 'effective' actually means less costly (2003: 96). The improved input/output ratio will be achieved by 'moving resources (money and people) quickly and easily' in 'a move away from fixed, long term teams towards project working' (http://webarchive.nationalarchives.gov.uk/20061209022624 /http://www.defra.gov.uk/corporate/how-do-we-work/index.htm), proving that enduring personal relationships become accepted casualties of flexible management and that relocating people or photocopiers when pursuing efficiency targets are equally detached business decisions by those able to distance themselves from the resulting human impact on employees. To underline this dismissal of concern, the workforce's 'enormous effort', mentioned in the lead sentences of the 2002 Minister's Foreword to put staff literally and symbolically in a place of priority (2002: 2), goes unacknowledged in the 2003 Foreword (2003: 6–7). Here they are demoted to the final paragraph where the 'difficult and challenging time' (7) contextualises but no longer recognises their contribution. All of this confirms that since Defra's work plan was renamed a 'prospectus' (a word generally reserved for shareholder offers) and departmental progress became described by the CEO-beloved metaphors 'vision' and 'journey' (2002: 5), the chosen route may be experienced very differently by certain sectors of the organisation.

Public sector employees are encouraged to embrace the ethos denoted by 'Changing', 'Reform', 'Customers', 'Business' and 'Challenge' in the Contents page (undated(a): 5–6) of Defra's 2004 five-year strategy supporting the aim to 'become a different kind of Department: one which relentlessly focuses […] constantly searches […] is outward looking […] is flexible and agile and understands the needs and behaviours of its customers' (undated(a): 84–86). However, the chameleonic behaviour and constant reinventions proposed in this postmodern position sit uneasily alongside Fordist, goal-oriented claims to be also 'planning for the long term as well as the present' (2003: 6–7), and are barely contained by the organisational effort to present a coherent and consistent image to stakeholders. The ambiguities signify the identity fracture of the Department and its staff, and yet the organisation desperately holds to its own myth of unity.

Superficial meaning, hidden contradiction

A key linguistic technique declaring coherence against all evidence is the use of the corporate 'we', a magical pronoun that co-opts and excludes at will. When it is claimed that 'Defra has developed an ambitious but widely-shared set of values [...] living up to these will mean changing the way we work,' the plurality of 'Defra' and 'we' appears to implicate everyone. However, the majority of employees had no hand in writing a set of categorical values – Diversity, Empowerment, Focus, Relationships, Accessibility – whose acronym too neatly packages its contents, and they may not necessarily recognize the corporate reality claiming the organisation embodies the qualities of recognition, authority, trust, courtesy and consideration, openness, honesty and integrity. In fact, many might see the only value truly enacted is the literal and symbolically central 'Focus' that claims the organisation is geared to 'efficient service to our customers' (Defra, 2002: 17–18). This indicates that the 'widely-shared' values extend between corporations and the market and not between corporations and employees. Sentences using 'we' or 'Defra' presume an unproven unity and intimacy that is fouled by the comment that 'the Defra family will be examined for potential rationalization' (Defra, 2003: 105), an emotionally detached statement whose passive construction carefully avoids pinpointing the responsible agent(s).

This linguistic dexterity is evident elsewhere in Defra's corporate language, where it obscures rather than clarifies meaning. The following examples, taken from a growing body of HR stress management output, testify to the increasing attention being paid to the psychological difficulties experienced in today's workplace. The analysis shows how meaning is lost in linguistic imprecision, how sense disappears beneath the gloss of formulaic phraseology and how passive verbal clauses are a grammatical technique used to sidestep having to name or locate any particular agent or agents responsible for what is being said. The first sentence of a public sector *Stress at Work: Policy and Guidance* booklet illustrates the avoidance of authority. It reads:

> This policy and guidance aims to:
> - ensure that all staff are aware of the factors that can produce stress and to take [sic] preventative measures to avoid creating stressful situations.
>
> (*Stress at Work: Policy and Guidance*: 1)

The policy and guidance can make staff aware but it cannot take measures. Without indicating 'who' is 'to take preventative measures', the implication is that an impersonal (unnamed) agency will enact the policy. The solecism indicates an unwillingness to name such agents (even by occupational post), showing how responsibility disappears at critical points in the management process or else it exposes the failure to allow sufficient time for professional proof-reading (if 'to take' is amended to 'take', then the staff would be the active agents). Here, the image of the caring organisation does not extend to care taken with its messages to staff.

The leading paragraph of the stress policy introduction is an interesting structural example of how corporate-speak attempts to handle the wider irresolvable tensions between business needs and those of its employees. The sentences have been separated and are numbered for identification purposes.

1. A stimulating and supportive working environment can have a positive effect on mental health, but adverse situations can have a negative effect (see Section 5).
2. Dealing with stress is not just about individual coping mechanisms but also about looking at the causes and developing corporate approaches to the problem.
3. Defra is subject to financial and other resource constraints, as are other similar organisations.
4. However, good management practices and concern for staff go a considerable way to reducing excessive pressures on individuals.

5. The aim of this booklet is to provide guidance for managers and staff to assist them in recognising and dealing with stressful situations.
6. It is in the interests of Defra and all its staff that harmful levels of stress should be minimized.

(*Stress at Work: Policy and Guidance*: 2)

The six sentences are thematically linked through the idea of stress. However, there is no strong logical argument or narrative line dependent on the current sequence. Sentences 1, 2, 5 and 6 are separate, semantically discrete statements, but although each is internally grammatical, they bear no critical relationship to each other and can be placed in any order. Unlike these entirely separate statements, the conjunction 'however' refers the 'management practices' in sentence 4 to the 'resource constraints' in sentence 3. In this way the central two sentences are interdependent and their meaning lies in their logical sequencing, while the other four sentences can be paired in any way to provide the outer casing either side of the inner sentiment.

Sentences 3 and 4 are the critical, literal and metaphorical heart of the matter, and it is worth looking at their content and logical pairing. The first part of the third sentence, 'Defra is subject to financial and other resource constraints', indicates cost-dependency, while the second part of the sentence, that Defra's constraints make it 'like other similar organisations', locates responsibility outside itself and, significantly, obscures the distinction between the public sector organisation and public shareholder companies. The next statement (at the beginning of sentence 4), that 'good management practices and concern for staff go a considerable way to reducing excessive pressures on individuals', is a rhetorical expression which acknowledges the benefit of personal interaction and support but, given that 'resource constraints' are going to heavily influence 'management practices,' the extent of 'concern for staff' looks set to diminish. The 'considerable way' leaves unspecified what else needs attention for the elimination of stress, including responsibility for locating the precise causes of the admitted 'excessive pressures on individuals'.

Ironically, these two sentences appear to be written in Plain English but their very simplicity is the linguistic poverty of a presentational style that prohibits full understanding and conceals irresolvable paradox beneath a gloss of openness and clarity. Their placement at the *centre* of the paragraph is significantly metaphoric, as the linguistic elision is a symptom of contradictions emanating from the heart of the organisation. The sentences appear straightforward, individual and incontrovertible (and uncontroversial) statements of fact, but they are emblematic of the way structural fragmentation conceals ideological contradiction. In fact, the organisation of the paragraph reflects and represents the organisation itself: the site of contest for opposing ideological ideas; apparently coherent but actually structurally fragmented and internally riven; tensioned by the public sector's incorporation of corporate business ethics; using communication that ostensibly informs and comforts but truly perplexes understanding and so prohibits question; employing indirect grammar to shift responsibility away from itself; and calling on its management professionals to reconcile contradictory objectives of concern for staff welfare with cost-cutting priorities. Such contradiction seems very much like O'Neill's 'incompatible or barely compatible requirements [that] invite compromises and evasions' (2002: 54). The textual avoidance bears witness to the need to speak clearly about something that cannot be spoken. It results from a market-oriented focus which has to subordinate the needs of employees to corporate success but which it tries not to acknowledge openly. It is evidence of a continuing (Blairite) agenda of public sector cutbacks *and* accountability that sit uneasily together and prove Bauman's view that 'the prime technique of power is now escape, slippage, elision and avoidance' (2000: 11). The sub-surface tensions arise in Defra's communications by the attempt to negotiate and reconcile the competing organisational priorities through what Jameson calls 'imaginary or formal "solutions" to irresolvable social contradictions' (1981: 64).

Flux, fragmentation and narration

It is not insignificant that a deliberate bid for presentational consistency is made in the late twentieth/early twenty-first century just as the organisation of business becomes fragmented and dispersed, that complex organisations adopt monolithic identities – global branding – in which the single name and ubiquitous logo are unifying ciphers at odds with the diverse business interests of varied operations occurring in several different locations. During the twentieth century, economic, political and technological developments saw the Fordist stabilities associated with one aspect of modernism give way to the systemic fragmentation and eclecticism characteristic of postmodern forms[7] and the unifying effort through branding can be seen as an unsurprising attempt to re-establish the surety associated with an earlier model by disguising the fragmentation of the current one. The challenge of change is nothing new to business. Elton Mayo in the 1930s noticed:

> how profoundly the social structure of civilization has been shaken by scientific, engineering and industrial development. This radical change – from an *established* to an *adaptive* social order – has brought into being a host of new and unanticipated problems for management and for the individual worker.
>
> (Pugh, 1997: 360)

However, the acceleration of change since 1975 has been marked and remarked upon (Bell, Harvey, Hylland-Eriksen, Hochschild. Bunting, Ross, etc.). Today's adaptive order is, oxymoronically, a permanent state of flux, where the only constant is change, the only order, disorder. Instability and fluidity present both opportunity and threat; in business terms they characterise a market model of rapid turnover and quick profit far removed from the governing conditions of Fordism, in which organisational structures and worker behaviour drew on the stability required for long-term investment. The defining trait for the profit-conscious is now speed.

The conditions allowing 'flexible accumulation' (Harvey, 1990: 251–272) require corporate immediacy and responsiveness to convince investors that the company can beat its competitors in getting a product or service on to the market. The organisation of work within this efficiency model is structured around temporary affiliations of cost centres and specialised workstreams with companies that amalgamate and divide, form and reform in the pursuit of profit. It is a state of high contingency in which the workforce finds itself dependent on short-term contracts, serially threatened by corporate engineering (cost-cutting redundancy programmes) and with short-lead goals led by fluctuating customer demand.

Consequently the corporate workplace prizes very particular behaviour in its workers – speed, responsiveness, the will to change, to be mobile, adapt and keep up to date – traits that reflect its own structure and character organised for quick hits and immediate gain. However, while the inanimate corporation, characterised in this way, accrues financial benefit but can suffer no psychic ill effect, the effects on the human agent are serious.

Corporate flexibility and immediacy have two effects. First, the workers in this rapidly changing world are urged to transform along with it, encouraged to 'become a quick change artist', to mould their character and identity to mirror the 'organisation [that] will keep reshaping itself, shifting and flexing to fit our rapidly changing world' (Pritchett, 1997: 2–3). The problem with rapid changeability is that life experience becomes discontinuous and fragmentary and, like the textual examples analysed above, cannot be organised into forms of logical or coherent narrative. In identity terms, conditions of disorientation, of chance and uncertainty, mean self-definition in an individually created future must play off against the problems of achieving a consistency in circumstances of transience and contingency. When 'who we are' is replaced by 'who we want to be' and is addressed in the language of potential, one never really 'is' but is always 'becoming'. Flexible responsiveness in a human character is fundamentally a failure to situate oneself as a subject in cosmological and phenomenological time (Atkins, 2004: 341–366). Or, as Jameson (1984) puts it when relating temporal organisation to formal properties, it is the inability to conceive of ourselves as beings in relation to all past and future moments and events, to see some continuity of our state from 'then' to 'now' and 'what will be'. In his view this results in cultural productions of incoherent, random and unrelated ' "heaps of fragments" and in a practice of the randomly heterogeneous and fragmentary and aleatory' (Jameson, 1984: 71) as demonstrated in the foregoing communications examples.

Second, in the move to Daniel Bell's predicted 'post-industrial society', the 'information age' (Bell, 1973)[8] in which telecommunications and computer technology enable the shift from time- and location-based manufacturing to a time- and location-free knowledge/service economy, management became depersonalised – the hands-on foreman giving way to the time-and-motion overseer and later to bureaucratic and computerised forms of control. This allows management to distance itself from responsibility for the impact of the organisation's efficiency operations (Bakan, 2004: 60–84). It claims that 'the system' and, later in the march to capitalise on fluidity, 'change', is the responsible agent and presents itself as powerless by virtue of an overwhelming external uncontrollable force (Sennett, 1998: 114). Similarly the phenomenon 'recession' has become the force by which bank executives, fund traders, government regulators and others distance themselves from the effects on individuals of their (in)action. So at the same time that business embraces fluidity, responsiveness and mobility for profit-making and claims this empowers the individual to self-manage and develop, its agents are able to eschew responsibility for any of the unfortunate impacts of this model, as though their past actions and decisions have no bearing on what employees experience in the present and may suffer in the future.

While the bottom line creeps inexorably upwards by business managers exploiting the inevitable opportunities of chaos and uncertainty (until boom turns to bust, stock market trader frauds are exposed and banking institutions crumble when more evasions are uttered) the subject, unable to narrate itself logically and coherently, finds itself without an element as essential to human psychological survival as food, shelter and security are to physical survival. At this point the personally satisfying narrative forms able to counter the formal instabilities of the postmodern, late-capitalist workplace, to achieve psychological ease, to reclaim a more coherent identity and to resist corporate discourse are sought elsewhere and not in the cleverly termed 'portfolio' careers that now describe discontinuous work life.[9]

Empowerment and voice

The importance of employees' self-expression is demonstrated by two historic examples of industrial relations – Taylor's scientific management and Mayo's Hawthorne Experiment. Both show the workplace as contested terrain, the site of a power struggle between opposing human and corporate interests. In Mayo particularly the antagonism between the corporation's voice and that of the workers exposes the importance of discourse to identity, and identity to participation for securing productivity.

Frederick Winslow Taylor's time-and-motion experiments caused worker dissent because his efficiency measures took too little account of the needs of the human operator. As a result a raft of benefits was offered to quell unrest. However, Elton Mayo's Hawthorne Experiment discovered that such practical benefits were the lesser spur of efficiency. Instead, employee response improved when attention was paid to their psychological needs. Specifically, Mayo's staff interviews allowed workers to voice their opinions and concerns, which, being essential in maintaining the employee's sense of self, also paid dividends for production. Worker satisfaction came not so much from the opportunity to comment on physical conditions of work but in what that occasion signified – acknowledgement of the workers' mental, intellectual and imaginative capacities and the chance to comment *per se*, to be heard, to contribute to the organisational story. Mayo writes, 'It was as if workers had been awaiting an opportunity for expressing freely and without afterthought their feelings on a great variety of modern situations […] to give expression to ideas and feelings.' It is notable that workers used this participation to express 'feelings' along with 'ideas' and to correct what they saw as management misconceptions of their character and identity (Pugh, 1997: 360–362). Verbal contribution therefore seems as much a chance to determine themselves as to influence working practices. Speaking here is specifically allied to self-creation. Interviewees 'tell' themselves and surrender confidentiality as if the wider their story is told, the better the self-affirmation. Equally important, Mayo's 'interviewing programme closely resembles the therapeutic method and its triumphs are apt to be therapeutic' (Pugh, 1997: 363). Thus 'telling' is a form of recovery.

However, by attention to the non-physical capacities of the worker the 'whole' person, body and soul, is co-opted more fully to organisational requirements. Mayo's humanitarianism, superimposed on Taylor's rationalism, effectively marries the former's system of qualitative evaluation to the latter's quantitative measurement of output to ensure the predictability and dependability on which business continuity and increased production rely. While Taylorism required the productive capacity of the undifferentiated automaton, Mayo's psychological appeal to the individual's humanity is the means by which 'the "soulful" corporation demands the worker's soul, or at least the worker's identity' (Edwards, 1979: 152). In addition, though Mayo's experiments initially seemed to benefit both the corporation and the worker – the elusive win-win situation – the organisational concession to humanity resolves immediately (and ironically) into bureaucratic forms of control via personnel management. Management becomes encoded in 'job categories, work rules, promotion procedures, discipline, wage scales, definitions and responsibilities', and is more effective over *all* levels of personnel, including managers formally in charge of process compliance. Paradoxically, though born from acknowledgement of humanity, personnel processes 'allow the supervisor […] to detach his own feelings from his capacity as a supervisor', and claim that it is not he but company policy dictating the regime. Such control, divorced from individual responsibility, linguistically encoded, systematically disguised and applied, is less visible but just as alienating, damaging and external in origin as older forms. In it 'we can begin to perceive the repressive essence of modern structural control' operating as strongly as older hands-on management, as systems of checking focusing on 'compliance with the rules' extend organisational interest from production to 'work behavior'. Moreover, 'what distinguishes bureaucratic control from other control systems is that it contains incentives aimed at evoking the behaviour necessary to make bureaucratic control succeed' (Edwards, 1979: 131–152). It thus elicits cooperation by playing on the individual's concern for personal and employment security. The Defra-speak analysis above shows the continuing application of this technique.

Dominant discourse and the language of dissent

Where identity is concerned, official corporate narratives invite employees to adopt similar language, attitudes and behaviours, to express their own characters as types open to change, mobility and flexibility. In practice, the increasing volume of employee-directed corporate communication is a means of not just supporting but *driving* organisational change management programmes, while the market vocabulary used for this endeavour makes it hard to see how the individual agent retains any power over self-expression. Indeed, it can be argued that employment seems more a constant individual struggle to resist an identity that would be thrust upon us by a language that Amernic and Craig call CEO-speak (2006) than a choice to form it in ways that are privately articulated and personally acceptable.

Musson and Duberley's fieldwork reported in *Change, Change or Be Exchanged: The Discourse of Participation and the Manufacture of Identity* (2007) recognises both the role of workplace 'discourse in targeting and moulding the human subject' (148) and the efforts made to resist it. Looking specifically at 'employees positioned in the middle of the organization', they chart how those at the very top fully reflect the organisation's values through their self-narratives while those lower down more commonly challenge the corporate story with reference to selves existing outside the corporate purview (151). This suggests that while 'organizational control is accomplished through the self-positioning of employees within managerially inspired discourses about work and organization within which they may become more or less identified and committed' (Alvesson and Willmott, 2002: 620), total control is never achieved. Status and salary can certainly incentivise compliance, but at middle levels where employee rewards alone are not sufficiently satisfying, narrative resistance is the mark of retained autonomy. Thus while upper management's loyalty is an outcome of 'control through covert disciplinary power, a playing out of panoptical surveillance techniques (Foucault), designed to promote self-surveillance and self-discipline in the manufacture of the "ideal" identity' (Musson and Duberley, 2007: 157), self-making and self-management within corporate culture require a degree of complicity from the employee; buy-in is for those seeing advantage in being bought (and many do), and, paradoxically, those lower levels subject to the most formal management control, by virtue of their narrative resistance, appear the most free.

However, workers are led to believe that that developing in certain directions and adopting organisational values and perceptions of reality is in their interests for it will ensure their own and the organisation's survival. The master-stroke played by the agents of corporate conformity in the public sector is to categorise buy-in to the flexible behaviour demanded by neoliberal economics as 'successful' while employee resistance is commonly dismissed, not as political or ideological challenge, but as the inability of 'soft' (meaning undisciplined and second-rate) workers to get to grips with the 'hard' reality of market demands. Critically, opposing the corporate call for a market-prized 'can do' attitude carries heavy identity and acute self-esteem implications for the 'can't do' or 'doesn't wish to' worker.

Where compliance is achieved, a staff's mimetic, recursive acts reinforce a hegemony that operates to 'make certain ways of thinking and acting possible, and others impossible or costly' (Musson and Duberley, 2007: 145, quoting Phillips *et al.*, 2004). This is shown in Defra's benign rhetoric claiming 'to increase its professional capacity while achieving its efficiency […] targets through the business planning process, natural wastage, controlled recruitment and redeployment' (Defra, 2005: 264) that actually translates into staff outflow, with higher workloads and greater surveillance to ensure remaining staff become the appropriate change agents and contributors. Staff transformation is managed and measured through personal development plans and annual staff appraisals, both devolving much of the surveillance administration to the employee. The message is clear, buy in or be off, shape up or ship out, transform from rigid to responsive or you will be transformed from employed to unemployed. As a result the parameters of personal growth are so heavily circumscribed in neoliberal organisational discourse that self-development according to other principles, to alternative values congruent with one's personal ethical code, is effectively outlawed and devalued. In addition, the threat of job loss is a coercive pressure stressing 44% of public sector workers today who, according to a CIPD November 2010 survey (www.cipd.co.uk/pressoffice/_articles/Employeeoutlook291110.htm), feel they must grin and bear increasing stress levels from spending cuts that will only get worse in the future.

Continuing employment is not assured even for the acquiescent, as evolution towards responsiveness and flexibility allows more highly skilled and better-paid employees to be replaced by what is commonly called (younger) versatile talent. The exit of knowledgeable and experienced staff has a twofold effect. It preserves the fiction that every problem is new in the fast-paced workplace, and saves the cost and effort necessary to employ and manage time-serving skilled professionals. Experienced staff spell trouble for the new-breed manager whose confidence is built on the shifting sand of potential rather than on the rock of past achievement. Potential is an abstract concept denoting an ever-expanding capacity to grow (see Sennett,

2006: 115–130), as capitalism requires, constructing all workers as super-entrepreneurs rather than treating them as here-and-now, real human persons with finite capacities and differing abilities. Thus, ironically, corporate expressions valuing self-development and diversity arise alongside a programme of homogenisation that uses competency-based training to produce functionally interchangeable parts and seeks to encourage in *all* its employees the duck-and-dive behaviours of the street market trader who makes a good pitch, grabs a quick profit and moves on quickly when it is expedient to do so.

This wholesale determination is anathema to those whose own notions of self-development, albeit within the workplace, lie with a different model. For the middle-ranking public service professional, it creates an acute dilemma. They must give up stable, secure employment for a more precarious existence, trade their quality service-giving to citizens for providing a cost-paring, quantitatively measured product to consumers, and cede learning that leads to knowledge, experience and understanding for training that grooms them for versatility. Not everyone is willing to do so or to confuse wheeler-dealing with success. Many despair at the idea of progress and achievement where none seems to be made. Some hold out for other kinds of being. The evidence is that, despite penalties, resistance continues: today's conference circuit is awash with events aimed at securing the necessary employee engagement because, according to Kotter (1996), over 50% of change programmes fail.

Those recognising and wishing to resist this linguistic form of corporate power may do so by deliberate agent intervention. Resistance may take a behavioural form (absenteeism, sabotage, work to rule, etc.) but a key tool at the worker's disposal to disrupt discursive determination is language itself. Though conformity is incentivised, the organisation cannot control all spontaneously arising stories that contradict its preferred version of itself. For the non-compliant, resistance is marked by competing modes of expression. Contradictory or marginal voices, failed expression, silences, using the dominant discourse ironically or mockingly are all means of signalling dissent. So too are those speech acts giving voice to a reality that is imagined as 'other' to the official one, particularly stories of stasis, fixity and steadfastness countering the dominant narrative of change, mobility and flexibility which arise as the subversive utterance of a workforce that in formal situations expresses the official line. Or allegiance may be proclaimed to a different reality outside of the organisation in an attempt to neutralise the influence of the organisation's interpellation by casting it as irrelevant, taking 'the view of life outside work as "more important... more real" and where there were "real people" ' (Musson and Duberley, 2007: 159). These counter-rhetorical acts represent an imaginative leap from the sanctioned model by using language in a contextually fresh, untrammelled or unfashionable way to enable entirely 'other' forms of creation, to establish different conditions and denote survival *against* the determining power of the dominant stories. At work, the production of selves thus takes place within a nexus of competing discourses, in which identity is an effect of choosing a mode of expression. Thus the autobiographical act, which is the focus of this study, is its fullest form and can be the strongest, most complete form of resistance through self-expression.

We next investigate the literature supporting employees' efforts to be successful in the new economy workplace and to which they might turn when trying to cope with the psychological distress brought upon them by their employment experience.

II: Manuals of becoming: self-help for the failing

Introduction

Onora O'Neill (2002), confirming the stresses facing professional public sector employees, points out that 'during the last fifteen years we [education and health professionals] have all found our reputations and performance doubted as have millions of other public sector workers and professionals' (43). Those seeking help when their identity and usefulness is impugned find, unsurprisingly and ironically, that the market provides the solution in the form of popular business self-help literature specifically aimed at workers struggling to 'change or be exchanged' (Musson and Duberley, 2007). However, these manuals do not offer any workable alternative. Instead, they purvey the market way in distilled and insistent form. The advice is clear. The market is good, change is 'natural' (Clarke *et al.*, 2007: 13), technology is increasing its pace and, for success, you must work on yourself in a similar spirit of constant renewal and quick turnover. Paradoxically, we shall also see that the appeal these products make in formal literary terms relates particularly to coherence, autonomy and linearity – all qualities on which Atkins (2004) claims successful and continuous identity depend. Evident also are a number of other contradictions that disclose the flawed ideological foundations of the market argument.

The challenge of commitment in a changing world

Business self-help literature is polemical and didactic. It aims to turn workplace losers into corporate winners by presenting itself as a source of authority and experience – ironically, the professional qualities now less evident and little valued in the flatter organisation. It functions as a persuasive tool reinforcing the incentives and sanctions that work to define the ideal late-capitalist employee as flexible, able to cope with chaos, acquiescent, self-motivating, self-training, self-reliant, uncritical, committed and willing to bend her or his whole self to the needs of the business. The new economy character is presented nowhere better than the chapter headings of *The Employee Handbook of New Work Habits for a Radically Changing World. 13 Ground Rules for Job Success in the Information Age*:

> Become a quick change artist; Commit fully to your work; Speed up; Accept ambiguity and uncertainty; Behave as if you're in business for yourself; Stay in school; Hold yourself accountable for outcomes; Add value; See yourself as a service centre; Manage your own morale; Practice Kaizen; Be a fixer, not a finger-pointer; Alter your expectations.
>
> (Pritchett, 1997)

Appeal to the reader's vanity is made to elicit commitment by crediting those adopting the entrepreneurial attitudes with intelligence and smartness, and labelling those not demonstrating flexibility and responsiveness as unreasonable or dumb.[10] Though the intelligent and smart only stay employed by securing serial short-term contracts or by avoiding redundancy in the next round of corporate resizing, business gurus (ironically) still talk of career planning, even when admitting to the malign circumstances of new economy employment. For example, Pritchett's workplace is a tough arena where only the fit survive. Commitment to change causes 'grief, anger and depression' though confusingly it is 'therapeutic too, an excellent antidote for stress and a fine cure for the pain of change [...] a gift you should give to yourself' (Pritchett, 1997: 2, 7). Job security and pay increases should not be expected 'even if you perform well' because the 'era of entitlement is ending' and no company 'owes' a loyal worker continued employment (50). In fact, 'organisations actually do treat people unfairly at times [...] but employees don't seem to deserve any higher marks for how *they* treat employers' (38–39). Such antipathy and admissions of stressful conditions and ill treatment ignore that 'entitlement' refers not to choice but to right and obligation in which the stronger party owes a moral duty of decent conduct to the weaker in what has always been an unequal partnership.

Indeed, the market as a place of equal competition and fair exchange is highly false. One myth is that globalisation and technology allow small producers to compete on equal terms with large producers, that people have the power to choose to buy or not, that workers can take their labour elsewhere. None is entirely true. Frank (2000: 323–324) tells of a controlling media group using its power to squash small producers; enormous influence is wielded over buyers through advertising and information control, and employees marketing *their* skills, paradoxically, find the contractual arrangements leave power on the side of the buyer, and that when the labour market shifts or contracts for its own purposes, there is no 'elsewhere'. This is what happened, according to Ross (2003), to 1990s IT software developers on whose typical behaviour today's valuable independent, creative and committed worker is patterned. In the scramble for in-house jobs following the late 1990s crash of new media business, the market seized the opportunity to (re)employ these creatives on short-term contracts with little or no contractual benefits, relishing the ability to grow and contract by hiring and shedding workers as the business climate suited. Thus was self-satisfying autonomy appropriated and transformed into corporate subservience in which the humane was traded for the unjust and flexibility primarily benefits the organisation, not the individual.

Corporate empowerment rhetoric urging employees' self-responsibility allows the organisation to externalise any unfortunate outcomes of its actions, locating fault in individual weakness, and if not there, in some unnamed and impersonal force outside any control, as we have seen is often the case where management avoids taking responsibility. For example, Pritchett (1999) claims the bad luck of redundancy makes the loser 'a victim of circumstances' because the 'world' is forcing our hand' (14) and 'the world puts hard limits on how loyal an employer can be in return [for loyal service]' (Preface). The 'rapidly changing world that deals ruthlessly with organisations that don't change' (14) is therefore an overarching, impersonal, all-encompassing, uncontrollable power presumably above the market and separate from organisations. Accountability is dodged again when claiming that 'careers just don't work as they used to [but] that's not really anybody's fault' (42), particularly where treating employees unfairly 'doesn't mean that whoever is in charge should carry the burden of responsibility'. Now the employee is accountable, being 'far better off to assign to [her/him]self personal responsibility for attitude control' that does not resist, complain or expect emotional hand-holding (38–39). However, granting individual responsibility but excluding 'whoever is in charge' highlights the slippage that occurs in the corporate 'we' between the point at which 'personal' becomes 'corporate' responsibility – a legal difficulty debated in cases of corporate negligence.

Nurture and forced growth

While Pritchett's hard-line buy-in-or-be-on-your-way philosophy puts employees' failure to thrive down to their lack of commitment, other management gurus take a more subtle line, echoing current HR practice by pledging to development and 'wholeness'. Roy Bailey's *How to Empower People at Work: A Guide to Becoming a Green-fingered Manager* (1995) approaches its audience in a spirit of nurture, appropriating the language of growth from its original horticultural to its now-familiar investment context. This is noteworthy given that some are returning to activities in which it resumes its original connotations. In contrast to Pritchett's harsh coercion, Bailey's advice is overtly about 'changing attitudes' to secure improved performance (Bailey, 1995: 12) through reassuringly therapeutic Performance Counselling because 'people matter [for] as human beings we all have feelings' (11). Though Bailey quotes Herzberg's motivation-hygiene theory (Watson, 1995: 48), thus acknowledging the higher-level satisfactions necessary for commitment, he then undermines this humanitarianism by praising Lee Iacocca, who made Chrysler 'a number one player in the world stage' (noting here that business and the world are now synonymous).

> [Iaccoca] realized how to get the best out of people. He was tough. He axed jobs. He was demanding. He led by making difficult decisions. But he did something else. He inspired people to go beyond their roles. He reached the whole person. People at Chrysler gave more than what was expected. They were more than simple role occupants riding out the act of making Chrysler successful.
>
> Iacocca was not a bully but a person who had found in himself the resources to shape up the troops at Chrysler. Authority and fear had motivated Chrysler employees. Even though there are disagreements about whether Iacocca was a leader or a louse, he was a phenomenon - the first hero manager. At the same time, he made many enemies. And when he wasn't 'minding the store' there was always the threat that people would slacken off their great efforts to compete with Ford and oppose the Japanese invasion of vehicle markets in the USA.
>
> (Bailey, 1995: 74–75)

None but the uncritical or partisan could take this example of robustness and firmness as entirely positive. Nothing in this extract hints at the concerned management that could construe Iacocca's 'reach[ing] the whole person' in the positive Herzbergian sense. Bailey would have us believe this is not dictatorship but directorship of an 'organisation that casts its players into clear roles with snappy scripts' (74), the unfortunate theatrical metaphor confirming total control of action.

The commitment achieved by a CEO who 'was tough [...] axed jobs [...] [and] made many enemies' is clearly undermined by the coercion required to achieve it and by the need for constant 'minding the store' surveillance. This leadership style of a 'hero manager' seems unlikely to motivate other than by the predictable response to militaristic command and control underpinned by xenophobic rhetoric. Iacocca's way of preparing 'troops' to fight the 'Japanese invasion' relies too obviously on the disavowed 'authority and fear' rather than on the voluntary giving of 'more than what was expected'. This story of business efficiency will not stand as an example of the humanitarian nurturing or empowerment Bailey's book title – *How to Empower People at Work* – suggests. Performance here is no different to Pritchett's exhortation to 'add value' and 'contribute more than you cost' (1997: 30, back cover), a call for workers to take on additional work that subsequently becomes a new norm. This euphemistic concept of role extension (overload without reward) has certainly reached the public sector. Recent civil service performance management included guidance that exceptional ratings, which trigger bonuses, should be given rarely, when logically, if everyone is stretching as the organisation wishes, many more should receive bonuses. Such management is clearly not about judging and rewarding performance, but avoiding payment for the improved productivity extracted from employees who find at appraisal time that 'their commitment is exploited by government without fair reward' (Noon, 2007). Bailey's interpretation of Iacocca's role merely attempts to market bullying by selling it as an example of heroic success based on the qualities of toughness and resilience with which it can seduce employees because in other circumstances, such qualities are laudable.

Inevitably, those slower to adapt in this system of occupational Darwinism will suffer from problems of self-esteem, having to recognise themselves as neither tough, resilient nor powerful. In fact, increasing numbers of stretched performers are failing and business is worrying far more about the cost of ill-health than it used to. One of Bailey's scenarios presents an employee's personal concern that 'STRESS COST THIS COMPANY £500,000 THIS YEAR' (uppercase original) (Bailey, 1995: 87). Certainly, because of the negative economic effect, stress figures are grabbing the attention of government. In a 2004 HM Treasury public policy document, Richard Layard (2005) acknowledges the scale of the problem of declining mental health and, in his recent bestselling book *Happiness*, presents evidence showing the increase and high incidence of depression and unhappiness in the postwar period (Layard, 2005: 35, citing Fombonne). However, the debate centres on economic, rather than humanitarian concerns – £0.6bn spent in the health service would save £7bn in lost tax revenue (*Today* programme, 19 June 2006, http://cep.lse.ac.uk/research/mentalhealth) – and Western economies are unlikely to follow Bhutan's measurement of national wealth in terms of Gross National Happiness.

Masterful education – magical tales of success

Significantly, management self-help manuals offer expert help using two key stratagems – authority, which has disappeared from the 'youthful' workplace, and story, which is now disrupted by fragmented work experience. The writers claim both knowledge and experience, and deliver their advice through narrative vignettes in which recognisable authority figures, social situations and story-types are used to blend the real with the imaginary. Typically a teacher/student relationship is set up with the pupil told that poor ability causes time pressure (rather than work overload and too-short deadlines). The familiar 'blame yourself' terms (Bliss, 1993: xiii, 8; Blanchard and Lorber, 1994: 77) shift responsibility away from work conditions and on to the worker with 'slowness' used to indicate intellectual and/or performance failure. In one story a child comments that if 'Daddy can't finish at the office... why don't they just put him in a slower group?' (Blanchard and Zigarmi, 1994: 42).

Another struggling pupil (employee) visiting an effective 'One Minute Manager' (OMM) finds him staring out of the window having finished all tasks, about to go home on time and announcing that working at home is unnecessary or counterproductive (Blanchard and Zigarmi, 1994: 58; Blanchard and Lorber, 1994: 10–11). The presentation of this imaginary situation, this alternative reality, shows a magical 'One Minute Manager' apparently having turned time-poverty to time-plenitude. It seduces by attaching mystery to authority. The Director's freedom from pressure seems contained in his upward/outward gaze that implicates some remoter source, thus still evoking an older-style divine right authority from the ultimate, otherworldly power *even as* management promotes employee empowerment. What the Director seems *not* to represent is Fordist hands-on management or a real-world example of how-to-do, which is what Bauman (2000) says the miserable seek, if not as authority, then at least as comfort 'to know how other people, faced with similar challenges, cope' (63–68).

However, the gaze also reinforces the schooling theme in which managers must apply a 'behavioural reminder' aimed at 'getting good performance from your staff when you're not there'. This is achieved by understanding that three 'secrets' – goal-setting, praising and reprimanding (which semantically shift to present as incentives not-to-do particular actions) – can ensure acceptable conduct, 'otherwise people will revert back to old behaviour' (Blanchard and Lorber, 1994: 33, 35). Trainees are informed that 'You can expect more if you inspect more' (72), proving that compliance is achieved by both Pavlovian training and Foucauldian self-policing, a correctional regime contradicting the Director's relaxed and non-coercive style.

The manuals also appropriate the power of myth and magic through the cultural referent of the fairytale. The rhetorically powerful number three is regularly employed, as it is in fairytales, to note the number of 'secrets' and the successive and progressive nature and stages of the quest, though in reality the magical effect is brought forth only by hard work and application. The endgame of the training is that the pupil will discover a wonderful world in which all problems are solved. Bailey (1995) ends with:

> a journey through Aladdin's cave. You know there are some enchanting gems of personal empowerment to be found and developed. Aladdin had a genie in the lamp that produced wondrous results and achieved fantastic goals. But first Aladdin had to work at it, and find out how to release the powerful genie. [...] You can achieve undreamt-of results. [...] But to make it work, and work well, you have to be like Aladdin. You need to work at polishing your lamp. The more you polish it the more your genie will appear. [...] Set aside one period each day [...] to deliberately and consciously put into practice your abilities as a green-fingered manager. At first you may feel awkward and embarrassed [...] [but it] gets a little bit easier each day and that bit more exciting as you see the difference it makes to people and their performance.
> (Bailey, 1995: 127–128)

There is more than a little masturbatory fantasy of male power in this passage that goes on to describe a fecundity whereby the one manager grows into a group of managers, which in turn proliferates into several groups, until the entire business, or at least a critical mass of the organisation, is initiated into the brotherhood. The visionary goal is one of total compliance with no disruptive or resistant employees. A similar fruitful example describes how:

> The entrepreneur went back to her company and told all the people who worked directly for her what she had learned and they in turn told the people who worked for them. Pretty soon the inevitable happened: The entrepreneur became a Situational Leader.
>
> (Blanchard and Zigarmi, 1994: 102)

At this point the reader supplies, also inevitably, 'and they all lived happily ever after!'

Further use is made of authority figures when writers position themselves as messianic and godlike, adopting the hard-line language and symbolic power of what Amernic and Craig (2006) term the 'Corporate Chieftain Incarnate' (74–75)[11] handing down from on high prescribed values and tough behavioural lessons to create obedient subjects. Indeed, 'in a society flirting with agnosticism, atheism, and hedonism, the CEO warrior chief has become a surrogate religious icon' (139–140). One could even argue that business culture proposes a new theology through its mission statements, its endless practice of the rituals of observance and its rhetoric, all designed to mould character in its own service, though ultimately this produces a hollowed-out spirituality that fails in providing solace for the disciples of its doctrine. In this religious analogy the initiation through the text, symbolically the Word, turns manager into priest with the role of maintaining the faith and ensuring others keep to the one true way.

Bailey (1995) uses this metaphor, warning against those 'who will try to persuade you to give up', advising one must follow those who 'will excite, motivate and astound you' (129) so that his route to success, though not quite a pilgrimage, certainly draws on the storyline of the quest. Bailey urges his disciples to repeat rhythmically the mantra 'the prize is worth the price', invoking the meditative practices of Eastern faiths or CBT (cognitive behavioural therapy) techniques taught by counselling psychologists. Protagonists in the illustrative examples are cast as seers, prophets or visionaries, or embodied in roles as priest, doctor or teacher, as holders and passers-on of wisdom to readers constructed, in turn, as pupil, penitent or patient. It is noteworthy that this form of secular and psychological healing through authoritative narrative appeals when the actual provision of corporate in-house doctors and welfare staff has diminished, when electronic communication of dubious provenance has mostly superseded word-of-mouth, and when there appears a new need for help from charismatic and knowledgeable individuals.

Heroic and competitive concepts are used regularly in business self-help manuals. The familiar metaphor of the quest or journey (now overused by contestants in reality TV programmes) take advantage of this powerful cultural referent with Bailey drawing on real-life icons such as Scott (whose fateful *mis*-management and bad planning will not be seen by all as an example of heroic and effective leadership) and Amundsen to stress the status and acclaim awaiting those able to overcome challenge. These paradigms metamorphose into the more prosaic version of the workplace winner in a contest typically constructed as a power struggle involving the intellect. In one example, an established manager, Frank, known for his pranks, decides to catch out a newly arrived executive of good reputation. Frank holds a live bird in his hand, shows the new man a glimpse of feathers and asks him what is in his hand and whether it is alive or dead. Twenty onlookers, poised to see the outcome of this contest, give the scene a dramatic edge. If the new man says 'alive' then Frank kills the bird, if he says 'dead', Frank lets the bird fly, in either instance proving the newcomer wrong. The new man answers the obvious 'what' question by saying it is a bird, but in reply to the alive or dead question says, to the amazement of the onlookers, 'I think the answer to that lies in your hands.' Frank exclaims in a somewhat astonished tone:

> 'My my, it is true what they say about you. You really are fair and you do know how to help people at work.' From that day on Frank never played any more pranks with managers. Instead he spent many hours telling the story about the bird and the wisest manager he had ever met.
>
> (Bailey, 1995: 100–101)

Leaving aside judgement on the suitability or relevance of the example to management, this narrative clearly presents an instance of competitive advantage such as is required in market transactions. The new manager is a supercool, James Bond-like hero, reaching for a secret weapon, a nugget of management knowledge, to secure his triumph. The story has one more time-related edge: being set as a contest between 'clever old' Frank and the 'new' unnamed manager, it places a new, smarter, sharper knowledge as triumphant over an older, outdated kind. A further observation is that the 'old' *is* frank, and like old management is transparently manipulative, whereas newer modes of power are nameless, less obvious but more effective.

In these stories of success we see again how newer-style management is merely the (re)presentation and application of an older-style authority. Though employees are urged to change themselves into 'winners' (with fierce competition lauded as the means to identify and blame 'losers' and lack of self-responsibility blamed for failure), power relations remain untransformed. Ironically, those consulting self-help manuals *are already* self-responsible by having identified themselves as in need of instruction. Those currently feeling stuck or willingly acknowledging their failure desire progress and are thus both susceptible to tales of heroism and success with which they would rather identify, and seduced by narratives of mysterious power and magical knowledge, which they willingly acknowledge is presently out of their grasp.

Marketing the message – the authority of the text

As with all literature, authors may write to convey a particular truth but can never fully ensure that meaning is received as they would wish. The space for interpretation always leaves understanding as much in the hands of the reader as in the intentionality of the writer. What seems fairly certain is that readers of business self-help literature are willing to look to experts for instruction, and writers of this genre take great pains (some might say too much) to convince that they are the authoritative agents. Validation comes in several forms – testimonials, qualifications, associations, previously published work, board membership of blue-chip organisations and global acclaim in their roles as educators or trainers. Citation descriptors include 'internationally known', 'has written extensively', 'recognised expert' (Blanchard and Lorber, 1994: 94–95) and 'leading authority' (Pritchett, 1997: 66). Most claim PhDs, often in psychology, (though not all state the awarding institution) and some call on the respect afforded by a string of letters – in Bailey's case, 'PhD, MA, DACP, MIPD, AFBPsS, Dip EHP NLP, C Psychol' (1995: outside back cover).

Pritchett, recognising the charge of academic elitism lurking in the qualification-validation approach, intersperses business-sourced quotes with those derived from celebrity – comedians, actors, pop stars, sports personalities – as well as from popular songs and comics, to signify his rooted, man-of-the-people status. This bid for wider democratic appeal, made by co-opting the populist backlash to elitism (Ehrenreich, 1989: 125–128; Frank, 2000: 29) shows also in other mass-marketing features: the easy-to-read large typeface, the sparse content (double-page spreads with fewer than 50 words, e.g. Pritchett's booklet contains fewer than 5,000), pages printed with only a single easy-to-memorise aphorism and fatuously simple diagrams. The lack of sophistication indicates the expectation of the childlike, uncritical intelligence that Thomas Frank believes marketspeak creates and relies upon, and is underlined by the lack of academic rigour he finds generally in 'meaningless diagrams and home-made master narratives' that characterise Management Theory 'bullshit' (Frank, 2000: 176).

However, educated readers (even those failing to acquire competitive flexibility) are likely to feel patronised or alienated by this type of presentation and by the once-upon-a time tone of the stories, the simple short sentences and early learning level phrases like 'then the busy manager brought his book home', the very basic mnemonics of the 'ABCs of management', and the audit-culture advice to deal only with what can be observed and measured as 'thoughts and feelings are complicated' (Blanchard and Lorber, 1994: 18, 24). They may also baulk at the polarising of good and bad that avoids complexity and insults the reader's intelligence or, as they come to realise, is more worryingly marketed at a level to meet it.

Nevertheless, two significant, universally applicable elements of the self-help stories can be seen as a providing solace for those failing to thrive in new economy conditions whatever their education or status – the comfort of coherent narrative and identifiable authorship by those claiming direct experience. The reader response to the stories works on a culturally ingrained recognition of the satisfaction afforded by the simple tale with a beginning, middle and end, progressively linear with a situation evolving through crisis to denouement. The 'bird' story cannot work in any other way. You cannot shuffle the order of its events, rearrange its sentences, start with the end and work towards it, or use any other structural effects now familiar to readers of sophisticated postmodern creative, or new-economy corporate writing. Even where the content and context of these particular stories renders them problematic, the effect of story *per se* is not diminished. Neither does the inappropriate use of a hero undermine the attraction and cultural relevance of the role. In fact, its use and misuse in trite and superficial business tales, by contrast, makes the original conception of moral hero and survivor all the more powerful and attractive.

In addition, for the middle class, one needs to consider the cultural significance of *Robinson Crusoe* (see Conclusion) the early hero-survivor story expressed in the (essentially bourgeois) form of the novel. This tale of capitalism and survival associates individualism, in which one controls one's life, to the first-person narrative in which one also controls the writing of one's story. The authorial projects go hand-in-hand: the development of character through action intimately linked to the story it produces. For these readers, self-help manuals crassly marketing the not-so-changed fast, flexible and responsive business model as a form of necessary progress from an older (and by implication slow, rigid and unresponsive) model in which was found a comforting certainty and identity, prove uncompelling. When business stories fling out versions of heroism, survival and winning in the inglorious context of corporate survival, or when slippery corporate-speak skates on the surface of underlying truth, severing any connection between form and content, presentation and meaning, the impulse to remake those stories and re-establish those associations becomes a very strong one (see Watt, 1974).

This chapter has described how the importation of private business values by the public sector fundamentally alters the working culture for caring professionals. The adoption of a lean business model, organised for responsiveness to facilitate higher production, relies on constant change that also brings with it structural instability, time-pressure, management avoidance of responsibility and the requirement for the staff's behaviour and attitude to meet the flexibility, mobility and immediacy of the corporate character. The demands of this state of constant flux cause the inability to construct a coherent and sensible narrative, whether this is the progressive story of an individual's career or the coherent presentation of the corporate image. The failure of narrative is reflected in corporate communication as the organization tries to negotiate its way round the contradictions, uncomfortable truths and human effects of its chosen mode of operation. In an effort to avoid the personal confusion and disorientation brought about by these developments workers may seek support in self-help manuals which, while only selling the new economy faith in distilled form, employ some narrative strategies that prove comforting to those seeking some form of anchoring structure and surety.

In these circumstances, far from feeling empowered middle-class professionals are pitched into an occupational identity crisis by the loss of respect for their status, knowledge, experience and quality-based output that finds no place in the fast-paced modern business environment. In addition for this group, the loss of autonomy together with the push to adopt unattractive characteristic values drives three potential outcomes, two of which gravitate towards the cultural extremes described by Ehrenreich in *Fear of Falling* (1989), which appear to offer some form of safety from the abyss lurking beneath the uncertain middle ground. The first is selling-out to elitism – doing whatever is necessary to climb up the corporate ladder with the few that make it to the rarified heights of high office and a mega-salary, which in literary terms would be to embrace a form of artistic snobbery; the other is accepting a drop to less distinctive and distinguished forms of 'ordinary', non-specialised employment, to disappear into the herd defined by values associated with populism and the mass-market. Either direction requires a considerable shift in identity that the middle-class approach with trepidation. A third way, the argument in this book suggests, is to attempt to recapture a distinctive group identity by returning to older, more structured kinds of culture and other class-associated, narrative forms (autobiography) that counter the disorderly and fragmentary market conditions in which they find themselves defined by language, values and stories with which they cannot comfortably identify. The next chapter discusses more fully the particular political and cultural history of the middle classes that could drive them in this direction.

Notes

1. Liberal individualism is taken to mean the ability to self-develop towards personally identified goals unopposed by external interference. Where Amernic and Craig point out that the market model draws 'upon the rugged individualism of the North American entrepreneurial ethos' which presumes a political standpoint pursuing the 'maximisation of profit conceived of as the public good', this argument defines autonomy as self-direction allowing development in line with goals, desires and values that may be antithetical to profit-making.
2. Among commentators writing on the idea of corporate personhood are Ted Nace (2003) and Joel Bakan (2004).
3. See http://www.guardian.co.uk/media/2008/feb/28/itv.marketingandpr The headline for this article in the Guardian, 'New Labour-style rebuttal unit for ITV', shows how the US-imported form of verbal defence is associated with Alistair Campbell, who managed New Labour's communications.
4. Although Edwards (1979: 155) says that individual acts of resistance have not brought capitalism to its knees, the proliferation of print, broadcast and internet channels endows the individual with a disruptive power unequalled in earlier times, e.g. Bradley Manning and Julian Assange.
5. Over this period, DfES rebranded as (lower case) 'education and skills', DTI became dti (department of trade and industry) to be joined by dcms (department of culture, media and sport). At this time also, the Ministry of Defence's web pages showed the lowercase legend 'defence' but the Chancellor's presence retained HM TREASURY in full capitals. Some government websites have been redesigned since departmental restructuring following the 2010 election, though dcms and defra still retain their lower-case presence.
6. Defra has since carried out three Voluntary Early Retirement and Voluntary Early Severance schemes, the latest in June 2011.
7. I do not assert any easy parallel development between cultural and business conditions, or suggest that the move from Fordist stability to post-Fordist instability implies a similar sequencing of modernism to postmodernism. I am sensitive to arguments about whether postmodernism succeeds or is merely an aspect of modernism and aware of David Harvey's argument (1991) that the modernist movement encompassed both stability and instability, and that its artistic production, according to Baudelaire, was a contradictory project encompassing the 'the transient, the fleeting, the contingent [with the] eternal and immutable'. Whereas the history of modernism 'wavered from one side to the other of this dual formation' and many writers dealing with the 'overwhelming sense of fragmentation, ephemerality and chaotic change' believe that 'the only secure thing about modernity is its insecurity' (10–11), the history of business development does witness the disappearance of operational stabilities associated with Fordist organisational structures (though this thesis argues the power on which they rested still exists) and their replacement by less stable forms. See also Elgaard

and Westenholz, 2004: 148. Paul du Gay (2007) parallels post-Fordism with postmodernism even while arguing against an epochal stance that views an earlier period as distinct and different to a later one.
8 The accompanying social, political, cultural and aesthetic effects are taken up by Jameson (1984: 53–92) and Harvey (1990: 14), both of whom analyse the eclecticism and diversity of rapidly changing forms. Also Eriksen (2001: 14) disputes that post-industrial society is synonymous with the information age and Maurizio Lazzarato says we have moved beyond this now into the age of debt (Critical Management Studies Conference, Naples, 11–13 July 2011, plenary address and www.senselab.ca/inflexions/volume_4/n3_lazzaratohtml.html).
9 Jameson (1984: 55) deliberately uses the term 'late-capitalist society', rather than Daniel Bell's 'post-industrial society', to maintain attention to 'the omnipresence of class struggle'.
10 See also Hamilton (2003: x). Hamilton would find irony in this discourse of insanity for though 'downshifters [outsiders] frequently ... are dubbed '"crazy" to reject higher incomes... it may transpire that those who are the prisoners of overwork and debt, and find themselves beset by stress, ill-health and family strain, may come to be seen as the "crazy" ones'.
11 The term describes Jack Welch, the CEO of General Electric, 'dubbed "Neutron Jack" for his ability to eliminate people and their jobs'. He 'exerted significant influence over his own company and a whole generation of corporate leaders in the US and abroad, writers in the popular business and general press, and academics'.

2
Identity
Sink or swim: the dilemma of the failing middle-class professional

Introduction

This chapter contextualises the work-based identity insecurity experienced by middle-class professionals in the public sector among the general identity-making problems of postmodernity and other cultural determinants of the group. The aim is to illuminate how the call to adapt quickly and constantly to the changing demands of the profit-hungry and cost-effective market impacts on this class with particular intensity. It lays out the theoretical foundations on which assumptions concerning a failing, work-based, middle-class identity are formed, and provides three reasons why the professional sector in particular might seek remedies in which well-being is related to the inherent values of practical activities and self-expression.

The first is that the diversity of type covered by the middle class classification, which already weakens their wider group identity, means that any further threat to aspects of differentiation on which their particularity rests is more critically undermining. The second is that a recent polarisation of wealth creates a void at the centrally occupied position presaging a choice of moving up or down socially. Third, the group's historical tendency to radicalism, and their social and financial capital and entrepreneurial spirit, fits them well for the kind of political response made through a 'slow life' in which activities involving creativity, nurturing, distinction and progressive improvement signify the effort to retain, or reconnect with, certain disappearing virtues and values that hallmark their class. It is then possible to understand the increasing popularity of autobiographic narratives over the period since 'new capitalist' philosophy became dominant, particularly where these are able to capture and reflect identity in self-created and coherent forms.

Subjectivity, identity and character

The problem of achieving a secure identity from among the instabilities of modern life has exercised many contemporary theorists. In fact, according to Bauman (2001), 'no other aspect of contemporary life, it seems, attracts the same amount of attention these days from philosophers, social scientists and psychologists [,] [...] "identity" has now become a prism through which other topical aspects of contemporary life are spotted, grasped and examined' (140). Where the hegemonic ideology convinces us we can choose anything and everything, the making of identity becomes a key responsibility but not one without problems. As Donald Hall (2004) observes:

> We are widely led to believe we have the freedom and ability to create and recreate our 'selves' at will, if we *have* the will, but at the same time are presented with a suspiciously narrow range of options and avenues that will allow us to fit comfortably into society and our particular gendered, regional, ethnic, sexual subset of it.
>
> (Hall, 2004: 1)

This statement, indicating that subjectivity (i.e. the state of being subject to various forms of influence) impacts on identity, acknowledges that 'the subject is powerfully *subjected to* forces outside itself' (Robbins, 2005: 14; emphasis original). However, the extent to which such forces determine the self is also the cause of much philosophical debate making subjectivity, like identity, a highly contested state and their meeting doubly problematic.

At one end of the scale it appears possible to be an entirely autonomous and sovereign self (therefore hardly 'subject' at all); at the other is a state of wholesale determinism by which the self appears as what Gagnier (1991) terms (admittedly theorising an earlier historical period, but still relevant today) an 'effect of institutional practices'. In this latter position, for theorists such as Lacan,

Althusser and Foucault, as Gagnier so neatly puts it, 'the *I*, the apparent seat of consciousness, is not the integral center of thought but a contradictory, discursive category constituted by ideological discourse itself'. If this is so the challenge is to understand 'how subjects mediate (i.e. transform) those discourses in their everyday lives, or how subjects see themselves to the extent that they are not entirely identified with those institutions' (Gagnier, 1991: 8–10).

Theorists such as Williams, Giddens, Thompson and Bourdieu appear to reintroduce agency, allowing the individual some power of transformation over 'structures and systems, including systems as large as the language and the State'. Thus, as Gagnier says, ' "the self" is not an autonomous introspectible state – a Cogito or a unique point of view – but is instead dependent upon intersubjectivity, or the intersubjective nature of language and culture' (11). These sociological theories are formed on an understanding of dynamic interaction between self and institution admitting that each modifies the other. They insist on the scope for individuals to understand instrumental forces in a way that enables their own action in respect of those forces, and the identification of common perspectives that would permit concerted action. However, intervention is only possible where one agrees with Judith Butler (1997) that 'being' is precisely 'the potentiality that remains unexhausted by any particular interpellation' (131). Though we may be hailed as subjects by what Althusser terms are various Ideological State Apparatuses, there still remains capacity to take deliberate action. All of this means that discourse may define us, but our individual or collective power of influence over discourse marks the extent to which we may alter the terms within which such definition takes place.

Contemporary identity-making based on continuous flexibility and change seems to imply that such terms may be infinitely extended or altered. Such potentiality was not the case in earlier times when categories such as class and gender provided a normative structural framework for identity against which non-conformity could be recognised. In the post-Fordist conditions of fluidity it is presumed that there are no normative categories, that among the vast and ever-increasing options for selfhood, predestination is replaced by 'a compulsive and obligatory *self*-determination' (Bauman, 2001: 140–152). Hall may hint that social categories still provide defining roles, but Eriksen (2001) writes that 'the fragmentation of work, consumption, family life and the public sphere brings us to a world beyond ready-made "identity packages" ' (140). Ulrich Beck (2001) has theorised modern identity formation in these fragmented and flexible conditions as 'reflexive individualization', meaning that self-creation is no longer a 'given' but a 'task', one carried out over and over again as we identify and seize opportunities in the attempt to quell the 'biographical uncertainties' resulting from the compelling call to choose our 'self' from among a vast and quickly changing range of options.

There is an evident theoretical difference between identity-formation in relation to stable identity categories and identity-formation as the continual and opportune making and remaking of the self in conditions of permanent flux. However, in conceding some agency for the subject, and recognising also that selfhood is constituted in and expressed by action, there may be little practical or ethical difference in choosing to act in relation to a stable category or a series of changing ones. In either case the subjective experience involves 'being' at a moment in time (in fact, in both cases at several successive moments through time) and acting in alignment with some personally adopted (however generated) values. Whether choosing to act in accordance with, or resistance to, a predetermined social category, or opportunely creating temporary, continuously modified, serial identities, the issue is as much one of understanding how personal agency relates to the motivation and gain directing one's choice as it is of operating within a stable or unstable context.

If the self is the mere coincidence of a moment in a postmodern world of infinite interpretation and remaking, we could expect such contingency to produce a single person with widely differing performative identities – say, one moment extrovert, money-conscious and studious, the next shy, spendthrift and lazy. This is rarely the case, unless there is some deliberate role playing (stage-acting or similar) or psychosis. Rather we see persons acting within a fairly narrowly defined sphere, and in a mostly coherent manner within boundaries that are personally and/or socially determined. Remembering Atkins (2004), acting is always acting *towards*, which supposes there are reasons for acting. Arguing from Marya Schechtman, Atkins holds these motivations to be first-personal concerns of 'self-interest, compensation (receiving benefits or losses in the future for one's actions in the present), moral responsibility and survival', and that these are the same concerns that make personal identity matter and motivate psychological continuity (342).

Self-making in a fast world

There is, however, an aspect of modern life that poses a great difficulty when identity-making. The exhortation to 'be who we want to be' presupposes the time to decide what actions must be taken to become that identified self. It is pertinent to question one's capacity for deliberate action when modern life is characterised by an accelerated pace and the ever-changing conditions brought about by the short-termism and quick turnover demands of the new economy. At the very least, in addition to the discursive influence of market terminology, speed compromises the time available for reflective thinking in which deliberate action is conceived.[1]

The lack of reflective thinking is problematic for, according to Atkins (2004) quoting Catriona MacKenzie, reflection is the self-consciousness needed for the making of ethical choices:

> Self-consciousness is the reflective capacity to call into question our beliefs, desires and motives; it is the reflective capacity to ask ourselves whether these constitute reasons for us. Reasons are impulses, perceptions and desires that have withstood reflective scrutiny. The capacity for reflection, then, is the source of normativity; it gives us a choice about what we should believe, what we should decide, how we should act.
>
> (MacKenzie in Atkins, 2004: 362)

It follows that without the time to reflect, the power to choose is compromised and our actions are in danger of becoming ungrounded, unfocused, automatic and unethical. The modern individual, as we have seen, is characterised by choice but they must:

> choose fast, must – as in a reflex – make quick decisions. Second-modernity individuals haven't sufficient reflective distance on themselves to construct linear and narrative biographies. They must be content [...] with bricolage-biographies in Levi Strauss's sense. The non-linear individual [the person whose life is characterised by

discontinuous relationships and fragmented, rather than accumulative, experience] may wish to be reflective but has neither the time nor the space to reflect.

(Lash in Beck, 2001: vii)

Three key commentators support the view that the combination of accelerated pace, continual change and mobility impacts critically on identity-making and ethical choice. Richard Sennett (1998) identifies that trust, loyalty and commitment are casualties of fast time and its associated conditions. Such qualities, he says, need to be demonstrated across time and before an enduring witness (Sennett, 1998: 21, 24). Thomas Hylland Eriksen (2001) in *The Tyranny of the Moment* agrees that anything time-consuming no longer 'has a snowball's chance in hell of surviving as an element in the personality formation of the majority' (Eriksen, 2001: 152). According to Beck (2001) quoting Bauman, the pressures for an individual's motivation appear today to originate in a 'vagrant's morality' by which the ethically rootless person perpetually identifies goals as new ones present themselves and, finding each unfulfilling, moves on to the next in the hope of greater joy (Beck, 2001: 2–4). In this aimless behaviour it is easy to understand why so many feel life is pointless and do not develop the ability for the continuous commitment required either for managing oneself towards longer-term character development or for managing other human relationships through difficulty.

In being 'peremptorily invited to constitute themselves as individuals', people are required to make 'decisions, possibly undecidable ones within guidelines that lead into dilemmas' (Beck, 2001: 3–4). Such decisions, one finds, might include wanting a work/life balance when life is, of economic necessity, all work: balancing responsible parenting with the need for two incomes; or trying to eat healthily when time pressure forces recourse to fast food. For Beck 'the deep layer of foreclosed decisions is being forced up into the level of decision-making' so that the comforting routine actions of the social everyday, the ordinary activities once founded in habit and custom, now demand conscious handling and decision-making. Whatever decision is made within the ' "precarious freedoms" that are taking hold of life as modernity advances' (Beck, 2001: 6), the dilemmas are settled only temporarily as the individual engages in the task of trying to impose order on their world on each and every occasion in an effort to achieve psychic ease.

Despite being thrust into insecurity by 'biographical uncertainty', Beck finds, paradoxically, that self-making occurs not as an entirely free choice but rather under very evident and identifiable constraints. Like Thomas Frank, Beck (2001) sees that '[d]ependency upon the market extends into every area of life' and continues:

> The individual is removed from traditional communities and support relationships, but exchanges them for the constraints of existence in the labour market. In spite of these new forms of constraint, individualized cultures foster a belief in individual control – a desire for a 'life of one's own'.
>
> (Beck, 2001: 203)

In other words, there continue to be many who experience the 'deep layer of foreclosed decisions' as still deep and still foreclosed; the apparent opportunity to choose is in large part just that – apparent, an illusion, a diversionary dance played out on the surface of a capitalist economy whose various interests it serves. Though we are sold the idea of freedom to create our 'selves', that does not necessarily mean we are become more powerful or that the institutions selling the idea have loosened their grip. Indeed, the universally employed market discourse of freedom of choice over everything (and its workplace equivalent 'empowerment') has become and remains powerful not least because the anxious population it maintains, whose mental capacities are so fully engaged in trying to secure their identities, status, careers, homes and relationships, are by that occupation disengaged from political action, and instead assuage their anxiety by quick-fix consumer spending. As Bauman (2001) puts it, 'shopping expeditions fill the void left by the travels no longer undertaken by the imagination to an alternative, more secure, humane and just society' (151).

There is clear evidence for a widespread, influential and disabling marketism (nevertheless claiming to empower through choice). First, choice is illusory. As Bauman acknowledges, fast-moving, changeable conditions can produce opportunity *or* threat, for in unpredictable circumstances, 'anxiety and audacity, fear and courage, despair and hope are born together'. However, stating also that 'the proportion in which they are mixed depends on the resources in one's possession' (142), he confirms that though conditions might be universally affecting, individuals are differently placed to respond to them. Those who – for whatever social, cultural, economic or personal reason – draw anxiety, fear and despair from unpredictability are thus *pre*sently determined as ill-equipped to chase the opportunities open to those able to respond with audacity, courage and hope (which, incidentally, define the market-preferred entrepreneurial character). The freedom to choose for the fearful, anxious and despairing is very much narrower, is indeed foreclosed, in scope if not entirely. In addition, where such individuals are identified, not as belonging to some already classified group, but ranging across group boundaries, then it is the disability itself that forms the common factor and must be examined in its relation to social conditions to decide what is causing a growing negative effect. The argument here suggests today's social reality is one in which the increasing domination by an overarching market economy, by virtue of a recursive dynamic which continuously maintains its effect, disables ever-growing numbers and causes a widening divide between those able to function in its unpredictable conditions and those who cannot. In other words, while the confident and audacious become more so, the lack of surety felt more usually by the socially disadvantaged, disqualifying them from opportunity, affects those members of the middle classes now also made fearful by having their social and occupational status undermined. Professionals repeatedly forced by the public sector's adoption of new-economy values into choosing between what they consider is the 'right' action (care-ful work producing a quality outcome) which carries a penalty, and its opposite, the 'cheap' or 'quick' option, which *apparently* does not, face a particular conundrum. In their case, action taken either way compromises one or more of those first-personal concerns (self-interest, compensation, moral responsibility and survival) on which their identity and psychological continuity depend. Choosing 'cheap' and/or 'quick' ensures survival and continuing compensation in work, but in eschewing moral responsibility, ultimately harms self-interest and psychological continuity. Choosing 'right' maintains moral responsibility, ensuring psychological continuity, but damages chances of survival and continuing compensation in work and so also harms self-interest.

Second, individualism disempowers. According to Beck (2001), previous sociological categories have been broken down by modernity, i.e. a fracturing evident in the fragmentation of family life and class affiliation, and in the diversification within communities over which there is less and less commonality (13–14). In fact, individuals increasingly represent only themselves when interfacing with institutions as today it is *supply events* 'from pension rights to insurance protection, from educational grants to tax rates' that characterise 'modern thinking, planning and action' (2). This segments the population not by social categories but by marketing categories.[2] Not only are we thereby constructed as consumers, but being constantly encouraged to think of ourselves, think *for* ourselves and choose for ourselves as individuals weakens the collective impulse. Evidently, if challenge to institutional power is made by the strength of one person alone, such a manifestly unequal fight is often abandoned, leaving the abiding power inviolate and the individual feeling weak and alone. Similarly, in the workplace a middle-class public sector employee ethically rejecting new-economy values may also feel impotent, particularly where union membership to redress this power inequity is absent.

Next, speed and fragmentation lead to a weakened psychic state. In new-economy conditions there is the problem of situating the self so that one's choices make sense – that is, so one is motivated toward something in particular. A commonly held view is that as a consequence of accelerated time, 'individuals haven't sufficient reflective distance on themselves to construct linear narrative biographies' (ix). However, paradoxically, as shown in business literature, 'if they are not to fail individuals must be able to plan for the long-term and adapt to change; they must organize and improve, set goals, recognize obstacles, accept defeats and attempt new starts' (4). This places the individual in a position of impossible contradiction: facing forward believing in some form of continuity (otherwise how can planning for the long term make sense?), while behind them the evidence of frequent change piles up, indicating there is only discontinuity.

A different way of looking at the situation is that the future is always by definition unknown, but even if the past appears littered with discontinuity, the single-person perspective is the element that holds these fragments together as a sequential, albeit sometimes erratic, unfolding. The risk in refusing the concept of continuity is that one accedes to the possibility of being flyblown by events, for where time pressure replaces a thoughtful and purposive reflectivity with an instant reflexivity, planning is redundant. Without a space between stimulus and response, one is never able to change one's reaction to a repeated event, or chart a course and attempt to keep to it. That is, no learning can result from experience and our so-called choosing is merely the superficial effect of a deeply affecting but invisible systematic determination that has reduced human response merely to merely Pavlovian reaction.

As Atkins (2004) says, arguing from Schechtman, narrative continuity it is what gives us a reason for caring about personal identity. It allows us to think of ourselves as the same person (albeit a developing character) at different times (Atkins, 2004: 355). Continuity makes reflection on the past part of planning for a future, and so gives us a sensible means to guide action and prevent reflex action diverting one too far from a desired path. In short, continuity gives shape and focus to a life and provides us with reasons to act. Without these, the individual becomes overwhelmed by both the number of decisions to be made and the variety of options presented for each decision, and lacks any guidance for making a purposeful choice. The capacity to posit long-term goals and work steadily towards them typifies the middle class, but holding to that approach is much more difficult when life is experienced as fragmentary and discontinuous. For those already feeling unsure, the total and weighty responsibility for defining the self through action, without a compelling reason to choose any particular direction, would result in the inability to move forward at all, which is the paralysing state of neurosis or identity crisis. Continuity thus supports the maintenance of psychic health.

Bauman (2001) tells us identity crisis is the term Erik H. Erikson applied to 'the confusion suffered by adolescents', likening their condition to that of mental patients who had 'lost a sense of personal sameness and historical continuity' (148). It is clear therefore that, on a personal level, there are serious psychological implications for a population embracing conditions of plasticity where all identities, roles and lifestyles are permanently up for trial and selection. However, Thomas H. Eriksen (2001) sees the benefit of this quasi-adolescence state for employers:

> In every society, adult life is associated with responsibility, predictability and stable commitments. [...] the young (or youthful) person is flexible and ready for new challenges. Who would not rather employ this kind of individual than a predictable person who is certain of his priorities?
>
> (Eriksen, 2001: 135)

However he confirms that subjection to this cult of youthfulness is disastrous 'in other spheres – family, arts, personal development' as it means we 'happily return to square one, priding ourselves on the ability to "remain young", and maturity becomes an outlandish concept' leading only to an increasing number of 'immature and unfixed Peter Pans of both genders often well into their thirties' and beyond. Perma-youths are 'unfixed, uncertain, playful and have an experimental view of life' (131–132). This not only makes them perfect employees for the responsive new economy; it also makes them avid serial consumers with malleable appetites, kept in a state of childlike awe and wonder by advertising, says Thomas Frank (2000: 56, 230–234). Small wonder that capitalist economies requiring ever-growing demand have welcomed the development. Unfortunately, such flexible attitudes are disastrous when applied to changing life partners, treating people like consumer goods to be exchanged once the initial novelty and excitement of 'possession' has dimmed. This group's failed relationships are proof enough that trust, commitment, loyalty and responsibility prove too challenging. In the private sphere the market-valued ability to 'move on' quickly (and uncritically) from failure when things go wrong validates a form of high turnover that compromises the time, attention, maturity and accumulative learning required for successful intimate relationships and self-development. These wider-ranging impacts show the power of the market story for creating and validating our unsettled existence, but these circumstances also threaten traditional family life which, for so long, has been a cornerstone of middle-class existence.

The problem of large numbers existing in immaturity is that most of us can manage well when audacious, courageous and hopeful, but it is another matter entirely to handle anxiety, fear and despair. The underdeveloped adult has no adequate response to difficult and debilitating emotions, and may respond with aggression, avoidance or silent withdrawal. Full character development never occurs if one always instinctively vents one's emotions or is driven on, like Bauman's vagrant, by 'disappointment with the last place he stopped at, and the never-dying hope that the next, as yet unvisited place, or perhaps the one after that, will be free of the defects which have spoiled the ones up to now' (Beck, 2001: 3, quoting Bauman). Managing negative emotions requires the development of different strengths of character whose acquisition involves much longer and harder work. If everything, every identity, every lifestyle is (theoretically) possible but some are easy and some difficult, the question of what route is chosen devolves into one of character – has one developed or can one develop the qualities to attempt the difficult, especially when so much else about life is fraught with anxiety and the hegemonic interest is in keeping the population forever youthful and uncritical? Never has there been greater need to undertake the conscious project of progressively improving and strengthening one's character than now when the serial inhabiting of multiple identities and the accelerated pace of life makes that project seem all the more impossible.

A true choice over who one is – how to live, when to change course and what direction to follow next – is a matter for sound judgement. Yet often, in frenzied modern life, these critical points are reached in a debilitated state without the capacity for such judgement. While both Beck and Bauman would construe any escape as nothing more than just another lifestyle selected, another temporary stopping place, it appears that a fundamental advantage is being looked for when a move beckons – the most critical of which is well-being. Thus when Beck claims that 'time is the key' and 'at the centre of a new ethics is the idea of the quality of life', (2001: 212) he validates that a pause is required for good, ethical decision-making and acknowledges those opting for a slow life may indeed be seeking longer-term happiness.

Ethical identity-making, character development and self-narration

So middle-class family life is threatened and structural dissolution makes individualism a state of confusion, aloneness and fearfulness, which diminishes the confidence by which opportunity is identified and grasped. In addition, accelerated time and the denial of any connection between past, present and future makes forward planning, deferred gratification and belief in control over one's destiny a nonsense and makes narrative continuity (on which psychological health depends) an impossibility.

To understand further the negative impact on middle-class professional identity, it is worth considering the influence of liberal individualism on the group, how its hegemony settled the fault lines of certain dichotomies and where philosophical, economic and ideological development has begun to have effect. Hegemonic models exert considerable power because they are the products of power and therefore carry cultural and social value. Thus, for the middle class, the bourgeois liberal ideal of a self-creating, autonomous, economically accumulative self, characteristically associated with the active, rational, public, male, makes action in accordance with it more probable (especially by those already aligned or willing to align their personal value system to the dominant) but not always possible (it excludes or marginalises some sectors of society, most notably women) and not entirely predictable (because action may be taken in rejection or resistance). In operation, such models variously inform, enable or restrict action and, by determining prescribed and proscribed behaviour, they encourage reinforcement and prompt resistance, but they cannot be said to be universally adopted or applicable and are rarely unequivocally espoused and expressed.

Nevertheless, four key areas of opposition (outlined below) operate through liberal ideology as defining elements of the middle class and also form the matrix of contention with which the texts analysed later in this study engage.

First, the *rational* is opposed to the *emotional*, a conflict expressed also in the clash between *mind* and *body* and the competing authorities of the *intellect* and *heart*. The disembodied Cogito, prioritising the rational, thinking (normally male) individual who gains knowledge and understanding of the world through the process of intellectual enquiry (Descartes), has by default defined emotion, feeling and intuition as (female and) less valuable, as 'un-reasonable', and the bodily or physical as base. Consequently intellectual, abstract work is valued higher than manual work that produces tangible products serving mankind's baser, fundamental needs for survival.

Second, where the *individual* is opposed to the *collective*, the authority of the *self* contends with that of the *self-in-others*. The complex interplay of these oppositions occurs because man or woman does not live alone but in social conditions and her or his needs and happiness must be negotiated with others (Locke) unless they accede to being governed (Hobbes) and/or willingly trade individual freedom for common good. However, through the dominance of individualism, self-mastery and self-sufficiency are prioritised over interdependence, while total dependence is utterly devalued as being typically associated with immaturity and low social class.

Third, the *home/work* dichotomy places the authority of the *self* in opposition to the *corporation or employer*. Social and technological changes occurring at the Industrial Revolution divided the domestic self from the working self, the rural from the urban, and agriculture from business. As mechanisation and automation compromised personal autonomy (Kranzberg and Gies, 1975), a false dichotomy opened between employed (bought) time and leisure (free) time (Adorno ed. Bernstein, 2006). Though accumulation was acceptable, the Protestant ethic valorised work and for those wealthy enough, promoted investment over hedonism. Thus reward was deferred with the greatest return occurring in the afterlife as a result of earthly restraint.

Finally, the *secular*, which rests power with the *state*, is divided from the *sacred* that grants authority to *God or the church*. With the transfer of power from the sacred to the secular, trade disentangles itself from a moralising church that might hamper its activities. Valuable action becomes defined as purposeful, economic and material, thus downgrading the religious and spiritual (Ward, 2003). More recently the authority of the state and church has further diminished and corporate authority has increased.

These elements of liberal ideology form the deep cultural root of the middle class. Founded on values and behaviours associated with the rational (male) independently minded individual, he who worked hard to support his family knew that whatever he accomplished through toil in trade or business would be of credit to him now and in the hereafter. Furthermore, all of this was under his control providing he could demonstrate the character, drive and restraint that would achieve it. All seems possible to the individual working within stable and secure structures, because he feels confident and positive about negotiating those unchanging forms. However, the particular nature of free market politics and economics underpinning the liberal model today is delivering some members of that class into a state of destabilised confusion and impotence. When the fluidity on which business now operates dispenses with those knowable and negotiable forms, casting the individual adrift, independence turns into less comfortable aloneness, insecurity and separation. On the other hand, scientific rationality, once providing the secure anchorage of knowledge, now becomes a binding chain in its guise of mathematical auditing applied to production through the now ubiquitous personal development plan. Another conundrum arises when the demands of home and work become utterly incompatible. Then, the middle-class parent is faced with the dilemma of betraying one's family values or compromising the career prospects on which that family depends. Furthermore, when secular economic endeavour and conspicuous consumption fail to deliver sufficient differential status and well-being, the hollowness of consumption and accumulation bought at the entire sacrifice of free time is all too evident and yet heaven as a reward is gone too. Thus is the bedrock of middle-class life called into question.

A weakened value system leaves the individual without guidance for considered action for 'when we reflect upon our situations and look for reasons to guide our actions, we appeal to those beliefs, feelings and ideas that have the capacity to move or motivate us' (Atkins, 2004: 362). It is these values, having stood the test of time, that inform planning and so give shape, focus and direction to a life, but if they seem no longer possible or profitable to hold, the basis of one's identity is threatened. Workplace pressure for a radical shift of ethical position and the confusion of flexibility's chaos can leave one feeling extremely uncomfortable and out of personal control. Generally, changes to one's value schema are made by a more deliberate and thoughtful, internally directed process. We are acculturated to the social and cultural values of the personal circumstances we are born into (Bourdieu, 1984), and in the growth to maturity, by virtue of reason and imagination, and through the development of critical faculties and experience, we question, keep, modify or reject these values. In effect, this is a process of evaluation whereby one prefers, adopts and constantly tests certain values against others. By choosing one 'good' over another either repeatedly or differently in a change of direction, individual identity is always a present reflection of sets of (consciously or unconsciously) adopted values that are used as a measure of consistency, for the guidance of future action and as a model for continuing, coherent selfhood. Thus one might consider oneself rational rather than emotional, active rather than passive, and so on with the opposing traits subdominant rather than erased.

Thus one's 'set' of personally adopted values guiding (moral) action can never be totally coherent (or consistent). Any held position is always under threat from opposing forces and, under duress, fractures to expose its own contradictions, which, if both evident and strong, cause existential paralysis. Conflict occurs through engagement with other systems, including those personified by other individuals, when one's defined relationship to a schema of meaning created through experience is shown by further particular experience to be erroneous. When the 'story' one tells oneself about the world and the self – one's worldview – is radically disrupted or challenged, or in some way 'cannot hold', the moment essentially signals a point of critical transition or development; a potential for revolution rather than evolution.

At such points we become Hamlet. When opposition presents with equal validity and force, the negotiation that affects resolution stalls and the self becomes confused and immobile. The problem turns over and over in the mind and the agent exists in a perpetual present – in stasis and unable to act – unable to 'move on'. This is classic Freudian trauma. Importantly, its symptom is a lack of ability to articulate; its cure is essentially an act of narration that is able to accommodate the disruptive event into a rearticulated and once again coherent view (Mukherjee, 2001). Narration, then, is essentially the means by which order is imposed on life (even an individual life) as it is on literature. The coherent story is like the coherent self – well structured and affording the comfort of order imposed as the *apparent* remedy of contradictions which are still under the surface and there to be uncovered by analysis or challenged by criticism.

The reflective moment is necessary for critical judgement and the key tool is objectivity: the self as it sees itself, or the self presented with external data that is used as qualifying information, i.e. the other life as a measure. It is the reflective structure of consciousness that (time permitted) allows self-criticism of a kind that can direct action and facilitate deliberate authoring and narration of the developing self. Without that moment for judgement (which is now compromised by accelerated time), the self is static, either in neurosis as described, or locked into a loop of repetition where nothing is learnt from experience. A fully developed and dynamic identity is achieved in and through time. It is a project of continuity having antecedents in something recognised as the past that forms the basis for reasoning and hope in an imagined future. With reflection before action, the loop becomes a spiral so that even when experiences are repeated, one is already further along the path of learning than when a similar situation was last encountered. Action in such circumstances is not reflexive but recursive.

Autobiography makes concrete that reflective moment while those texts resting on continuity and coherent narrative are also the bid to counter the impact on identity of modern life's 'biographical uncertainties'. The deliberation and developmental action witnessed through autobiography is possible because:

> in writing or self-representation (like autobiography), the *I* is the self-present subject of the sentence as well as the subject 'subjected' to the symbolic order of the language in which one is writing – the subject is subject to language, or inter-subjectivity (i.e. culture).
>
> (Gagnier, 1991: 9)

Taking this to imply that writing is the point of intersection between subject and the institution of language – that it is indeed produced by the dynamic relationship between self and structure – it is therefore a medium within which challenge to institutional order can be made. At the very least, writing is the bid to lever a space between the subject and the means by which that subject is subjected (language); it is a way to impact on or even change the discourse, even if it is not a method of freeing oneself from it. Both autobiography and novel writing began as bourgeois forms, and even where realism has taken the latter to the murky depths of the ordinary and everyday (and surfaced in the hyper-real of soap operas), writing is still the reflective surface of inner consciousness, is an external form that allows the objectivity necessary for evaluation. As such it is no surprise to find these forms, particularly autobiography, which is singularly fit for purpose, being used by middle-class authors to grapple with and settle questions of identity while at the same time providing a counter-narrative to the over-determining corporate-speak discussed in the previous chapter.

In summary, current ideas of inter-subjectivity suppose a dynamic relationship between self and structure, each having power to modify the other. The self is neither entirely institutionally determined nor self-determined, but is continually created and recreated at (and as) a point of convergence of (mostly unknowable) external influence and its (equally uncertain) interplay on genetic make-up and personal experience. Identity-making in today's fluid conditions is no longer referenced to the normative categories afforded by structure and relies ultimately on the agent acting in accordance with a personally adopted value scheme. The problem is that fast and flexible life diminishes the opportunity for the reflection and forward planning required for deliberate action towards identified long-term goals. Accelerated time presses us to act quickly and reflexively, making an almost unthinking response, while overstretch across all areas of life can recommend the easy route as the only practical possibility. Beck thinks action conceived from within old social categories is likely to be habitual and customary (2001: 6), but it is actually more likely that the instinctual responses made under circumstances of confusion and duress will be reflexive and non-developmental.

Despite the biographical uncertainties resulting from the supposed freedom of choice over identity it is evident that constraints, originating in the labour market, still bind, not least because those so thoroughly engaged in the effort to maintain their security by keeping the plates of life spinning withdraw from political action. Flexible conditions might well offer opportunity, but not everybody is equally placed to take the advantage, while the individual who is marketed to as a constituency of one is likely to feel not independent, but separated and alone. Where fragmentation and immediacy concentrate attention on the present moment, an appreciation of historical time and narrative continuity is required for psychic health. Without a means to establish continuity, one suffers an identity crisis and can remain in a position of neurosis and/or arrested character development. In classical psychological theory, an act of narration is required at this point as the means to clarify identity and maintain good mental health.

In recognising that self-development comes through deliberated action but is subject to various forms of influence, the force with particular resonance and authority for the middle class in Western economies is the liberal hegemony. However, the certainties once supporting its ideology have been modified, and the structures that once upheld them dissolved, creating insecurity and challenging the bedrock concepts of rationality, independence, satisfying and purposeful work and secular endeavour leading to heavenly reward. At points of such destabilisation, there is a danger of neurosis and/or identity crisis that is harder to handle by those whose proper self-development to maturity is arrested by the market's creation of persons made ready for mindless consumerism. Recovery to a defensible, stable position where action is ethically guided comes only when the subject is able, with reflection to settle the contradictions (at least apparently and temporarily) through the creation and belief in an acceptable 'story' about the self and the world. Thus the autobiographic act is, at once, the formal effort to secure that identity and a challenge to the discourse that caused the original trauma.

The plight and flight of the middle-class professional

Another difficulty facing the professional lies in the prospect that any threat to the distinctiveness on which their middle-class identity rests also threatens their position of privilege and power. This is more critical than it might at first appear, because the solidarity of their class is already problematic before the wholesale breaking down of categories occurred. Most commentators agree that the British middle class cannot be conceived of as homogeneous, though it is possible to identify certain sector interests that oppose the concerns of other sectors within the middle class or those of other classes. Alan Kidd and David Nicholls, in *The Making of the Middle Class?* (1998), state that the category:

> is stratified, with enormous differentials in the power and influence, income and status, between the *haute bourgeoisie* at one extreme end and the *petite bourgeoisie* at the other [...] the differences are compounded by religion, education and politics [...] further complicated by the fact that individuals do not live out their lives within neat, homogeneous social categories.
>
> (Kidd and Nicholls, 1998: xxv)

Michael Savage *et al.* (1992) see the difficulty with definition as a problem of a number of antagonisms – anti-Thatcherist versus pro-Thatcherist, public versus private, and entrepreneurial versus professional versus managerial interests (Savage *et al.*, 1992: 186–187, quoting Mallett, 188, 194). King and Nugent (1979) believe this diversity within the middle class leads to internal contradictions, e.g. a public servant concerned with job security would oppose the independent entrepreneur's call for less state intervention (13). In the US, Ehrenreich (1989) considers 'the very ubiquity of the professional middle class makes it vexingly difficult to write about *as a distinct class*' (5, original emphasis).

Much commentary, therefore, concerns itself with attempts both to disentangle the complexities of stratification and to characterise sectors sufficiently to identify subdivisions that are workable for the purposes of analysis. Two of the more readily understandable and enduring ways of categorising the middle class are by occupation and motivation. The types of occupation are generally held to include 'the professions – business men, managers above the grade of foreman, most farmers, the majority of the public service, most shopkeepers, a substantial number of clerks, other non-manual workers, and some independent craftsmen', and the key motivations are the desire for independence and deferred gratification (King and Nugent, 1979: 9 quoting Lewis and Maude, and Hutber). So workplace over-determination by new-economy values reliant on ever-greater volumes of consumption is particularly problematic.

Two further connected circumstances contribute to middle-class vulnerability. The first concerns the reducing differentials between middle and working class caused by a 'growing proletarianisation of middle-class jobs' and a dilution of middle-class ranks through recruitment to its numbers of those from working-class origins (Savage *et al.*, 1992: 187). Linked to this loss of distinction, and of key relevance to the middle-class professional, is increasing management control and the downgrading of professional work, both of which affect autonomy and status. By 1979, structural changes had already brought middle-managers 'under much more meaningful control of the top echelons of management' (Edwards, 1979: 141, 182):

> for middle-layer workers [...] the loss of control over the labor process has been as complete as for the other fractions of the

working class [...] Workers superficially have more autonomy [b]ut their situation fails the test of true autonomy, since such workers cannot decide anything about either the product of their work or their labor process; control over these fundamentals passed out of their hands when they became wage (or salary) workers. Instead, bureaucratic methods foster indirect control or 'self-control'. For they function in the interest not of the worker but of his or her employer.

(Edwards, 1979: 193)

In addition, new-economy rationalisations begin to affect middle sector professionals as well as less skilled employees. In the 1980s, when lower-status workers were ' "peripheral" and "numerically flexible" [...] employed on temporary contracts and easily dispensed with', professionals were, temporarily, 'insulated from the external labour market' by their specialist skills (Savage et al., 1992: 62). However, a work culture prizing flexibility ultimately devalues specialism. Certainly, in the public sector, developing employees to a set of HR-regulated competencies, effectively making them functionally interchangeable, has all but eroded the difference on which specialist knowledge and particular worth depend. In addition, where quality gives way to cost, government departments and public institutions are replacing professionals with cheaper, white-collar workers or other alternatives – PhD students substitute for fully qualified academics, nurses for doctors, teaching assistants for trained teachers, and temporary, self-tutored agency staff with carefully crafted CVs for every specialist functionary. The fuller embedding of new-economy principles make professionals equally subject to the market's vagaries by having their work downgraded, their specialist functions diluted, their positions reduced in number and their work outsourced. Where they do remain, the professionally qualified are pressured by demands from two directions. They are expected both to do work above their pay grade *and* to take on demeaning and routine administration and secretarial work, absorbing these functions and their separate associated costs within the same hours and pay contract, with overload covered by the addition of imprecise catch-all clauses requiring 'such additional duties as may be required from time to time'. Not equipped in managerial terms (or unwilling) to join the organisational power coalitions, and too specialised, and therefore expensive, to use as numerically flexible labour, their midpoint position is one of precarious ambivalence.

This insecure middle position is the second factor of note. King and Nugent say the traditional Marxian division between 'the bourgeoisie – the owners and controllers of productive property – and the working class, who sell their labour power to these capitalists' appears to define the middle ground as void (King and Nugent, 1979: 10). In fact, where the middle-class professional is concerned, the increasing polarisation of the *haute bourgeoisie* power elite above, and other white-collar workers without specialist knowledge below, creates a culture divided principally into market winners and losers, metaphorically erasing the middle ground on which that professional is located.

Who am I?

In *Fear of Falling*, Ehrenreich (1989) also argues that the unstable and contradictory central position creates a crisis for those occupying it. The dynamics of Western, post-Fordist economies present them with a stark choice – absorption into the undifferentiated realm of 'ordinary' waged labour, or the prospect, for only a few, of obtaining a footing in the higher echelons of an elite upper management where they cream off high status and high pay far in excess of that which all professionals used to enjoy.

Ehrenreich defines the professional middle class as having 'economic and social status based on education, rather than the ownership of property or capital' (Ehrenreich, 1989: 12). Once seen as the 'universal class' having 'a culture everywhere represented as representing everyone' (4), they were distinguished by achieving their protected status and above-average income through effort rather than inheritance and by their cultural assets – home ownership, enriching travel, lifestyle and consumption experiences – which indicated their 'taste' and ensured no mis-identity with lower-class types (14).

However, in the 1960s they became categorised by authentic hardworking citizens as an 'isolated elite, pretentiously liberal and despised', and by their own offspring as a class that doesn't really 'do' anything (because visible poverty showed their political failure to be socially instrumental and Taylorism had abstracted managing from producing) (143). In the New Right backlash that followed, the traditional antagonisms between professional intellectual independence and the business interests of the corporate elite took new impetus. Defence of that professional autonomy persists where 'professors may risk firing to express an unpopular opinion, [and] executives occasionally blow the whistle on an unsafe product or unethical procedure' (157). In the yuppie era, professionals could either sell their services to business to maintain their economic position (as Ehrenreich puts it, abandon 'sociology and public service for banking and management' (158)), or face the downward economic spiral as a middling income no longer made possible the kinds of differentiation on which their specific identity rested. Even if yuppie hedonism served to compensate for the 'loss of an intrinsically rewarding profession' (240), it brought with it the guilt of intemperance. The difficulty through the 1980s was maintaining a clear identity uneasily balanced between the hard work and discipline that secures affluence and the excessive self-indulgence such wealth allows. Letting up threatened social and economic decline, while the spectre of indulgence brings a fear of 'going soft', so 'whether the middle class looks down towards the realm of less, or up toward the realm of more, there is the fear, always, of falling' (15).

Where the dominance of market enterprise makes market 'winners' into a kind of human elite, all other values are subordinated to the economic imperative. Professionals unwilling or unable to trade up on their talent to stay ahead find wider-spread affluence leaves them without the differentiation on which their economic, social and occupational identity rests and with the falling relative income that Layard considers contributes to unhappiness (Layard, 2005: 41–53). In all, this class is facing hazards on many fronts. It is therefore unsurprising that when these identity pressures manifest through workplace reforms in which some 'lose their places' (either literally in redundancy or figuratively in weakening professional status), the result is a devastating blow to self-esteem and self-assurance. Add the overwork caused by lean efficiency, the surveillance of auditing and personal development processes, the stress of a groaning email inbox and the preferment of youthful responsiveness over mature knowledge, and it is easy to see the sources of currently increasing psychological confusion, poor mental health and the drive for identity security.

Back to the future – putting the 'self' on a firmer footing

For those whose identity rested on the stable footings of older organisational models, the replacement structures, practices and institutions of the new economy may indicate what one is *not* and does not *want to be*. As discussed more fully in Chapter 1, many middle-class professionals who have hung on to a residual sense of their position and social contribution in the institutions of public service now find this threatened by private business values that introduce a fundamental contradiction – a market culture incompatible with the service ethos through which much of their satisfaction of work derives. For this sector, 'buying in' to the market ethos is the flip side of 'selling out' the values inherent in their class, professional status and public office.[3] At the same time, buy-in is encouraged by vast amounts of corporate literature that effectively silences or drowns out opposition. CEOs wielding 'immense power over us, and over management control systems that structure the working lives of countless employees' decree that 'conformity with the ideological values of the CEO [...] is compulsory for those who wish to retain their positions' (Amernic and Craig, 2006: 81, 138). So, for continuing employment, professionals find themselves, at once, without autonomy, threatened with erasure through a lack of distinction from other workers, standing out by virtue of their unwillingness to participate, and with an uphill struggle to voice resistance effectively against the corporate communication machine.

Musson and Duberley (2007) acknowledge how participation discourse directing employees 'to develop self-images and work orientations that are deemed congruent with managerially defined objectives, [...] bears down on actors and actions [...] targeting and moulding the human subject' (148). They note also the various strategies used to resist this pressurised moulding (silence, alternative discourse, superficial performed compliance, compartmentalisation). However, they say nothing about how the 'internal inconsistencies' (148, quoting Knights and McCabe) so produced are handled by the subject, beyond stating that understanding 'the impact and importance that life outside the work environment can have on the way that individuals interpret the work role' (162) is needed. Indeed, interviewed employees 'in the middle of the organization' (145) 'almost always linked [their responses about participation] to discussion of who they were' (150), which suggests that employees' interaction with managerial discourse still centres on a consistent, self-controlled and self-expressed identity crossing the work/home boundary (as was the case in Mayo's experiment), and that dissonance is unacceptable.

However, the need for a consistent selfhood seems to counter theories of identity as 'always relational, produced within a specific context for a specific purpose' (147, quoting Karreman and Alvesson). Certainly, Musson and Duberley quote a number of commentators who claim that a belief in identity as an 'amalgam of multiple, diverse and sometimes contradictory narratives' must necessarily 'challenge the accepted belief that people strive to be consistent and produce a definitive identity narrative' (147). This is not so. Those subscribing to multiple identity theory do no more than observe and understand that we have become adept at reading the nuances and coded requirements in various complex social situations in order to behave acceptably and appropriately (Goffman, 1986). This study suggests that the need for coherent self-narration extends beyond temporary fixes and indicates that people do indeed 'strive to be consistent and produce a definitive narrative', that this consistency is guided by personally held, enduring (even if dynamically developing) values able to direct action and express identity at work, at home and in various other social situations.

The bid for definitive narration indicates that the extent to which we will bend is constrained by what aspects we *are* willing to accept as a characteristic of our self and what we will not. In fact, one is acutely aware and even uncomfortable when one is required to perform a role that is too far removed from what one knows of oneself; the performance is often poor and evidently false. Even organisational identity fails when its external presentations are at odds with its inner self (public relations, as opposed to spin, works on a required correspondence between 'show' and reality). However, where the inanimate organisation has no emotional or psychological response to dissonance, human agents required to perform a role at odds with values they know or own (i.e. to act out of character) certainly do.

Those who rise up the management ladder are one of two types: either what the organisation requires of them is what they require of themselves, in which case they are, in effect, truly suitable for high corporate office, or they survive on a daily basis by bringing into play strategies to cope with the dissonance. There are a number who can neither manage the dissonance nor find the management role to their liking, and still more not willing to align with the corporate values or to adopt expressions of flexibility, change and future orientation that define them as new economy company men and women. It is possible that their middle position, in which 'they do not align themselves with the shop floor workers, but neither do they define themselves as "management"' (Musson and Duberley, 2007: 155), poses a dilemma of allegiance at work that parallels and magnifies the growing insecurities already felt in their perplexed central class and social position. The fact that they are generally held to be the cohort most resistant to organisational change could also indicate how much is at stake if they are made to declare partisanship either way.

If neither option is acceptable they may opt out altogether; may hold on to traditional notions of autonomy, hanker for stabilities rooted in place and time, and seek fulfilment in different modes of work. Trading their ever-eroding status and pay for a lifestyle espousing alternative values at least has the merit of being an active decision about identity rather than a passive acceptance of one imposed by a corporation. Capturing that choice and subsequent identity development would almost be second nature to a sector once having ubiquitous influence on a culture 'in which it both stars and writes the scripts' (Ehrenreich, 1989: 6).

Resistant response

The fact remains that it is possible to express a more coherent stable identity in a variety of ways, so the question arises about why this social sector, in particular, seeks to articulate their need through more practical, creative and artistic activity (discussed in later chapters) and take, sometimes, a rather radical step to do so. For the answer, illumination is provided in the observation that Marx's binary formulation nevertheless 'recognises both the persistence of the "old" middle class of farmers, artisans and professionals, and the development of the new middle class of white collar employees, managers and administrators with the growth of the state and large corporation' (King and

Nugent, 1979: 10). The migration of many from the working class taking up white-collar employment and the increasing administration devaluing professional skills are problematic issues for those already occupying the middle ground. However, surely the recognition of a 'persistent' category of 'farmers, artisans and professionals' presents an uncanny coincidence for a study claiming disaffected professionals find solace in horticulture (farming), baking and writing (artistry)?

It is even more surprising to find that a public sector professional's preference for resistant action is supported by research on occupation and voting profiles which finds that 'in terms of political alignments the public sector professional middle class is increasingly isolated from other middle-class groupings and is attracted to a more radical politics' (Savage *et al*. 1992: 218). In fact, a fault line occurs between 'private sector professionals [...] clearly distinctive as an up and coming group [...] of professional specialists [...] attracted to a "post-modern" culture [...] consistent with a generally Conservative political orientation' (195) and 'the "creative and welfare professions" as a relatively more radical group' (194) who Savage *et al*. define as 'public sector workers [...] consistently less likely to vote Conservative' (195). In addition, the habitus of the public sector middle class can already 'be seen as simultaneously a product of deliberate choice (one rejecting competitive individualism and marketplace values) while at the same time being a rationalisation of their comparatively low incomes' (110).[4] Savage *et al*. identify also that 'cultural assets may be the basis for distinctive political profiles', claiming that 'the significance of the "creative and welfare professions" as a relatively more radical group within the service class [...] suggests that the "ascetic lifestyle" goes hand in hand with a relatively radical politics' (194). Indeed, their conclusion distinguishes the 'conspicuous extravagance of the private sector professionals, who indulge in new types of sports and fitness regimes along with exotic holidays and luxury consumption' from 'the old cultural distinctiveness associated with the public sector middle class where there is a close reliance on traditional creative forms of "high culture," such as classical music, art, literature and so forth' (212–213). Given these alignments, doctors, teachers, lecturers, vets, social workers, civil servants and others of their ilk seem rather well prepared historically, culturally and politically for exactly the resistant response described in this study.

So in all, for those of the public sector professional middle class who confront a number of stark contradictions in relation to their work and social identities, four elements converge to predispose their interest in creative activity associated with an alternative slower, land-based lifestyle. These are: the importance of particular artistic cultural assets for this sub-sector; their affinity as a displaced group along with farmers and artisans; their growing radicalisation; and, not yet mentioned, that 'the progressive nature of the politics of this class is frequently illustrated by reference to its involvement in "new social movements", especially the environment movement' to which the various 'slow' movements are allied. As a result of the 'profound ramifications for middle-class politics' when 'Thatcherism [...] moved towards a market-oriented, anti-statist politics, seen by some as linked to the development of a "Post-Fordist" economy' (Savage *et al.*, 1992: 207, 202), and because studies of middle-class political activism show that diversity within the class has prejudiced collective resistance (King and Nugent, 1979; Savage *et al.*, 1992), small-scale, even individual, acts of resistance are unsurprising. These uncoordinated individual responses are entirely in keeping with an ideal of middle-class self-reliance. They mark the impulse to realign one's daily actions with a personal code of ethics while the interest shown in lifestyles able to capture and express in a creative and literary form the coherence and distinction is the effort to preserve a failing identity through a new form of cultural, as well as social and economical, distinction.

The downshifting phenomenon

There is evidence that the experience of employees in competitive Western-style economies is linked to the downshifting phenomenon in which the disaffected reject the empty promises of consumerism in favour of other lifestyles. Research by Breakspear and Hamilton (2004a) on Australian downshifters confirms a profound dissatisfaction with the stressful pace and values of the workplace. Respondents, who speak of their relief from a malign culture characterised by 'bullshit' and 'worries, stressing about it, plotting and planning and scheming, writing all those lists about how to achieve', are evidently happy to distance themselves from the misery, unethical behaviour and the pressure to succeed in the particular way defined by late twentieth- and early twenty-first-century work (Breakspear and Hamilton, 2004a: 18). Similarly, in the UK, while downshifters come from a variety of social grades and make a number of resistant responses, the drive to opt out comes invariably from experience of the relentless pace and all-time-and-mind-consuming pressures of the market-driven work environment that compromises individual fulfilment and personal health. In fact, the increasing burden of work that overwhelms 'all other life goals' means that 'among executives a breakdown in health is often the only factor that will cause them to reassess their working lives' (2003c: 8).[5] Hamilton's statistics (2003c) show that of the Western-style economies, Britain had the highest proportion (25%) of downshifters aged between 30 and 59 over the previous decade, a figure considered 'remarkably high and much higher than previous estimates' (vii). The principal pull for lifestyle change (in descending order) is the feeling that 'more time with the family and less stress, rather than more income, would make them happier', or wanting 'to gain more control and personal fulfilment' or achieve a 'healthier' or 'more balanced lifestyle' (19).[6]

According to Hamilton:

> [British] downshifters are spread fairly evenly across the social grades although with a slightly higher proportion (27%) amongst grades A and B [professionals, senior managers, business executives, bank managers, university lecturers, middle managers in large firms and senior officers in government organisations] and a lower share (23%) amongst social grade E [those on benefits and the long-term unemployed].
> (Hamilton, 2003c: 15, 23).[7]

With reference both to this social spread and the variety of ways that downshifters alter their lifestyles – including cutting hours but staying in an urban environment – Hamilton concludes downshifting is not confined to the 'wealthier individuals who [...] can afford to take the risk', and that 'survey results immediately dispel the widespread myth that downshifting means selling up in the city and shifting to the countryside to live a life closer to nature' (vii). However, those downshifting but remaining in urban areas still promote lifestyles gesturing toward values and timescales that are implicit in agricultural or horticultural living.[8]

While not disputing the diversity of these findings, interesting observations may nevertheless be made about the AB (middle-class professional) sector of society. In fact, Hamilton also pays special attention to the problems of identity for the AB group, noting that '[s]uccess in the United Kingdom is now powerfully associated with affluence and putting one's achievements on display through conspicuous forms of consumption' (1). However, conspicuous consumption has particular ramifications for the happiness of the middle class in a market culture, for:

> half of those in the richest income groups in the United Kingdom [...] are caught up in an endless endeavour to make their incomes match their desires for material success, and because their desires always outstrip their incomes they feel constantly deprived. This phenomenon has been dubbed 'a culture of middle-class complaint'.
>
> (Hamilton, 2003c: 25)

While this feeling of deprivation fuels the continued and increasing effort at work and the spending required to support a growing economy, the realisation by many that the levels they wish for are unattainable, and that affluence and shopping do not provide lasting fulfilment, is leading more to consider wealth to be 'far fewer things, a little more time' (de Blasi, 2004: 217) and to contemplate downshifting as a way to 'break the link between money and happiness' (2004b: 5).

It is the re-evaluation of what constitutes wealth and well-being that ultimately leads to the decision to live a different, less frenzied life in the search for fulfilment. This occurs when potential downshifters begin to account for the many losses incurred by earning enough to keep pace with a never-satisfied consumer desire, including the loss of freedom to self-define against market values and the loss of the personal relationships that make life worthwhile.[9] It is the misery and futility of an ongoing struggle towards a goal that is never achieved that has produced 'a large class of citizens who consciously reject consumerism and material aspirations [and] agree that the excessive pursuit of money and materialism comes at a substantial cost to their own lives and those of their families'. That cost includes 'those who are the prisoners of overwork and debt, and find themselves beset by stress, ill-health and family strain' (Hamilton, 2003c: x). Hamilton's research, therefore, supports the argument of this book that although the primacy of the economic good 'is an assumption rarely challenged' (1), many are discontented and stressed by the high work levels and fast production timescales that support a materialist culture in which 'money-hunger conflicts with their deeper values and preferences' (vii). In fact, 'Eighty-seven per cent of respondents believe that British society is too materialistic, with too much emphasis on money and not enough on the things that really matter' (3) and downshifters dispute (and ethically challenge) the values implied by a consumerist culture that encourages 'maximising incomes, often at the expense of other aspects of life' (25). When that dispute translates into escape from formal employment, those with substantial assets choosing the wholesale switch to a self-sufficient lifestyle abroad make evident to others the promise such lifestyles hold for any who disengage with free market living even on a more modest scale.

Middle-class complainers, who by virtue of an educational advantage (and consequent language skills) can consider emigration, are likely also to be most socially and culturally able for a life of self-sufficiency and self-making abroad, and most financially fit for the capital expenditure on property and/or land and the substantial (and typically bourgeois) risk-taking this 'foreign' life entails.[10] Certainly, those turning to writing make use of their social and cultural capital, such as the networking skills and familiarity with communications practices, practitioners and technologies that are essential advantages in getting published. This group may not be typical, but by studying emigrants who choose to live a life closer to nature, it is possible to see more clearly how natural rhythms of time operate as an attractive countermeasure to fast life, and to interpret what slowing down means for selfhood even for those who opt to downsize but stay in the UK and to read that resistant action in terms of ethical identity.

However, before turning to specific examples validating this claim, we look next at a novel by one of the UK's most renowned writers – Ian McEwan – to see how the concerns for professional identity of a fictional character working in the public sector are reflected in an item of mainstream cultural production.

Notes

1. See also Eriksen (2001: 121–141).
2. See the government portal, www.direct.gov.uk/en/index.htm, which represents the interface of the institution and the individual, and organises its communications by supply events. Age-related categories acknowledge linear, sequential time while a subsection directed at living abroad indicates that these days, migration or 'escape' is considered a more likely part of life experience.
3. Paul du Gay (2007) says selling out only becomes an issue where one's passions have been annexed to work identity. Older models of 'office holding' never infer that behaviour at work is anything other than role play.
4. Savage *et al.* also claim that Bourdieu's schema of cultural capital is difficult to pattern from the French to the English middle class, as he deals with the French middle class as a homogeneous group and does not distinguish between industrialists, managers and professionals, which are distinct sectors of the English system.
5. See van Gelder (1998). Schor sees overspending as a means 'to avoid dealing with ugly status and class issues' by those 'living at an incredibly high level of economic insecurity every day, whether or not they're consciously aware of it'.
6. The figure of 25% compares with 23% for Australia and 19% for US. See Parkins and Craig (2006: 45).
7. Though other grades (C1, C2, D and E) appear not far behind AB, Hamilton states 'It should be noted that these are reported social grades *after* the change in life so some downshifters may have moved down a grade or two' (emphasis added). This makes the bias towards AB more pronounced.
8. Though downshifting does not necessarily require a move to the country, the urban exodus is documented in books such as *Moving to a Small Town: A Guidebook to Moving From Urban to Rural America* by Levering and Urbanska (1996), while publications promoting simplicity and/or self-sufficiency in an urban setting, such as *Backyard Self-Sufficiency* (Jackie French, 2005), *Self-Reliance: A Recipe for the New Millennium* (John Yeoman, 1999) and *Living the Good Life: How One Family Changed Their World from Their Own Backyard* (Linda Cockburn, 2007) are still ideologically 'rural'. The narrower focus of this study on the AB group, which includes those more wealthy who do move to a rural (and sometimes overseas) environment, specifically facilitates analysis and comparison of the effects of temporality on identity under different conditions by reading through and across the characteristic dispositions of a particular class profile.
9. Layard (2005) found that, as we are social beings, relationships are key to our happiness. Socialising makes us most happy (after sex) (15), and separating from a partner decreases happiness by the greatest degree (64).
10. Once emigrants have left the country, their opinions are not available for canvassing. Their exclusion from UK national surveys therefore means the views of the disaffected are never fully captured and the number downshifting is almost certainly higher.

3
Trauma
Ian McEwan's *Saturday*: a tale of the vulnerable professional

Introduction

A number of the points discussed in the previous chapters concerning work conditions and identity security appear in McEwan's *Saturday* (2005). Part of the reason for examining them here is to demonstrate how the influence of the market economy is so pervasive, so culturally embedded, that the themes already identified and their effect on the public sector individual, are captured, reflected and (to some extent) normalised in mainstream artistic production. The argument presented is that Baxter's physical attack on Henry Perowne's person has a subtextual parallel in the assault to his psychic health caused by his work conditions. It starts with a discussion that contextualises the impact of contemporary work conditions and structural fragmentation on identity among historical, sociological and philosophical background. Next, narration is shown to be vital for psychic health, and story a key instrument by which we understand ourselves and construct our worldview. This includes a discussion of the fluid boundaries of fact and fiction that allow self-delusion as a necessary element of creating and maintaining a recognisable identity and the use of life stories as the measure, which by comparison, inform our own. Finally, analysis of the subtext illustrates a clash between self and institution in which professional insecurity indicates Perowne's bid for identity survival when time pressure and the demands of a flexible, responsive, new-economy business model threaten to overwhelm him.

The demands of business on identity

The institutional attempt to bend employees to its way of thinking and being is part of a well-rehearsed debate of industrial history (Hobsbawm, 1982). The human cost to workers whose efforts secured national economic growth but whose physical and psychic health suffered in the process is noted in Karl Marx's comment that 'the alienated character of the work for the worker appears in the fact that... in work he does not belong to himself but to another person' (Kranzberg and Gies, 1975: 123–124). It is tempting to think this an outdated circumstance, but incorrect given the strategies of corporate communication driving the new economy agenda and their mostly damaging effect on employees. However, the impact on public sector professionals flows also from the particular socio-historical conditions of their class, as seen earlier.

Through most of the twentieth century, occupation was a critical marker of identity and status. So fixed were the social structures that the work undertaken or professions joined indicated not only where we had 'got to' in life but often where we had come from. Admittance to the professions was by qualification and, until the mid-century when social mobility through education began to take effect, one of the key determinants was class. It was the middle class that aspired to, and entered, professions such as law, medicine and teaching, and having done so, felt secure in their personal value and social position. They could reasonably expect to remain so, provided they behaved ethically in accordance with the values of the chosen profession and, in gaining greater knowledge and experience, could expect to enhance that status and security further. This is no longer the case and what can be seen in *Saturday* is that contemporary business methods and processes threaten Perowne's professional identity and undermine both his status and security as he loses control over aspects of his life.

Any loss of autonomy is problematic because it is incompatible with the acculturating values of Western liberal individualism, which school the human subject to believe its achievement is possible. Williams observes that 'in any actual society there are specific inequalities in means and therefore in capacity to realise this process [of defining and shaping their whole lives]' (Williams, 1977: 108). Certainly, self-government appears more possible for the socially dominant sectors of society than it does for others, and historically, the professional and management ranks have used the philosophy of self-realisation to fuller advantage. This premise of self-management extends through a complex of attendant scientific rationalist principles that prioritise thinking over feeling, activity over passivity, independence over dependence or interdependence, and the economic and material over the spiritual and immaterial, affording individuals an understanding (and a measure of control) over their situation and sovereignty over their character. Moreover, the philosophy accredits individuals with the ability, through hard work, to shape their own destiny, and where this does not seem possible it remains an unfulfilled promise.

However, conditions of employment have altered greatly following the IT revolution of the late twentieth century and, as we have seen in Chapter 1, despite the rhetoric, the opportunities for self-management (unless in sanctioned directions) are limited. In fact, changes in organisational structure, from a known and negotiable hierarchical model to an amorphous horizontal one, together with demands for market-responsiveness, have created conditions of instability and disorientation in which one is required to jump from job to job and move on quickly and uncritically from failure. Other factors associated with this structural dissolution, according to Sennett (1998), are the loss of valid authority, risk taken without responsibility, the devaluing of knowledge and experience, and the replacement of defined gratifications with 'desire'. As a result Sennett has found 'a large group of middle-class individuals who felt their lives were cast adrift' (Sennett, 2006: 7).

Now that corporate practice is being adopted by the public sector, the subjectivity of an ever-widening group of white-collar workers and professionals is being negatively affected by a market-driven, technologically enabled capitalism whose by-products are an increasing pace, larger workloads and growing volumes of information exchange. In addition to stress, these conditions inhibit the necessary reflection required for self-critical awareness that enables deliberate action; thus self-determination and agency are compromised further. Any form of 'escape' from these conditions (either literally or imaginatively) is effectively an act of resistance by which the individual signals the importance of self-evaluation, self-definition and intentional action or agency. Literature plays a key role in this act of resistance. While reading any text provides temporary, imaginary escape, the proliferation of autobiographical memoirs presenting the possibility of other lifestyles based on productive, time-dependent, measured (as in rhythmic, not bureaucratically counted) labour is evidence of that resistance and of narrative self-making that simultaneously records the fulfilling work through which that self is brought into being. On the other side of that literary equation, McEwan's novel is a creative illustration of the forces that cause breakdown and make escape necessary, and of the role that story and particular types of activity play to enable recovery.

Narration and psychic health

There are two important coordinates when contemplating the reason for these autobiographical acts at this time. First, individuals are socially embedded and find that when the relational structures to which they are connected disintegrate, then identity similarly loses its coherence. In other words, as the subsequent textual analysis shows, the relationship between self and structure is an affective, dynamic one. Second, the inability to 'make a narrative of one's life' is a keenly-felt loss as 'our lives need to be recounted to be understood' and narration enables us to 'identify the relationships, roles and capacities that define and give direction to our lives' (Atkins, 2004: 346, 362).

Narrative's role in self-understanding is critical when considering the nation's failing mental health. Various trauma theorists, drawing on Freudian psychoanalysis, describe the traumatic position as one of stasis and silence in which narration is an *essential* vehicle for recovery leading to the capacity for action and psychological well-being (Mukherjee, 2001: 49–62, citing Caruth *et al.*). Notwithstanding the use of the term 'trauma' to refer mostly to highly dramatic and disturbing experience, it is defined more generally as something which occurs as the result of an experience that radically contradicts one's view of 'how things are' and 'who one is', with the traumatised state persisting for as long as this experience cannot be reasoned and assimilated into, or told as, the subject's personal history.[1] This understanding has great relevance when considering how more minor but still personally disturbing events affect us. In daily life, allegiance to a culturally conditioned position (our acculturated view of the world and oneself) makes one course of action over another desirable and possible. For consistent identity, one's orientation is consciously and unconsciously defended against threats to integrity that opposing positions or any challenging evidence represents. Thus, Perowne holds his consistent view of himself as 'rational', defining himself against the emotional characteristic of his children. Most challenge to one's self- and worldview is minor and resolved by slight adjustment of attitude and values. However, 'because a coherent identity is an achievement it can also fail' (Atkins, 2004: 347). Occasionally, challenges of greater magnitude or persistence require more radical referential adjustment and entail a transition from one position or state to another. These generally indicate moments of significant personal development and psychological adjustment with settlement achieved only when a perspective is reached from which one is able to contextualise the disturbing event. For example, when the corporate rhetoric of empowerment or a belief in personal sovereignty is contradicted by evident institutional control over one's conduct, the promise of self 'expression' becomes a non-sense, and some means is needed to deliver the subject from its confused state.

So, at a time of rising mental ill-health, the increase in cultural forms of self-expression, such as autobiography – particularly those using very particular types of coherent and ordered story to make sense of experience – is notable given that both psychotherapy and the maintenance of psychological health are concerned with narrative possibility, or more precisely the *control* over narrative possibility, which essentially is authorship. The human being must manage similar interrelated possibilities to those facing the literary author – for the former, selfhood in respect of action and structure, for the latter, character in respect of plot and form. In each case there is an affective dynamic between the elements. In the life world, structural instability is related to the meaningless and contradictory discourse it produces that in turn impacts the human subject (see Chapter 1). In the literary work, a coherent or fragmented form will in turn influence the artefact's expressive possibilities and the presentation of characters it 'contains'. The difference for the human agent is the belief of being able to act independently to affect that dynamic (whereas the literary character is under the control of the author).

Where structural instability or ideological pressure limits self-expression the ensuing identity crisis, brought about by the fear of over-determination, mobilises the fight or flight instinct. However, the odds in an unequal power struggle (self against institution) are stacked against fighting, so flight, withdrawal or escape presents itself as the only viable alternative. Escape thus becomes the attempt to make a narrative, to make a life, to manage the three elements of existence – selfhood (character), action (plot) and structure (form) – and direct a story in which one's character can both exist and freely develop. The narrative possibility is the life possibility is the literary possibility. This analogy makes literature's relation to the life world both complex and of prime cultural relevance to issues of subjectivity and experience. In this respect Ian McEwan's novel *Saturday* proves fertile ground for examining matters of authorial control, the literary/life world relationship, and the recognition of story as the connective tissue of experience and meaning that holds narrative as an essential instrument of understanding. That it also connects with the issues of power, work and identity with which my argument is concerned makes it doubly relevant.

Story as cognitive instrument

A connection between literary art and the life world is established by knowing that McEwan spent more than a year following a neurosurgeon to write *Saturday*[2] and it 'is his most autobiographical novel to date (Perowne's house is modelled on McEwan's own and the parallels between the surgeon and the writer are numerous)' (Childs, 2005: 151). It is imaginative literature but nevertheless its representation rests upon a thoroughly researched and recorded reflection of contemporary hospital work culture. It is not too fanciful to claim that the underpinning logic of *Saturday* is the interplay of the fictive and the life world and the nature of that connection (a matter still exercising literary theorists). In fact, meta-fictional presentation in *Saturday* draws attention to a cross-fertilisation that hints not at the simplicity of correspondence but at a much more complex relatedness and interdependence. The novel shows 'story' as ubiquitous, working as a critical unit of meaning relevant to the individual and his or her world, and manifest both as inscribed text and as a way of thinking about the self by placing order on events and experience through a process of interpretation.

In Henry Perowne's story, fact and fiction do not appear as sustainably watertight categories and the elements of the novel do much to perplex the relationship between the two. Within the novel Henry witnesses an event – a burning plane flying across the skies of London – and subsequently becomes fixated on how that unfolds as a news story throughout his day. Even as we contemplate that a news item (real or as portrayed within the novel) evolves as a narrative where factual events are journalistically represented in story form (with all that implies about both writer and reader's hermeneutic creation of 'reality') McEwan complicates the fact/fiction relationship further. When Henry possessively refers to the event, 'hoping that *his own story* [my emphasis] breaking at four-thirty might just have made the late editions' (2005: 69), we become aware that 'his own story' is also the narrative McEwan has written *about* Henry (a fictional character created by a fully informed living author). So where any novel starts with the conventional correspondence between the real and fictive worlds, this novel's use of historically specific, factually based situations – the idea of a burning plane over a city, the global insecurity following 9/11 and London's anti-war demonstration – and its attention to the role of interpretation involved in creating a narrative, thoroughly implicates fact with fiction and alerts the reader to their complex interplay as well as to the various narrative levels on which *Saturday* operates. Building on this *Saturday* is strongly intertextual, relating itself to other traditions of both fictive and factual writing through the topographically specific journey of a character through the period of one day (emulating Joyce and Woolf), to other referenced creative literature by Austen, Eliot and Bronte, and to a biography of Darwin (a story of a real person interpreted by another real writer) that the fictional character, Henry, is reading.

In this way escape into the novel, engagement with it at one narrative level (the story level) repeatedly refers the reader back outwards to the life world (the empirical level) to which it is ontologically connected. At its most simple level, the exposition makes apparent the referential correspondence between the life and the imaginary worlds on which all interpretation and meaning depends in mimetic or realist fiction. In addition, the interweaving of fact and fiction shatters the illusion of the self-contained narrative act. The boundaries of story are fluid, not fixed. This not only challenges generic categorisation, it proposes story as a hybrid, inter-referential structure operating on multiple levels of discourse, as one that refuses the 'intratextual confines' of form and exists instead within, between and around the 'multifarious extra textual factors' that provide the cross currents within which its meaning is determined (O'Neill, 1994: 109–117). Reading and interpretation, like writing, are therefore endeavours also situated within, and affected by, such determinants. By simultaneously erecting and dissolving the boundaries between fiction and fact, and between the fictive character and his real-world counterpart, these realms and their respective agents are so thoroughly implicated in each other that the division itself is no more or less illusory than the 'realities' that exist on either side of it. If the division is a construct then it has implications for literary theory, which investigates the nature of the relationship across the divide. Literary theory would matter only insofar as theory itself is a story, albeit a very detailed, complex and analytical one, telling its understanding concerning the relationship between art and life. Where that art is the narrative art, theory becomes self-referential, the attempt to know the status of its own self. This parallels the philosophical investigation of the human condition. In other words, a known correspondence between story and life, where both are subject to the same overarching determinants, makes the creation, reading, interpretation, investigation and understanding of the text and/or the self a like project.[3]

Narrative control as a means of authorship

An important difference concerns the powers of authorship that operate over the novel character and the human agent. While it is known that a writer determines characters in a novel, the character of the human agent is also subject to declared external, formally managed organisational narrative control (see Chapter 1). However, in the life world, though the corporate voice may diminish the employee's expressive power, the capacity exists for the worker to resist such power or generate a counter-narrative. This is significantly different from the novel world in which multiple narrative voices, including those of characters and narrator, cannot speak for themselves but emanate from an author whose own creative authority and intent is subject to much less readily discernible influence. Where corporate discourse and creative novel overlap is in the actual textual evidence produced by the attempt at narrative control, particularly where this generates a particular analysable effect, intentional or otherwise.

Although *Saturday* is formatted as 'a day in the life' narrative, it is not written in the first person. Perowne's thoughts and views are reported in the third person, and thus are mediated by a narrative voice, which, in turn, is mediated by the real-world author, McEwan, who inhabits the world shared (but not necessarily experienced in the same way) by the reader.[4] The important part of this layering is the use of a narrative voice separate from Henry Perowne's but which sees through the perspective of the main protagonist. This 'eye' is important because narration in the third person is thereby deliberately distanced from the 'I' that would signify the first person. The distance between the first and third person is something akin to the self-distancing we each make in reflective thought – the self viewing (and commenting on) the self. However, where the self-identical perspective of the 'eye' and the 'I' leaves no gap for self-awareness unless that self-knowing is explicitly expressed by the agent, the opening between first and third person makes clear the space for interpretation and evaluation that occurs whenever anything seen or experienced becomes the subject matter of subsequent stories told about the self or the world. In other words, the gap between first and third person more clearly introduces the concept of deliberate authorship.

Thus, in *Saturday*, insights into Henry's character and motives are made by a voice that implies an intimate first-hand knowledge of the subject, but is not the subject, so the reader cannot know how aware Perowne is of his own condition. Though we are told he leaves nothing unexamined, we do not know if his self-scrutiny provides accurate or useful insight. Neither do we know on what truth his beliefs are based. However, because we follow Perowne's day (apparently) from his visual perspective, the impression is of being inside Perowne's consciousness looking out. This effect is strengthened by the use of the present tense in the narrative inferring that the reader is accompanying Perowne in real-time and, being held at this level of limited consciousness, is by that made aware of the subconscious. So the movement symbolised by the text is a gradual one traced from the outer reaches of the world inhabited by a real-life author and real-life events, through a mid-point narrative voice that partly obscures its own mechanism of control, to the consciousness of a single mind reflected outwards again to the real-life reader. This whole movement is metaphoric of the process of translation and transformation that occurs, some of it by unknown influence, when stories are created and passed one to the other.

This layering is important not least because the external/internal/external move is reprised elsewhere in the novel's thematic content (see p. 89) as the fear emanating from the burning plane insinuates itself into the very core of Perowne's consciousness and subsequently affects his ongoing action. The layered movement is itself also a parallel of neurosurgical practice – the drilling down through membrane, scalp tissue and bone into the very inner workings of the human mind, even if, ultimately, a mystery remains about the processes by which the physiological (the concrete external workings of the brain) impact the psychological (internal mental state). It is this mystery that engages and energises both the writer and protagonist, for Henry, cast as a neurosurgeon, has the real-world author's curiosity about the working of the brain and how this relates to behaviour, particularly where this involves deeply complex and unstable mental processes, i.e. Baxter's Huntington's and Perowne's mother's Alzheimer's diseases, or indeed, in another of McEwan's novels, *Enduring Love*, Jed's de Clérembault's syndrome.

One might even say there are certain elements that story, society and the brain have in common. Each is an apparently ordered entity, stable and under control in certain conditions that disguise the chaos and complexity that can be brought to the surface under other circumstances, at any given moment – in story through interpretation, in society by riot and in the brain by malfunction. Similarly, the novel, like the brain, keeps mystery at its innermost centre, and the layering hints at the variety of creative and interpretive possibilities that exist as potentiality at every level.

However, perhaps the strongest parallel drawn is one between the novelist, who exercises control over the elements of his creation, and the neurosurgeon, who can do likewise over the character of a patient. In either case, the expert (or poor) application of skill determines the outcome but neither the writer nor the neurosurgeon can be totally sure that their intention will produce a particular result. All the novelist can leave on the page is a plethora of signs facilitating multiple meaning. The interpretation of those signs by others can result in faulty reading and skewed understanding but, undoubtedly, it is necessary for surgeon and novelist to believe, even if partly self-deluded, that '[t]hough things sometimes go wrong, he can control outcomes here, he has the resources, controlled conditions' (246), for this allows the operator to proceed when lack of self-belief will stop them dead. The novelist's pen (or computer) is the surgeon's scalpel, the narrative voice akin to an anaesthetic that allows the operation to proceed. The reader/patient is kept under a form of control for as long as the dupe/dope is consistently applied. Of course, in such a vulnerable position, the subject can be manipulated (as is clearly the case in *Atonement*). Vulnerability to external impact is evidently a point McEwan wishes his reader to note by quoting Saul Bellow in an epigram that asks us to question 'what it means to be a man. [...] Under organised power. Subject to tremendous controls' (*Saturday*, Frontispiece) and this applies as much to the socio-political as to the medical, narratorial or even managerial spheres.

Coherence, contradiction, and the role of illusion in the construction of meaning

Though McEwan's narrative voice clearly wants the reader to understand story's ubiquity and its function as a means of understanding events/the self/experience, Henry is cast to play devil's advocate and deny its importance. However, rather than deflating the case, his denial displays another shared condition of existence of the self and the text – that to produce coherence, the negotiation and settlement of contradiction is essential in both cases.

Henry is presented as a rational scientist whereas his two children, Daisy and Theo, typify the emotionally literate and artistic temperaments of poet and musician respectively. Henry believes 'this notion of Daisy's, that people can't "live" without stories, is simply not true. He is living proof' (68). However, beliefs and proofs are slippery in nature and even those adopted by scientifically inclined neurosurgeons sometimes have an element of illusion about them. In this instance, Henry's 'proof' that he *can* live without stories is countered on two narrative levels. In the empirical world, Henry *only* lives through McEwan's story that creates him, and the reader's belief (or the suspension of disbelief). In the fictive world, the story Henry regards as his own (126) (the 'factual' burning plane story) indicates his emotional, professional and imaginative investment in a narrative he overlays with his own fiction, creating for himself a part in the story treating the disaster victims and thinking his personal security is threatened by what he believes to be political terrorism. At this moment both meaning and his identity as active surgeon or passive victim depend on stories, part fiction, part fact, which are possible to uphold in particular surrounding circumstances or contexts.

Equally important is how understanding must alter when circumstances change. Henry's definition of the burning plane as a terrorist attack is informed by the context of the political situation and an impending anti-war march. When further information makes this view unsustainable, the comment that Perowne 'suspected the story was not all it seemed' (151) hints at the illusion involved in sustaining belief, and the adjustment required when the basis of that belief is undermined. News that the plane is merely a cargo carrier forces cognitive re-contextualisation producing an adjusted story consonant with the additional information. Henry's (and the reader's) understanding of his identity shifts also – active surgeon becomes citizen observer. Similarly, Henry's identity is also founded on a story he tells about himself to himself – that he is a rational type – and the stability of this identity relies on maintaining that belief, thus it requires him to reject Daisy's view of stories being essential to life. In order to 'be' himself, the contradictory idea that stories *do* have meaning and relevance to him must be suppressed (most evidently in his useful forgetting of how vitally connected he became to the 'plane' story). By avoiding contradiction in this way his self-coherence is not disrupted and the reader also believes in him because his story-world character presents with the kinds of consistency expected in a normal life-world character (Rimmon-Kenan, 1993; Porter-Abbott, 2002).[5] Both Henry and the reader need belief in illusion to keep the story meaning intact; for both such illusions function essentially to maintain coherence, meaning and understanding with regard to a worldview, its agents and its produced art.

Story and agency

Story is subordinate in Henry's system of rational value; likewise, his claim that he doesn't 'really want to be a spectator of other lives' (66) is part of a 'package of values' (Ward, 2003: 128)[6] associated with a rejected passivity. He enacts other values that he recognises as a reflection of his self, values of the acculturated liberal male that rates the active more highly. The next obvious enquiry concerns how the life-world character Henry represents is constructed and determined. In fact, the juxtaposition of imaginary and life worlds directly invites questions concerning how far a fictive character parallels a real-world counterpart, how far one world is analogous to the other. Fiction's difference to the real world, as much as its similarity, gives it a status of an object 'other', both intimately connected and critically apart, the linked separation facilitating its function as a system against which other experience can be measured and valued. So fictional Henry's lack of independent existence confirms the relative potential agency of his real-world equivalent, while his experience and character provides a reference against which readers can evaluate their own agency, experience and selfhood. Autobiography theorists believe it is these comparative possibilities that make us read other people's lives, but there is no reason why the autobiographic genre, in some respects, should be seen to function differently to any other story about life. In fact, the autobiography critic Nancy Miller (2002) quotes the epigraph in Philip Roth's *The Facts: A Novelist's Autobiography* spoken by his alter ego Zuckerman – a character crossing the generic autobiography/fictional divide and, like McEwan, problematising the fact/fiction distinction – as saying: 'And as he spoke I was thinking, *the kinds of stories that people turn life into, the kind of lives that people turn stories into*' (Miller (2002: xiii–xvi, quoting Roth; original emphasis).

The debate on the attraction and effect of narrative is as vigorous now as when it began with Aristotle, who saw the potential of 'art as a moral instructor and the artist as an instrument of moral instruction' (Halperin, 1974: 4). A. A. Berger (1997) says, 'We read to meet interesting people [...] to gain insights that will help us live better lives' and quotes Bruno Bettleheim as saying other texts 'provide us with ways to escape our personal preoccupation and open up to a broader sense of possibilities' (133). In effect, not just contemplating another's actions, but gaining access to another's mind, is an essential means by which human individuals attempt to see themselves as not alone; indeed to see themselves as having some recognisable similarity and commonality with others even while, or especially where, that information also denotes aspects of one's uniqueness. Literature's role in this is evident in McEwan's invitation to consider Henry's world and his experience as something that informs their own. McEwan says:

> I think we have probably not yet bettered a device than the novel for looking at what it's like to be other people, what it's like to be someone else. I think movies, for example, are fantastically crude in this respect – they can't give you consciousness, they can't give you life lived from the inside. Even, I have to say, poetry can never quite give you what it's like to be an individual moving through time over a long period of time in a society.
> (McEwan, 2005: *South Bank Show*)

Henry also displays a desire to understand others, a need to know about the motives and agency of other characters which is a common hunger acknowledged and fed by news journalism's human interest values.[7] His curiosity transfers from the incident of the burning plane to the particulars of the persons flying it, and their personal involvement, if any, in shaping the event in order to give meaning and value to his own experience and character. By recognising others as like or unlike what he considers himself to be, he is able to gain knowledge about the world in which he lives and those with whom he shares it, to orient his self relationally and gain insight about his own drives and potential agency.

What applies to Henry applies to any reader of *Saturday*. Henry (we) cannot escape story's implications any more than he (we) can escape its presence. Technologically enabled distribution ensures Henry's attachment to the story-event at home, in the street, in the gym, from radios and TV. Where story informs knowledge, and knowledge illuminates existence, to be affected by any story is to recognise that existence is impacted by mediating influence – by structures, ideas, and events outside of the self – and to some extent, is determined by that influence.[8] Though the degree and direction of that influence may be unspecified and unpredictable, story nevertheless indicates the connection of the subject to other human, institutional and artistic structures. Story itself, and interest in story, specifically acknowledges that the reality of any individual structure (organic, institutional or creative) is comprised of the same stuff and substance, common elements, arranged in, and presenting, endless variation through which each achieves uniqueness.

A key artistic metaphor used by McEwan in *Saturday*, Bach's *Goldberg Variations*, confirms this, by showing that the product of this dynamic is not merely postmodern superficiality, endlessly reproducing an ungrounded effect. Bach's *Variations* enacts form as a stable thematic entity which nevertheless develops and changes to differing contextual demands, displaying a whole range of keys, melodies, harmonies, styles, moods, tempi, performance techniques and oblique as well as specific connections, each variation a seemingly disconnected and unique presentation that, nevertheless, is built on a consistent structural blueprint of the original and held to it through an anchoring bass line. Importantly, an organic wholeness is indicated by the fact that each harmonic variation returns to the tonic and the piece, as a whole, returns at last to its original founding theme (Perahia, 2000; Gutmann, 2002).[9] The structure, while being a metaphor for identity, is paralleled in *Saturday*, which takes place over 24 hours, begins and ends in Perowne's bedroom, and holds to the stability of home and family as a place of return and anchorage against disturbing external events that signal the potential for personal change. Art is a metaphor for life because both are compound constructs under like influence. As Bal (1997) says, quoting Claude Bremond, 'the narrated universal is regulated by the same rules as those which control human thought and action' (188).

However, all apparently unified structures – artistic, human or institutional – entail paradox, contradiction or tension and Henry is no exception. He presents with all the characteristic qualities of the rational, cold and enquiring individual intellect paradoxically involved, by life itself, as a participant in a collective and intensely emotional social story in a material world. As mentioned earlier, the management of his self as a coherent entity requires him not to 'know' parts of the self out of line with his preferred value system, particularly the vital function of his imagination. Full conscious acknowledgement of that would challenge his self-coherence and identity. Likewise, the novel *Saturday* is at once an exposition of separate categories that are unsustainable (fact and fiction, reason and imagination, emotion and intellect, self and other, art and life) and unities, like the story and self-identity, which are fragile achievements liable to fracture by strong external pressure.[10] Thus while narrative has a vital role to play in imposing order and sense on our world and our selves, it also gives us a tool by which to measure our experience, our characters, our lives and the circumstances of our existence. It can provide the comfort of unity but at the same time, by exposing the potential for threat and fracture, shows what is necessary for that unity to be maintained.

In the next section, closer examination of *Saturday* will demonstrate that any apparent coherence is vulnerable to assault. Survival for the sentient is a matter of fight (of handling or in some way suppressing, though often not eradicating, potentially disruptive elements, or resisting challenge by some means or other) or flight (distancing oneself from the source of the threat) or, indeed, either willing or enforced capitulation. In respect of *Saturday*, the analysis shows how malign working conditions act as an undercurrent threatening Perowne's professional identity, mirroring also how widespread acceptance, suppression or ignorance of such conditions in society operates to maintain a flawed structure; how in a dynamic interconnectedness of structure what upsets the equilibrium of one part affects others also; how accelerated time and communication technology supporting business negatively impacts human relationships; and how story is the means of resolving the tension between dialectical elements.

Henry Perowne – the (dis)contented man and professional medic

Henry Perowne is described as a 'contented man' who also, contradictorily, is 'troubled by the state of the world' that threatens his family life (back cover). Certainly, much about Henry's life – his status, his possessions, his happy marriage and healthy children – ought to make him content but, as another reviewer claims, *Saturday* 'focuses on the moment when someone's life starts falling apart' (*Frankfurter Allgemeine*, frontispiece). It is possible to see Henry as both content *and* insecure, but only if one focuses, in turn, on his being in a personal, private, domestic capacity and then in a public, political one. The separate states would seem to indicate that the Henry in one sphere, is not, in some sense, the Henry in the other, when the evidence points to the spheres and the 'persons' being only categorically and not ontologically or hermeneutically independent.

In other words, Henry can be defined as (private) husband and father, and/or (public) surgeon, citizen, etc., but existence and meaning within these roles or selves relies on their relational interdependence, on the decisions, action and manner he makes in various situations. Thus we are told Henry, in his professional role, has 'an unassertive manner' but also that this 'unassertiveness is misleading, more style than character – it is not possible to be an unassertive brain surgeon' (McEwan, 2005: 20–21) hinting that Henry's character has a more stable cast to which his varying performative levels (styles) refer. Henry's management of characteristic traits finds him having to decide between what 'are contradictory terms, but not quite, and it's the degree of their overlap, their manner of expressing the same thing from different angles, which he [and the reader] needs to comprehend' (22). Importantly, it is Henry's ability to 'measure his voice and feelings against a stranger's' (23), to refer outside of his self, to compare and contrast, that helps define for him the enduring sense of who he is.

Henry is partly defined by his personal relationships (roles as a husband, father and colleague) and outwardly signified by his personal possessions, his home – several storeys of grandeur in a prime London square – and his car. His silver Mercedes S500 operates as an outer skin, anthropomorphised as another version of his self 'that breathes an animal warmth'. The car reflects his worth in economic terms. His wife 'encouraged him to buy it' because it 'was time for him to fill out', as if it would somehow augment his character and make him whole. Having now 'accepted himself as the owner, the master of his vehicle […] it's become part of him' (75–76) and its 'padded privacy' (121) functions as physical representation of his self, an outer casing of status and power, like his profession, that affords him a measure of protection and control. When Baxter's car hits the Mercedes, it is little different to the assault he makes on Henry's self, which Henry defends by calling on his professional identity for self-confidence and protection.

Henry's occupation as a neurosurgeon is central to *Saturday*, and being noted in the first line of the novel, is a defining factor of his identity. The opening statement describes him also as naked, coupling the image of professionalism with vulnerability. Formally, this professional status is protected by qualifications, knowledge and skills, attributes that indicate his level of authority. That authority is strong: for his mother, ' "what the doctor said" was a powerful invocation' (155–156) and at her care home 'Henry receives special consideration [from her nurses] on account of his medical connection' (158). This coupling of personal identity to employment is part of the codification, integral to all daily life, by which we negotiate our relationships with, and expectations of, others. Henry's occupation is a key factor in the novel's plot for its social currency is an element that defines him and guides his action and speech. To understand why an undermining of professionalism would devastate Henry, we can examine how he employs the power of his status in practice and see how his personal insecurity (raised by the enemy without – Baxter) reflects the macro-political fear of potential terrorism featured in the novel.

When verbally and physically threatened by Baxter, Henry finds himself making 'decisions' about how he will present himself, altering his language so that the full effect of 'standing on his professional dignity' (89) has the desired impact on his foe. His unsolicited, but correct, diagnosis of Baxter's neural disease imposes a doctor/patient relationship that Henry recognises as a 'shameless blackmail' (95) in which he 'senses the power passing to him' (95). Henry can depend on this approach to gain advantage because he is exploiting a cultural determination to which they are both subject, so is reasonably sure Baxter will bow to the power that the status of medical doctor confers. The same reliance on social coding is what wrong-foots Baxter, who thinks that a man 'dressed like that' (94) in a scruffy gym outfit constitutes an 'out of character' expression of the doctor identity. This draws attention to the various levels on which identity is held and expressed, and to the importance of the characteristic signifiers that endorse it, showing that where any are removed, identity begins to crumble. Without his white coat (a visual clue), Henry brings into play his title and displays his knowledge and experience of diagnosis (discursive clues) – that is, he expresses his identity employing more embedded characteristic signifiers. Understanding the power Henry is afforded by his profession makes clear what any threat to that identity will mean for his self-security.

Structural connection

Meaning dependent on order may be disturbed by disruption to that order. In *Saturday*, global and national insecurity indicates that a world whose order is changing cannot rely on values and behaviours generated and applicable in more stable times. The novel centres on destabilising forces in a number of arenas, which pose potential parallel danger: the political (national terrorism threat), the public (Baxter's assault), the professional (work pressures), the private/domestic (relationship tensions) and the personal (identity).

Specific instances of structural connection are given to show that what happens in one operational sphere impacts more widely in others. For example, the political unrest affects Henry personally for now his days now are 'baffled and fearful' (4) due in no small part to mass-media stories enforcing the reality of terrorist threat and random acts of violence that disturb his equilibrium. The psychological stress, resulting from 'not only his broken night, but the whole week and the weeks before bearing down on him', is materially manifest in Henry, causing a feebleness in his joints and muscles that limits his physical movement (36). Here the metaphoric link, made between the psychological and the physiological, dissolves the categorical distinction between mind and body as both are equally vulnerable, equally implicated, equally threatened. Interconnectedness over compartmentalisation, illustrated using the 'Russian doll' structural metaphor, indicates how the threat Henry first perceives in the sky advances to the street, on to his car, then into his home, and finally results in personal confrontation in which his very being is under attack. Once again there is an inexorable movement by which the external threatens the internal and the impersonal becomes personal. With Henry's car and home both signifying his identity, assault on those *is* a threat to Henry's self, as it becomes more directly in the unfolding plot. As a consequence of perceiving external threat, we see Henry trying to strengthen his own boundary, ensuring extreme home security in a bid for self-protection:

> three stout Banham locks, two black iron bolts as old as the house, two tempered steel security chains, a spyhole with a brass cover, the box of electronics that works the entryphone system, the red

panic button, the alarm pad with its softly gleaming digits. Such defences, such mundane embattlement.

(McEwan, 2005: 36)

With the connection clearly made between the physical and psychological, these measures operate as an image of imprisonment on both planes with withdrawal (flight) as a favoured defence against malign forces.

A further instance of dynamic interconnectedness sees Henry's work affecting his personal relationships. While professional training has honed the qualities of rationality, precision and objectivity that afford Henry success in the operating theatre, these identifying characteristics are more problematic in his personal life. During an argument with Daisy about the Iraq War, his objectivity contrasts with her emotional engagement and 'it doesn't help that he becomes calmer as she becomes more agitated, but that's his habit, professionally ingrained' (189). When Daisy uses the word 'scan' during a poetry discussion, thoughts on the cost of a new hospital scanner intrude on Henry's consciousness (199), so professional determination is again in evidence. In other words, Henry's associative response is made predominantly by reference to discourse that supports his work self. We are not seeing here merely a consistency of attitude that marks a stable character (against the entirely social-situational reaction that would signal a weak identity), but rather a hardening in one direction that indicates Henry no longer has the flexibility and sensitivity necessary for successfully relating in a number of social situations with a range of different people. Henry here appears dominated by work, programmed (to an injurious extent) by its discourse.

Causes of dissatisfaction at work

More problematically, Henry's workplace makes demands on him that are steadily diminishing the confidence borne from his professional status. In seeking an explanation for his malaise, Henry diagnoses his own mental state as being the 'consequence of extreme tiredness [having] finished the week in a state of unusual depletion' (5). He locates his weariness in 'this modern professional life. He works hard, everyone around him works hard and this week he's been pushed harder […] balancing and doubling' (7) in order to work simultaneously in three operating theatres. The descriptor 'modern' indicates emerging circumstance, one not yet fully accomplished. Thus there is a telling semiotic lag when he uses the as-yet unmodified language of old-style, 'iron cage' stability commenting on 'the discipline and responsibility of a medical career'. As there is also 'over much of it, a veil of fatigue' (28), the attempt to maintain traditionally recognised professional values in an increasingly lean and overstretched system indicates a performative conflict which ultimately causes the worker to tire and fail.

Here, 'modern professional life' (contrasting with orderly, stable, less pressurised *traditional* professional life) indicates instead the new economy's (oxymoronic) 'permanent state of flux' that can be interpreted in two ways: the perpetually edgy position of readiness that is the basis for the responsive action required to supply a demanding and constantly changing market; or as a transitional state without resolution known as the neurotic state of chaos in which competing demands result in a total inability to act. While Sennett identifies the 'confidence to dwell in disorder, [to] flourish in the midst of dislocation' as a characteristic of those successful in the new capitalist culture (Sennett, 1998: 62), the psychotherapeutic model, requiring resolution of contradiction and chaos for psychological welfare, suggests the certainty required for good mental health recommends against pursuing the kinds of rapid changeability now required for workplace success. While some are willing and able to immerse themselves in the seas of change, those mourning the old certain times are charged with previous generation nostalgia or seen as resistant to the adaptation necessary for survival. Existing among the fluctuations of new-economy conditions requires one to operate within its changeable currents for as long as that can be comfortably managed. When exhaustion ensues or if one stops, confused and directionless in eddying waters, one is sucked under – a method of natural selection in a system of occupational Darwinism by which those labelled indecisive or weak are identified as corporate losers and removed.

However, it is notable that hard work itself does not cause Henry trouble; the practical nature of Henry's occupation affords him fulfilment and he enjoys applying his skill to good effect, finding exhilaration in challenging work. It is the increasing bureaucratic demand of peripheral tasks making him deskbound that poses the problem. It is:

> the paperwork on Friday afternoon that brought him down, the backlog of referrals, and responses to referrals, abstracts for two conferences, letters to colleagues and editors, an unfinished peer review, contributions to management initiatives, and Government changes to the structure of the Trust, and yet more revisions to teaching practices. There's to be a new look – there's always to be a new look – at the hospital's emergency plan.
>
> (McEwan, 2005: 11)

The constant call for a new look is the 'fresh page' terminology that attempts to validate the changing policies associated with corporate restructuring undertaken in the too-frequent aim of cost-cutting. However, economist Richard Layard (2005) links 'change' to the rising tide of misery and believes 'we should [...] question policies of continuous change since they involve repeated losses' when any loss causes unhappiness greater than an equivalent gain would increase happiness (Layard, 2005: 141–142). The repetition 'there's always to be a new look' hints at the weariness of a repeated process that, if not creating loss, certainly yields no gain. A similar lack of progress and more direct loss of freedom are implied by the paperwork. With the relentless accumulation of the administrative load, work in the new economy, aided by information technology, replicates the psychic problems of industrial conveyor-belt automation – work needing attention arriving at a rate over which the worker has no control.

The name change from Health 'Authority' to 'Trust' is semantically interesting. Authority was once a guarantee that confidence could be placed in trained and experienced professional doctors. The alteration in descriptor occurs at a time when, according to Onora O'Neill (2002), 'Mistrust and suspicion have spread across all areas of life and supposedly with good reason. [...] Patients [...] in particular no longer trust hospitals or hospital consultants'. That the word 'trust' has replaced 'authority' is therefore deeply ironic (8–9). Instead of trust there is accountability, which, particularly in the public sector, O'Neill tells us, 'aims at ever more perfect administrative control of institutional and professional life,' bearing out the Weberian prediction that bureaucratic administration would triumph over specialist, professional knowledge. The constant scrutiny of professionals is pernicious.

> Professionals have to work to ever more exacting – if changing – standards of good practice and due process, to meet relentless demands to record and report, and they are subject to regular ranking and restructuring [...] many public sector professionals find that the new demands damage their real work.
>
> (O'Neill, 2002: 49)

Specifically, 'doctors speak of the inroads that required record-keeping makes into the time that they can spend finding out what is wrong with their patients and listening to their patients' (50). It is clear that Henry is less able to define himself as surgeon while vast amounts of his time are spent as administrator. His work conditions are eating away equally at his autonomy, authority and identity.

Like other aspects of his work, the administrative anxiety spills into his private life when following the car scrape, 'with rising irritation [...] he already sees ahead into the weeks, the months of paperwork, insurance claims and counterclaims, phone calls, delays at the garage' (McEwan, 2005: 82), so just when his characteristic clinical detachment could be of use, it fails him. This is perhaps because paperwork, requiring time he would rather devote to other activity but needing none of the professional skill and knowledge through which he experiences pride and achievement, seems fundamentally purposeless and unproductive. Unlike Henry's clinical work, ending pain and restoring function, these tasks do not 'make a difference'.[11] When Henry says of a litter collector he sees jabbing away at individual items of detritus, 'what could be more futile than this underpaid urban-scale housework when behind him [...] cartons and paper cups are spreading thickly under the feet of demonstrators,' the 'blizzard of litter' (74) on which the collector has little impact parallels Henry's paperwork, which is a similar form of useless toil, having little practical and no personal benefit. Situations like this in which one lacks control and achievement and the power to do anything about it is recognised as the classic condition of stress and depression (Layard, 2005: 68, 150, quoting Marmot).[12]

This passive position contradicts the view Henry holds of himself as active, particularly as the anti-war protest demonstrates a political route to effect change but there is no evidence that the more directly affecting work-related circumstances prompt collective action or resistance of any kind. Rather, the effects of contemplating the administrative list are absorbed internally and produce classic symptom of trauma – the lack of verbal facility, or in the words of the text, 'an unfamiliar lack of fluency' described as follows:

> Now he was stumbling. And though the professional jargon did not desert him –it's second nature – his prose accumulated awkwardly. Individual words brought to mind unwieldy objects – bicycles, deckchairs, hangers – strewn across his path. He composed a sentence in his head, then lost it on the page, or typed himself into a grammatical cul-de-sac and had to sweat his way out. Whether this debility was the cause or consequence of fatigue he didn't pause to consider.
> (McEwan, 2005: 12)

His inactivity, combined with a fixation on the unrewarding circumstances in which he is caught, exhaustion and the difficulty in externalising his thoughts, also warns of a locked introspection symptomatic of mental illness. That he 'didn't pause to consider' is as significant as it is uncharacteristic in one who 'leaves nothing in his life unexamined' (*Observer*, frontispiece) and prides himself on 'thinking independently' (181). The lack of thought suggests a pace that precludes reflection and pressures of a workplace culture so widespread as to be considered normal.

Authority, teamwork and working to win

Despite the evident lack of collective action in the workplace, the regular reassurance for a struggling worker is that he or she is not alone. In fact, the corporate 'we' covers everything from a team to the whole organisation in which, according to the rhetorical and theoretical model of modern business's flattened structure, everyone works together on the same level. However, experience often contradicts this, as Henry finds:

> In the past year he's become aware of new committees and sub-
> committees spawning, and lines of command that stretch up and
> out of the hospital, beyond the medical hierarchies, up through the
> distant reaches of the Civil Service to the Home Secretary's office.
>
> (McEwan, 2005: 12)

This description of a traditional military-style layered structure is anything but level, and its 'spawning' seems to indicate a growing mass of bureaucracy, while 'up', 'out' and 'beyond' evoke the finger of remote power being brought to bear on the individual through centralised, government-devised policies. O'Neill believes:

> an unending stream of new legislation and regulation, memoranda
> and instructions, guidance and advice floods into public sector
> institutions. [...] a look into the vast database of documents on the
> Department of Health website arouses a mixture of despair and
> disbelief. Central planning may have failed in the former Soviet
> Union but it is alive and well in Britain today.
>
> (O'Neill, 2002: 46)

Moreover, the Health Secretary, not the Home Secretary, is at the top of the medical chain of command. If this is Henry's slip, it is another uncharacteristic, unthinking mistake; if it is the narrator's or McEwan's error (whose reliability we have no reason to doubt), the authority of the text is questionable. Or, perhaps, the mismatch deliberately reconnects issues of 'health' with those of 'security' (as they used to be joined administratively in the Department of Health and Social Security) or indicates the personal stress involved in 'contingency planning' to which all organisations now subscribe in their state of ever-readiness. This is a never-ending task, as Defra claims in wearied tones:

> Our aim is to be fully prepared. Since the Department was formed
> in 2001 we have strengthened our emergency planning arrange-
> ments. But there is still some way to go and the programme
> will never really be complete: this is an area which is constantly
> evolving.
>
> (Defra, undated(a): 83)

Complaint is forestalled by corporate discourse that makes clear requests for less pressure appear as the cry of the weak, of losers, of uncooperative employees who leave their colleagues to shoulder the burden. In the contemporary workplace the concept of 'teamwork' serves to pretend that 'employees aren't really competing against each other' (Sennett, 1998: 111). Henry finds the reality different for senior consultants. Mutuality is not much in evidence if one lives in a 'watchful, jealous world in which reputations are edgily tended and a man can be brought low by status anxiety' (McEwan, 2005: 130). Personal insecurity is no asset in managing relationships and it is perhaps for this reason that 'Henry doesn't actually relish personal confrontation' even though he has been partly prepared for it as:

> clinical experience is, among all else, an abrasive toughening process, bound to wear away at his sensitivities. Patients, juniors, the recently bereaved, management of course – inevitably in two decades, the moments have come around when he's been required to fight his corner, or explain, or placate in the face of a furious emotional upsurge. There's usually a lot at stake – for colleagues, questions of hierarchy and professional pride.
>
> (McEwan, 2005: 85)

The workplace threat to his professional pride is intensified by the altercation with Baxter in which also 'self-respect is on the line' (86), so that the game of squash he plays immediately after with his colleague, Jay Strauss, becomes a means of reasserting a strength of character that he fears is in danger of being annihilated. So much so that when 'he fought back from two games down, and believes he's proved to himself something essential in his own nature, something familiar that he's forgotten lately', he wonders 'they've never had anything like this before. Is it possibly about something else?' (115). This makes clear that identity is worked through other aspects of experience, for Henry's game assumes the intensity of a bid for survival as 'there's only one thing in life he wants. Everything else has dropped away. He has to beat Strauss' (107). His need to dominate Jay and his comfort operating on immobile, anaesthetised patients entirely under his power, literally in his hands, leads to the conclusion that the particular types of contact that unsettle and challenge Henry are those that involve the real skill (rather than the workplace charade) of human communication and intimate contact. In the absence of the emotional intelligence to handle directly the personal confrontation he dislikes (85), Henry avoids it or uses sport's mediated opposition to displace the anger and frustration that is accumulated, but not expended, elsewhere. This projection is a way to handle the competition at work that cannot be openly recognised, though Henry's wondering about his aggression shows how deeply recognition of its cause is buried.

Time and IT

Henry's emotional withdrawal may result equally from the prevailing work culture, his training and genetic make-up, but it is also impacted by the management and experience of time. Global capitalism involving the control of business in remote centres is enabled by new means of communication, by technological advance that has caused growing volumes of e-communication. Henry's mounting pile of email not only defines him as an administrator, it also entails a great deal of office work and overtime:

> Perowne dictated monotonously, and well after his secretary went home he typed in his over heated box of an office [...] At eight in the evening he concluded the last in a series of e-mails and stood up from his desk where he had been hunched since four.
>
> (McEwan, 2005: 12)

Described here, the vastly increased, technologically enabled information flow imprisons Henry, compromises his home life and sets him in a foetal protective position.

Henry's wife, subject to the same punishing hours and the same technologies, also works on Saturday (199) so, ironically, as actual physical contact between them lessens, their relationship is conducted through electronic connection as 'once a week, [...] they line up their personal organisers side by side, like little mating creatures, so that their appointments can be transferred into each other's diaries along an infrared beam' (23). While always in touch, face-to-face (personal) conversations are replaced by face-to-screen (impersonal) contact, and the organisers replicate the sexual union compromised by a punishing schedule. In addition to removing the signifiers of voice, tone and facial expression that generally aid understanding, the immediacy of e-communication contracts the time between stimulus (message) and response, limiting the operation of the truly human capacity of interpretation and imagination to something closer to animalistic Pavlovian, instinctive or reflexive reaction. The rhythms of organic life are disturbed in other ways also. The difficulty of leaving work behind is because the boundaries between the working week and weekend, or between home and work life, are porous. 'The city's appetite for Saturday work is robust' (48) and Henry's own 'free time is always fragmented […] by the restlessness that comes with these weekly islands of freedom' (66). Henry's unease in the small spaces of his free time is a symptom of a twenty-four/seven work culture that, in leaving room for no other aspects of self-expression, means his professional identity has almost become all of him because:

> in ambitious middle life it sometimes seems there is only work. […] For certain days, even weeks on end work can shape every hour; it's the tide, the lunar cycle they set their lives by, and without it, it can seem there's nothing. Henry and Rosalind Perowne are nothing.
>
> (McEwan, 2005: 23)

The acknowledgement here, also, is that working life is relentlessly ordered by clock time, which overrides the less regimented ebb and flow rhythms of the natural world.

Historically, before industrialisation, work and home life were not divided, a situation often seen (retrospectively) as idyllic. Theoretically, a reintegration of work and home life would seem desirable, and is at the heart of much of today's home/work balance rhetoric. However, with circumstances of work so radically altered, this rhetoric merely attempts to formalise and validate work's invasion of the domestic space. For an employer, current work-at-home arrangements are a means of cutting costs and extending and concentrating economic effort,[13] not facilitating family or social communion. For workers, attention to work/life balance is more often prompted by an experienced loss of free time and a recognition that, in practice, 'flexible' full-time work operates more in favour of the employer and is incompatible with domestic and relationship needs.

Speed, failure and ethical conduct

Where hurry and speed are endemic and performance measuring means moving on quickly from project to project, the worker has no time for reflection and learning from mistakes, so leaves behind an unending trail of imperfection. This prevents any sense of achievement in the completion of a job well done, any improvement to process or to the development of their practical or personal skills. Work survivors both dwell in chaos *and* must accept a level of stasis in their personal development, however much corporate communication says to the contrary. Vital to this attitude of 'moving on' from failure is the attempt not to construe it as failure at all.[14] So the opportunity to forge the kind of character that learns to cope with failure (which is so much harder than dealing with success) evaporates with the very circumstances of workplace hyper-competitiveness that creates its need.

In Henry's profession, mistakes are more critical than the marketing of faulty software or a lapse of customer care in service industries. 'Moving on' without completion or learning from mistakes has serious life and death consequences for him and for his patient-products. Where trust has been replaced by accountability, professions traditionally reliant on trust face particular difficulty. If 'most people at their first consultation take a furtive look at the surgeon's hands in the hope of reassurance', it is because by putting their lives in his hands the literal gains metaphorical weight. Significantly, those not liking the look of his hands 'are placated by the reputation' (19) that today is generated by the audit culture's PR and league-tables in which the personality (or even celebrity) element of some professions captures and references an individual's performance as a basis for placing personal confidence, though reputation easily built on scant short-term evidence is as quickly demolished by a single failure. There is also a subtle, but vitally important, difference between placing confidence, as opposed to having trust, in one's surgeon. Placing confidence is a matter of belief in competence and sureness of touch whereas having trust extends this to an underlying faith in moral character.

While it seems entirely reasonable to allow prospective patients to access information regarding a surgeon's reliability based on the consistent performance of skill and knowledge over time, it is not acceptable for institutions to require the collection of such data by the same surgeons in a burdensome manner that makes their necessary demonstration of such diligence ever harder. This unreasonable requirement marks a performative contradiction that undermines the very standards it seeks to measure. Moreover, it gives the medic an ethical dilemma in addition to the logistical one and denies that some valuable things to do with quality of care – the nurse's hand-holding, the doctor's kind words, the teacher's support of a pupil – just cannot be easily measured even though they contribute to good performance and controlling costs. According to O'Neill (2002),

> the new accountability is experienced not just as *changing* but […] as *distorting the proper aims of professional practice* and indeed as damaging professional pride and integrity. […] professional and public servants understandably end up responding to requirements and targets and not only to those whom they are supposed to serve. […] If [accountability] is working we might expect to see indications – performance indicators! – that public trust is reviving. But we don't. […] the real focus is on performance indicators chosen for ease of measurement and control rather than because they measure quality of performance accurately.
> (O'Neill, 2002: 50–54, emphasis original)

The flexibility and mobility required of workers in organisations or social situations, the constant changes of location and function, the responsiveness and the competitiveness do not allow for social bonds to develop in which one can build or demonstrate relationships of trust.[15] The result in the twenty-first century is a climate of vulnerability and suspicion of the type that unsettles Henry even if his patients, equally unsettled and suspicious, have no choice but to rely on him. (O'Neill, 2002: 3–19). In total, *Saturday* paints a portrait of the socially insecure professional, whose imagination is heightened by vulnerability and suspicion, whose private time is diminished by a growing bureaucratic workload that also devalues his status, authority, knowledge and experience, who sublimates the ensuing impotence and lack of self-esteem in competitive sport, whose compromised personal relationships are both caused and managed by information technology, and who ponders a world in which ethical conduct is difficult.

Restitution

Henry's contentment is thus compromised by a heavy time-pressured workload, the difficulty of managing his personal relationships, and the ethical dilemma and identity crisis brought on by 'conceptions of accountability, which superimpose managerial targets on bureaucratic process, burdening and even paralysing many of those who have to comply' (O'Neill, 2002:18). Being a 'habitual observer of his own moods' (McEwan, 2005: 5), it is through reflection when walking – a slow (organic) form of travel – that Henry finds Theo's musicianship is:

> a reminder of the buried dissatisfaction in his own life, of the missing element. This feeling can grow when [...] [he] decides to go home on foot and reflect. There's nothing in his own life that contains this inventiveness, this style of being free. The music speaks to an unexpressed longing or frustration that he's denied himself an open road, the life of the heart celebrated in songs.
>
> (McEwan, 2005: 28)

Henry yearns for this creative and emotional freedom that would make him complete – the heart that would complement his head. His regret is clearly stated as envy of Theo's agency in choosing a lifestyle by 'boldly stepping where his parents didn't dare [...] *taking charge of his life*' (36, emphasis added). Moreover,

> musicians touch something [...] beyond the merely collaborative or technically proficient. [...] This is when they give us a glimpse of what we might be, our best selves, and of an impossible world in which you give everything you have to others, but lose nothing yourself.
>
> (McEwan, 2005: 171)

The highly individual but collaborative effort of making music is a version of the utopian community, 'the workers' paradise', the impossible dream made real (171–172).

The moral and restorative force appears also when Daisy reads poetry to defuse Baxter's knife-threat after he enters Henry's house and holds the family captive. When Henry sees this effect 'within the bounds of the real' (221) (though the reader may need to suspend disbelief to take this at face value), he is forced to re-evaluate the emotional power of art. With his arguments against the uses and value of literature partly invalidated, he is able to recognise and appreciate that:

> to do its noticing and judging, poetry balances itself on the pinprick of the moment. Slowing down, stopping yourself completely, to read and understand a poem is like trying to acquire an old-fashioned skill like dry stone walling or trout tickling.
> (McEwan, 2005: 129)

This recommends the literary arts and other slow craft activities as an antidote to the pace of modern life precisely because, like learning to play an instrument well, they cannot be accomplished quickly. The 'pinprick of the moment' here suggests not the tumultuous succession of many ephemeral moments such as are implied by an ever-pressing immediacy, but rather a savouring of the merest segment of time. Thus Henry's reading, that he worries could be 'slowing down his mental processes' (67) and could harm his ability to work, rather presents itself as an activity that, like walking, creates a pause for reflection that might rescue him.

Life-writing has already drawn Henry's attention to earlier times of less frantic activity and greater intimate connection. Darwin's biography makes Henry 'comfortably nostalgic for a verdant, horse-drawn, affectionate England' because it is evocative of a time when one's transport literally 'breathe[d] an animal warmth' (6). The backward glance draws attention to how the real animal on which one used to sit now appears only as the leather covering on the seats in Henry's 302 horsepower Mercedes, making comment on the superficiality, commodification and increasing pace of modern life where a pause for thought on its evolutionary direction is sorely needed but unlikely to occur. When Daisy 'throws herself back into another century' to recite a poem, it is the 'quiet rhythm' and 'meditative, mellifluous and wilfully archaic' lines in Matthew Arnold's 'Dover Beach' that restore calm and evaporate Baxter's threat. In effect, the slowing of time allows the full moral and practical implications of one's impending action to become conscious. For the irrational Baxter brought to new understanding, poetry seems not a step away from reason but a step towards it. In this moment, Baxter chooses life (his own and that of Henry's family) over death.

Two activities in Henry's life replicate this meditative quality and it is worth focusing on each, as they illuminate the contributory circumstances of Henry's happiness. The key notable point is that stillness of mind need not necessarily require a stillness of body. In fact, 'activity' that joins mind and body often allows a centring of the self that only occurs in pure repose by those well practised in cognitive meditative art. The activities Henry finds satisfying – operating and cooking – are not, in this respect, as dissimilar as they first appear.

In cookery he finds 'a release from the demands of the theatre. In the kitchen the consequences of failure are mild. [...] It occurs to him how content he is to be cooking. [...] He isn't thinking about work, he wants to cook' (176–178). Cooking is one of those 'old-fashioned skills' Henry mentioned that, like gardening, animal husbandry and self-sufficiency, have been the subject of a revival of interest in recent years. Cooking is a labour with a spiritual and moral dimension being both the basis of a secular communion and producing benefit to others as well as to the self (see Chapter 4). Cooking is precisely one of those activities 'in which you give everything you have to others, but lose nothing yourself' (171), unwittingly fulfilling the lack Henry has identified but believes is practically unattainable. Having both a material and spiritual dimension, it stands close to the harmonies and satisfactions found in Henry's operating work, activity in which knowledge, skill and experience are applied to good practical effect such as when his intervention means 'three years' misery, of sharp, stabbing pain, ended' (7) and good moral purpose when operating to save the life of the man who tried to kill him.[16] It is a selfless act in which object and subject are agreeably joined.

Henry's intense pleasure when operating on Baxter is described as a near-ecstasy, obviously indicating a secular replacement of religious experience now that (as Daisy reads from Arnold's poem) the 'Sea of Faith' is only a 'long withdrawing roar/Retreating'.[17] Like Theo's music, operating is 'a form of hypnosis, of effortless seduction' (28). When reflecting on the operation, Henry realises:

> For the past two hours he's been in a dream of absorption that has dissolved all sense of time, and all awareness of the other parts of

his life. Even his awareness of his own existence has vanished. He's been delivered into a pure present, free of the weight of the past or any anxieties about the future. In retrospect, though never at the time, it feels like profound happiness. It's a little like sex, in that he feels himself in another medium, but it's less obviously pleasurable and clearly not sensual. This state of mind brings a contentment he never finds with any passive form of entertainment. Books, cinema, even music can't bring him to this. Working with others is one part of it, but it's not all. This benevolent dissociation seems to require difficulty, prolonged demands on concentration and skills, pressure, problems to be solved, even danger. He feels calm, and spacious, fully qualified to exist. It's a feeling of clarified emptiness, of deep, muted joy. Back at work and, lovemaking and Theo's song aside, he's happier than at any other point in his day off, his valuable Saturday.

(McEwan, 2005: 258)

This is Henry happily absorbed in activity of his own choosing, directed towards an outcome he feels he can control. When operating, like the author, Henry has power over life and death, for 'here is one area where Henry can exercise authority and shape events. He knows how the system works' (278). It is not a wasted effort, nor one without a clear purpose or product or valid practical and ethical challenge, though Henry's act is not purely altruistic because '[b]y saving his life in the operating theatre, Henry also committed Baxter to his torture. Revenge enough' (278). Whatever the moral complexities, the operation validates the trust that can be placed in his professional competence, in the long time taken to acquire his skill, knowledge and experience, and to use it to best effect. It is also testament to the rewards accruing to competency and the constantly improving self through professional work that effects a synthesis of the ethical, emotional, intellectual and the practical. In this, satisfaction is to be found.

If Henry notices that operating can also rid him of desire (24), then a further benefit accrues. As desire is the basis on which consumerism and capitalism flourishes, activities pushing aside the acquisitive desire (which ultimately fails to satisfy) function as overt forms of resistance. Thus the interest in productive forms of labour expresses both political disapproval of the dissatisfaction rendered by current dominant lifestyles and work practices, and a reaching for deeper spiritual and moral connection that can rebalance (Henry's) rationality and counter the sensationalism of postmodern life.

Conclusion

In Henry the reader finds a man whose character is inflected through the clinical requirements of his profession. He is rational, silent, contained, at times even remote. He is conscious that his clinical, professional identity has been instrumental in forging his character, qualities he employs deliberately to useful effect at times, but finds inhibiting at others, not least because it affects his relationships. His calm exterior disguises an inner turmoil that is anything but unemotional. His public image is authoritative, but 'the trappings of professionalism, of office, can assuage but do not disguise serious self-doubt' (141), which feeds on the political insecurities of a post-9/11 world.

Henry is also wearied by the ever-increasing demands on his time and energy made by bureaucratic control and administrative tasks that require more versatility and faster adaptability but do not require the application of his professional skills. The most productive and profitable time for Henry is when he can apply his skills, knowledge and experience to good effect, when the divisions between self and other, between physical and spiritual, emotional and intellectual, between free time and work time collapse. In his private life cooking (and sex) come closest to replicating this ecstasy. In Henry's surgical work he values the 'egotistical joy in his own skills or the pleasures he still takes […] when he comes down from the operating room like a god' (23). This 'feat of technical mastery and concentration' (44) yields the sense of progress, control and accomplishment lacking in modern work but found in craft activities.

As 'McEwan brings together public and private events, from the tiniest incident in the brain to the biggest street demo of our times, so that they form a troubled unity, as they do in life' (*Evening Standard*, frontispiece), we are alerted to the interconnection of individual human and larger social structure. So we see that Henry's anxiety, proceeding from external factors of national safety, manifests as personal and professional insecurity. Henry's sovereignty is reasserted by excluding the national, global and occupational from his vision, and by contracting his sphere of operation to the home, over which he feels able to achieve paternal, benevolent control. Resolution of the plot in this spatial contraction is less politically weak than it first appears, for Henry's altruism regarding Baxter indicates the willingness to extend responsibility and connection outside his immediate circle, an impulse countering the individual competitiveness defining much else about contemporary life.[18] However, the reader has no way of knowing the extent to which Henry and others like him will survive physiologically and psychologically against near-burial (literal and metaphorical) under a pile of mounting administration in a work culture organised for speed, flexibility, mobility, competitiveness and responsiveness that exhausts the employee, damages mental health and weakens professional identity.

Although Henry believes he can live without stories, his method of information processing, ironically, is a creative, narrative one. It is clear that a coherent and internally consistent narrative is the means by which he understands himself and the world around him, but distinctions between fact and fiction blur where meaning results from the interpretation of the fallible and imaginative mind. Though he denigrates reading as a passive activity, the presentation of other lives (like watching Theo) stands as a point of comparison to Henry's own and, paradoxically, prompts his nostalgia for a past in which 'old-fashioned skills' required a different sense of time, a slowing down.

The next chapter looks more fully at withdrawal or escape as a means of survival. It examines the media-generated role models that are capitalising on the twenty-first century hunt for the elusive Holy Grail of modern life – fulfilment, satisfaction, happiness even – and the recuperative potential of craftwork, whose slower and more reflective activities offer a measure of autonomy, the equal occupation and stimulation of mind and body, the possibility of improvement and mastery, and productive outcomes enabling different and more personally acceptable stories.

Notes

1 A prime example is the First World War soldier whose view of a civilised world, and of himself as able to take orders unquestioningly, is fatally challenged by the experience of the horrors of trench warfare.

2   McEwan discussed this 'In Conversation with Melvyn Bragg', on *The South Bank Show*, ITV, 20 February 2005.
3   Atkins (2004) corroborates the view that by means of a narrative identity we achieve a coherent sense of self, that 'from the practical point of view our relationship to our actions and choices is essentially authorial', that the narrative model alone can 'mediate and synthesise the diverse and heterogeneous aspects of life' (347).
4   Patrick O'Neill's (1994: 109–111) model of narrative nesting inserts a further possible level between the narrator/narratee and the real-world author/reader – the implied hypothetical reader and hypothetical author.
5   This idea of adjusting one's viewpoint, or rewriting one's story when previously held beliefs are undermined by emerging evidence is taken up and applied to identity-making and character-building in Chapter 2.
6   Ward cites Michel de Certeau: belief is believable, one story is accepted rather than another because the values associated with them are part of a rhetorically persuasive package.
7   See Bal (1997: 191), who acknowledges Claude Bremond's view that 'it deserves some thought that so many narratives hold the reader's attention by precisely some form of "human interest"'.
8   Layard (2005: 85–93) presents research findings proving the varying impact of media presentation on human agency.
9   See Chapter 5 on the relevance of home as an anchor.
10 See also *Atonement* (McEwan, 2001) in which a damaged Meissen vase signifies structural fragility. Incidentally, this story again uses musical metaphor – the multiple narrative voices of a family named Tallis (after the sixteenth-century exponent of the polyphonic form) in a text exploring themes of order and balance, symmetry and harmony.
11 Sennett (2006: 35–36) claims that workers can be unhappy with an institution and be still committed to it. I would nuance that workers are committed – not to the institution, but to the social value of the work they do under the auspices of the institution. For nurses, teachers and civil servants there is still an amount of social capital attached to their job, even when the conditions of that work cause trauma.
12 Social science research has found that low-status work produces higher levels of the stress hormone that curtails life expectancy, concluding that for labour to be fulfilling, 'the most important issue is the extent to which you have control over what you do'.
13 On 15 October 2007, a local government boasted of its new work-at-home telephony system 'which the council predicts can save 20% in office accommodation costs, resulting in estimated savings of £1.2million in the first few years [...] allow[ing] the council departments to remodel their business services based on flexible working options, therefore improving staff working practices, reducing fixed-desk occupancy and significantly reducing costs'.
14 Sennett (1998: 118) calls failure the 'modern taboo', whereas it can be a necessary learning step to improvement.

15 See Layard (2005: 81) citing R. Putnam (2000) on the decline in individuals' social and political affiliation.
17 In one sense, operating on Baxter is both a moral *and* an unethical act. A surgeon would not be permitted to operate on a patient with whom he has connection of any kind.
18 Matthew Arnold's, 'Dover Beach' from *Norton Anthology of Poetry*, fifth edition (2005: 1101).
19 Layard, pp. 223–236. Layard identifies the happiness found in narrowly social relationships (friends and family) as the basis on which to recommend the cultivation of wider relationships in order to extend those effects throughout society and achieve the Benthamite 'common good' of the greatest happiness of all. This would increase trust so that the society 'out there' becomes less threatening.

4
Escape
Heaven, heroes and horticulture: the search for solace and meaning

Introduction

In the era dubbed late-capitalism, the market-driven requirements of flexible accumulation produced particular social, cultural and political conditions in which a sector of the middle class became increasingly destabilised. Until recently the working middle class retained both the privileges and distinction of occupational status and a sense of differentiation from the masses enabled by their relative wealth, their particular taste, their broader education and their social conscience (Gunn, 2005: 49–64). With that difference to an extent now levelled, their accumulated social and economic capital and acculturation to independence and self-sufficiency seems all that stands between them and identity crisis.

Feeling anything but autonomous, those out of kilter with market-dominated corporate ethics (after centuries of being ethically aligned to the hegemonic discourse) are experiencing the discomfort of seeing their own life narrative slipping from their control. One effect is that some are seeking active expression of their preferred identity through clearly demonstrated allegiance to alternative attitudes and behaviour, and the more direct 'expression' of that ethical realignment in stories they *are* willing to own. In relating narrative to identity, this chapter examines how a time-related structure forms a critical element of meaning when constant change and short-term market-driven goals deny the relevance of the past and make experience episodic rather than continuous. It also examines the rhythms and rituals of food-related activities through which it appears possible to attain the sense of achievement, fulfilment, stability and connectedness missing from today's accelerated culture and its associated forms of production, even if media-generated role models hijack those activities as means of both subsuming resistance to the market-dominated 'fast' life and disguising the current system's contradictions and discomforts.

Other stories

If, as a result of cultural change in public institutions, 'public servants are voting with their feet' (Bunting, 2005: 139), then where they are going and what they are seeking and finding may clearly indicate kinds of meaning and purpose critical to the well-being of our species. If the flexibility, fragmentation and impermanence characteristic of the new economy are corroding our character, the search may point to situations in which other more durable and desirable human qualities can be developed and demonstrated. If living to the work demands of a market-led global economy is causing us stress and making us ill, the modes of activity and the types of transaction being pursued instead might illuminate those contributors to human happiness we are in danger of losing if we continue uncritically along the road of entrepreneurship, competitiveness and individual independence.

It may be no mere coincidence that the last decade of the twentieth century saw the appearance and growing popularity of particular cultural forms centring around lifestyle choices (discussed later in this chapter and more fully in the next) that appear to rebalance the miseries, disorientation and instabilities of new economy working. Accompanying this trend, there has emerged an increasing body of critical academic work on the pace and nature of working and living in a society dominated by market values which depend on fragmentation and impermanence (Bauman, Beck, Ehrenreich, Eriksen, Harvey, Frank, Hochschild, Ross, Sennett etc.) and on the search for solace, happiness and well-being (Layard, Parkins and Craig, Schoch), in what is now being seen as a sick society requiring remedial political action. However, while Beck (2002) claims that the 'nexus of postmodernism, Thatcherism and neoliberalism, [...] involved the denial or abolition of society and politics' (22), it seems society and politics still retain an ideological charge, as the solutions sought both to rectify the sense of dislocation and to challenge the values and discontinuities of neoliberal ideology and postmodern fragmentation involve 'escapes' that are precisely a gravitation towards more social modes of existence and are effectively forms of political resistance. The irony is that such resistance is being made not as a collective solution, but rather as an individual impulse, remotely enacted, towards self-definition by a large number of people through what Ulrich Beck terms 'the paradoxically collective wish to live "a life of one's own" ' (53).

However, to live one's own life outside of paid employment requires an enormous effort of will and a dislocation of an entirely different sort (not to mention some kind of economic self-sufficiency, and financial and personal risk). This is because what sociologists refer to as the 'project of the self' has become entirely enmeshed with one's work. Bunting (2005) describes how it was that Maslow's ideas in the 1960s led in the 1980s and 1990s to the fusion of the work ethic with the 'growing preoccupation […] with self development and personal potential' (90). Ever since employers understood that employees' emotional commitment made a difference to the bottom line, a continuous effort has been made to co-opt the individual's mental and spiritual energies in the service of profit. So successful has been this corporate encroachment into the reserves once directed to one's personal and private life that self-actualisation is now seen almost entirely in terms of what one does for a living. The attempt to get workers to identify with the corporate brand is merely the final move in the formal effort to align personal and organisational goals, completing the 'seamless fit […] between the corporate requirement for highly motivated, highly flexible labour and individuals' requirement for a sense of self' (Bunting, 2005: 168).

Thus to disengage one's personality from a twenty-four/seven work culture, that through the market has colonised all aspects of identity and leaves no time for meaningful activity outside its ever-widening boundaries, requires a deliberate (if not almost superhuman) act. This is principally because the pace at which modern life is lived leaves little time for the reflection necessary to take an objective and critical stance to the circumstances of one's existence and future development. Some of those who feel that a number of valuable and fulfilling experiences are precluded by the speed of life today have been drawn to 'slow living' movements, such as Slow Food and Citta Slow, which recognise 'there is a positive potential in slowness as a means of critiquing or challenging dominant narratives or values that characterise contemporary modernity for so many' (Parkins and Craig, 2006: ix).

By far the largest group attracted to slow living is from the middle classes, though there is 'nothing conclusive about the proportional over-representation of the middle-class in new social movements as they are also over-represented in conventional political organisations' (Parkins and Craig, 2006: 34–35, quoting Nash). However, inasmuch as this class has the 'social resources for political mobilisation' (35), so too does their privileged social position fit them more easily for the particular form of self-management that is required of modern-day subjects.

It follows that middle-class professionals, with a habituated ability and developed sense of the goals and benefits of self-management, might find the corporate notion of empowerment overly prescriptive and at odds with their generally understood idea of autonomy. The professional who works faster and harder but feels less satisfied, and who also considers that the hedonism implicit in outright consumerism is at odds with the kinds of investment required for long-term security, might well find the idea of escape, of stepping outside the corporate purview, an attractive move.

Though Beck considers there are no 'biographical solutions to systemic contradictions' (Bauman, 2001: 150), directing one's life path is part of what he calls 'reflexive individualization', the process of self-making and risk-taking in which a person assesses and takes responsibility for actions and accepts their intended and unintended consequences. This results in a 'do-it-yourself' biography (Beck, 2001: 3).[1] If, as Lewis (2006) argues, this means the self-forming subject 'aims to map out a coherent consistent narrative of identity through constantly weighing up and assessing one's lifestyle choices' (475), this confirms that even with do-it-yourself biographies, the creation of narrative is both important and critically aligned to the creation of the self (Atkins, 2004: 345, 347).[2]

It follows that if an all-pervasive and overly influential market discourse, operating through employment, becomes the arbiter of selfhood, then the writing of selves comes under corporate management also. The attempt might be made to persuade employees they are 'empowered', but essentially the corporation as life-author is an omnipotent writer wielding control over a creation in which the corporate plot drives character. Dissatisfaction with such determination leads to a desire to avoid being the subject of 'clever corporations [that] offer a narrative for their employees' lives' (Bunting, 2005: 168), to resist being the type of flexible, highly motivated character that the corporate plot requires, to shun the models of corporate heroism offered by business gurus, and to reject management notions of empowerment in favour of the kind of control, autonomy and impact that effective agency affords. If being cast as a character in stories created and managed by 'clever corporations' is unsatisfactory, then there is a need to seek out and write other stories with different characters – in short, to reclaim authorial charge over one's own life. Only by wresting narrative control from the corporation is it possible to be the kind of person one truly wants to be, to become the author of one's own life story. Essentially, where the corporation is an instrumental author, the resistant employee must become an autobiographical one.

Character and the self – creating and owning the story

In order that employees may organise their lives in a manner that makes them author of their own life-story as well as characters in that story, they must discover or imagine and create another context outside the corporation in which such authority is possible. There is consequently a need to identify more acceptable and fulfilling activity in which values more consonant with agreeable self-determination can be enacted, activity able to counter the eschewed values, attitudes and behaviours associated with market-driven immediacy and flexibility. In this sense, by looking at the meteoric rise in cultural forms centred, for example, on gardening, cookery and building, one might conclude that a growing interest in activities that are inherently creative and purposeful represents precisely this 'alternative' impulse. Notably, such deliberately chosen activities, spawning a host of lifestyle and leisure pursuits, are both traditional (even nostalgic) and connected to the evident products of labour rather than the less tangible outcomes of the post-industrial information and service industries. As Hugh Fearnley-Whittingstall (2001) reminds us, 'vegetable gardening becomes the very definition of a worthwhile project: something that matures slowly over time; whose progress is visible and tangible;

and whose final rewards fulfil both a basic need – food – and one of life's finest luxuries – good food' (18).

Importantly, these kinds of activity are time-rooted and rely on knowledgeable practice facilitated by accumulated and transferable learning, even while allowing a degree of both creativity and innovation.[3] In traditional practice, within a community, these activities are often collaborative, rather than competitive, involving a sharing of surplus produce or a giving of labour. They are not wasteful, and when undertaken on a small scale they are 'slow' practices in which agents are able to demonstrate a level of care or mindfulness not possible in the fast-paced, technologically led, 'instant' world. Importantly, in their regard for slowness and for the seasonal calendar, gardening and cookery allow the agent to resynchronise with the time-rhythms and the organic cycle of nature. Hugh Fearnley-Whittingstall believes that 'our lives will be better if we can achieve some closeness to the natural environment, and some understanding of the nature and origins of what we eat, […] [for] a delight in the natural world […] can do the human soul a power of good' (2001: 356–357).

Fearnley-Whittingstall's *River Cottage Year* and Jamie Oliver's *Jamie at Home – Cook Your Way to the Good Life* (2007) are both reliant on seasonality as a basis for growing and cooking locally grown produce. In this concern for the local they exhibit a groundedness that contrasts with the mobility enabled by the phenomenon of time–space compression (Harvey, 1990). In all, these qualities make it easy to see how time-rooted labour presents an opportunity for the agent to resist the pace and shallowness on which business thrives by espousing characteristic attitudes, behaviours and values very different to the instantaneous flexibility and globalisation of the corporate world, and to discover work that provides recuperation from the stress its immediacy causes. Such action is 'a kind of opting out of the world as you're told it must be in favour of the world as you'd like it to be' (Fearnley-Whittingstall, 2001: 32). By this resistance, the agent effectively seizes narrative control to allow a different story, which plots life and experience as a progressive linear path that is also in tune with the pace and formal (cyclical) rhythms of biology and ecology. Further, this narrator-author who is also chief protagonist willingly self-identifies with the characteristic 'nature' and creativity of the 'work' that is at the same time labour, the self and, if the events are captured as a formal autobiography, a written text.

Religion and role models: the spiritual language of ideological heroes

Self-creation as an outcome of individualism and introspection within a predominantly secularised society poses a question concerning the image and likeness to which mankind aspires where 'the delusion that the self matters above all is a symptom of what happens when man lives without God' (Miller, 2002: 13). If one is to write the self, what guidance is there for ethical living and is that even possible when time is fragmented? A declining interest in formal religion and scripture leaves man without their rituals of practice, prescribed rules for ethical conduct or the models of selfhood. When mankind, at the top of the evolutionary tree, hubristically assigns primacy of being to itself, the traditions, laws and heroes must be sought within society. Beck's view on this is that 'having lost their faith in God, [most people] believe instead in the godlike powers of work to provide everything sacred to them: prosperity, social position, personality, meaning in life, democracy, political cohesion' (2000, 63).[4]

However, it is evident that paid work, for all its rituals of observance and its prophetic CEOs speaking of their 'vision' and our 'journey', is failing to fill the spiritual vacuum, and its managers are mostly unsuccessful in the priestly role. For the disenchanted, the search for spirituality becomes focused outside business but not, as will be shown, outside of the market. This is because the market is no exception to the rule that ideology is able to subsume forms of resistance to itself and so capitalise on its (apparent) detractors.[5] What happens when business heroes fail to enchant is that, ironically, the 'miraculous' technology responsible for producing the uncomfortable conditions of mobility and speed then markets, widely and in many formats, alternative iconic figures of celebrity as the antidote to its own sickness.

One explanation of the widespread appeal and production of particular cultural content is that it serves a real need in a secular society disenchanted by both religion and paid employment. Would-be pilgrims, seeking greater control over their selfhood and spiritual fulfilment, and a lifestyle change, find alternative ideals challenging the fast, immediate and flexible values, media-marketed through the iconic forms of such figures as Hugh Fearnley-Whittingstall and Nigella Lawson (to name but two), the god of self-sufficiency and the domestic goddess of home cooking. Many TV cooks trade on values such as slowness, deferment and stability or the real – i.e. authenticity – as a counterbalance to ephemeral and changeable postmodernity.

However, closer analysis of this cultural content discloses a problem rather than a solution. Cynically produced to capitalise on the desire for exit from the market hegemony, what these TV programmes, magazines and so on actually deliver is mythical forms exemplifying what is precisely unattainable in accelerated conditions. Just as business guru books make a leisurely management day and home by five p.m. seem achievable (see Chapter 1), Nigella appears to show the average woman that 'having it all' *is* possible. However, as we shall see, she truly presents a mystery every bit as unfathomable as a Virgin Mother, and her manipulated media image, combining nurturing, business success and sexiness, appeals precisely because it is *im*possible.

It is no mere accident that food-related activity has become a key vehicle for a new spirituality based on slower and more mindful 'earthly' living. In Christianity, food's nurturing and nourishing makes it a particularly sympathetic and universally applicable representation of the ongoing project of spiritual self-maintenance. To stay spiritually healthy and work towards heavenly perfection, the soul needs feeding with the bread of heaven, symbolised by the host. However, when heaven is dismissed, perfection becomes entirely earthbound. In the narrowing focus, mankind is locked in a wholly secular endeavour, and rather than awaiting the afterlife, seeks reward – material comfort and spiritual well-being – in the here and now and within the realm of the actual. Without heaven and without the host, food – real food – assumes greater symbolic importance as the nurturing and nourishing of the spirit becomes identical with its corporeal equivalent. This literal (re)translation sees the care and feeding of the body, enacted in the growing, preparation and serving of food, through their associated ceremonies of gardening and cookery, fully take on the 'project of the self' as an earthly, rather than heavenly, goal. Thus:

> when we even just think about going into the kitchen, we are both creating and responding to an idea we hold about ourselves, about what kind of person we are or wish to be. How we eat and

what we eat lies at the heart of who we are – as individuals, families and communities.

(Lawson, 2004: Introduction)

As food is reinvested with meaning, and the actions serving the body feed the soul also, the corporeal and the spiritual are brought much closer together, collapsing the distance between the literal and the metaphorical, the physical and the metaphysical. Further, the provision, preparation and serving of food become ritualised and the 'arcane and as yet unknown principles and processes' (Shelton, 2006: xxiv) once kept below stairs attain respectability and are able to be brought into middle-class drawing rooms. It is not so much that these arts become commonplace, for it is their mystery that fits them for spiritual purpose. As Shelton tells us in his autobiographical account *Allotted Time*, 'gardening should always be, in part at least, poetic and magical' (40). Thus gardening and cookery books promoting good nurturing and proper nourishment become the new scriptures, their attendant philosophies the new ideology, their practitioners the new saints and priests.

If business leaves us underwhelmed, then the CEOs and heroic examples of neoliberalism placed before us by business gurus will find us similarly unimpressed. However, if we have identified another activity whose characteristic values appeal, we may look towards that for heroes. Here the market's collision with technology and celebrity make it possible to establish new saints quickly and effectively via the media. No precious leisure time needs using for church-going. Devotion can be made from the armchair, and 'food for the soul' can be made in one's own kitchen (Allen, 2007: 11). Saint Delia, goddess Nigella, mother Rachel, cherubic James and sorcerer Heston officiate over the alchemy that turns base ingredients into divine food.[6] Even devilish Gordon has a role to play, while blessed Prue has scripted Kitchen, Meat, Fish and Vegetable Bibles. The *Nigella Kitchen* (2010) series and the linked publication, *Nigella Kitchen: Recipes From the Heart of the Home* (2010), drip religiosity likes candle wax: 'I didn't know whether to call it poached or braised chicken so I called it "praised" chicken because cooking and eating is an act of devotion' (30 September); 'the idea came to me in an apparition the middle of the night'; and again 'Lagerita – the idea came to me like divine inspiration from that great cocktail cabinet in the sky';

even the slightly inappropriate 'Japanese prawns give me a holy and virtuous feeling' (7 October).

Likewise, Rick Stein (2002), agreeing that for proper nourishment 'we need some heroes to turn to' (1–9), joins Hugh Fearnley-Whittingstall and Jamie Oliver as ideological crusaders, setting themselves up (or being set up by their promoters) as archangels guarding older values against a competing religion in which supermarkets and shareholders are cast as infidels. While Rick tells us 'profit is king' (8), Hugh elevates the language to the spiritual, claiming 'profit is their God, and the high priests of the temple are shelf life, consistency of supply and uniformity of size and shape' (Fearnley-Whittingstall, 2001: 24). If these 'new heroes of consumer culture make lifestyle a life project' (Hollows, 2003: 187), it is one that appropriates an otherwise redundant religious language, thereby making evident a thorough collapse of the spiritual into the material in which the latter carries the full weight of providing the meaning of life. Given this incorporation of the spiritual into the everyday, the heroic role models created both within and outside business function not as mere earthly representations of heavenly forms but as real life examples that contain the mythic within the actual. These icons place, within tantalising reach, the comforting idea that it *is* possible to manage the contradictions created by accelerated late-capitalism – it *is* feasible to embrace the fast-acting, hard-edged stance of the competitive, outstanding high-earner while at the same time resisting that value system by enacting the mindful, collaborative and nurturing attitudes required for a successful intimate life. Such models truly are 'fantastic' though many people, needing a way out of their predicament, willingly embrace the illusion.

Handling accelerated living

The effects of the frenetic pace of life caused by the technology-fuelled immediacy and flexibility of the late twentieth and early twenty-first centuries are addressed by a number of theorists (Bauman, Bell, Harvey, Hylland-Eriksen, Sennett, Ross, Leccardi, Parkins and Craig, among others), by many management gurus (Pritchett, Reich, Handy, to name a few) and by most writers of 'escape' narratives (Mayle, Shelton, Stewart, de Blasi *et al.*). Of these, the business writers eulogise speed for its role in pushing the endless corporate change that enhances profit and turnover rates, and hold the individual to account for any failure to adapt sufficiently well or fast enough to stay employed (see Chapter 1). The others, in varying measure, consider the fast pace a problem impacting negatively on the conditions of existence as the sheer proliferation of options breeds confusion and constantly changing demands diminish the opportunity for considered and meaningful action.

In particular, 'temporal acceleration' is the key to understanding the link between biographical uncertainty, institutional precariousness and 'the de-standardization of work and its consequences for personal life' (Leccardi, 2005: 139). Consequently, it is key also to understanding why biographical certainty might be sought through a culture engaging with greater institutional stability and more predictable, meaningful and autonomous types of labour. Flexible work practices not only preclude the kinds of satisfaction once afforded by professional employment, they also intensify the apparently irresolvable tension between work and home life. Though it is now possible to work from home and the opportunity is sold as an advantage to the worker, it is clear that the worker's Foucauldian self-discipline accrues benefit to the company and disadvantage to the individual. This is because ever-expanding workloads undertaken by fewer and fewer staff fearing job loss eat into the free time that was once expended on leisure activity and in maintaining happy and healthy relationships with partners, children and friends.[7]

The competing demands of work and home find us constantly juggling our priorities and discovering it is well-nigh impossible to maintain performance over the many areas of operation that we must manage on a daily basis. To commit to the work necessary to secure promotion and maintain an income (the familiar time-poor, cash-rich situation) means abandoning the family for whose benefit the effort is being made, farming out children and the elderly to care providers and relying on fast food. To devote the energy needed to succeed as a caring homemaker, parent and partner (time-rich, cash-poor) and provide nutritious home-made meals means facing a lack of progress at work or even unemployment.[8] Prioritising work brings spiritual emptiness while concentrating on home life can damage one's social capital and lower self-esteem. Late-capitalism may *appear* to offer a vast range of opportunities but managing their attendant complexities and incompatibilities means resorting to plate-spinning, short-term solutions that cause disorientation, exhaustion and incoherence.

In the face of such fragmentation and increasing demands on time, marketing the possibility of handling the speed and containing the fractures and contradictions resulting from postmodern life is merely another profitable business opportunity. Hugh and Nigella appeal because they *appear* as miracle workers, people having neatly solved the problem of managing time pressure, earning (more than) sufficiently and reconciling the work/home dichotomy, though the observer's belief relies on forgetting the huge advantage such rare examples may derive from social connections and undisclosed (emotional, practical and financial) support established as part of their already privileged lives.

Nigella, in particular, is a clear middle-class representation of Jameson's 'imaginary or formal "solutions" to irresolvable social contradictions' (Jameson, 1981: 64). Her form embodies a vision denying that, in the real world, for ordinary people, capitalist economics requires two full-time wage-earners to pay a mortgage and support a family, and the manifest result is deteriorating personal relationships because the time and attention is no longer available to nurture and maintain meaningful connection to others, let alone manage and overcome any other difficulties arising from the same time-poverty. Joanne Hollows (2003), writing on Nigella and on the cultural significance of food, 'suggest[s] that an identification with the position of the "domestic goddess" negotiates the opposition between the feminist and the housewife by offering a position that is only available in fantasy'. The position is one in which women can 'have it all', where competing female roles are wholesomely (if fantastically) fused in a single identity, where pressures of time scarcity disappear in an easy reconciliation of the contradictory demands of care and convenience, where the 'cultural omnivore' bridges highbrow and lowbrow culture, and the stressed reality of a difficult present is brushed away by embracing the simplicity of an imaginary past that uses nostalgia to evoke emotional memories 'as a source of social and psychological sustenance' (Hollows, 2003: 179–202).

The problem for self-esteem is that such unfeasible resolutions embodied in the real makes it seem, like the business self-help advice, that coping is a purely matter of personal ability. When Nigella appears always happy, always smiling, joyfully glancing as she opens a fridge door, leaves a room, or unscrews the lid from a flask of soup in the back of a black cab, despite an over-full and ultra-busy life, then maybe the magic you are missing in your life can be found in her books. In her the audience is presented with a model of kitchen-bound, domestic fidelity fused not only with the feminist but also – not mentioned by Hollows – with the bedroom temptress. In this she trumps Hestia, the Greek (virgin) goddess of hearth and home, whom she represents by adding yet another dimension to an already impossible combination. When she enters the kitchen in red satin nightwear, to whip up and eat a plateful of doughnut French toast, we are being asked to believe the culture of excess has no ill effects. Not only can you have it all but you can *be* it all – indulgent, sexy, successful and dutiful to yourself and others and relaxed even while juggling various demanding roles. The danger in falling for the illusion is in missing the manipulation used to convince an audience both that she is real and that the solution she presents is achievable.

The fantasy is craftily hidden also in Lawson's 2007 book, *Nigella Express: Good Food Fast*, which strives to appear fully grounded when taking on the problem of time pressure. On the jacket she is seen with mobile phone in one hand, a fistful of spaghetti in the other; the inference is that keeping up relationships, attending to business and producing a feast is all possible at one and the same time – providing of course, as told by business gurus, that one understands the secrets of success, all of which can be learned by purchasing the publication.[9] So clearly is this book marketed to address the problems of modern fast living that its introduction is worth quoting at some length:

> This is, as the title makes clear, a book about fast food, but it is a book about fast food for those who love eating. Perhaps that's self evident: how could I write any other sort? But I start with this premise because so much is written about the need to reduce the time we spend cooking it's as if the kitchen were a hateful, unsafe place, and that it must be only reasonable for us to avoid it. I love food, I adore being in the kitchen and I am happy to cook. But here's the problem: the day doesn't have enough gaps in it for me to do much shopping and the evening – what with battles over

homework, the still unchecked-off things I was meant to do, the calls I was supposed to return – doesn't yield much time to cook. But I must eat, and I must eat well – or else what is the point of it all? And then there are the people that need to be fed. I don't mention them grudgingly, either, I love to feed people, and rare is the person who comes into my home and leaves without a foil parcel of something from the kitchen.

I have had to adapt. I manage [...] within the confines of a timetable that is disorganized, busy, full of things I want to do as well as things I don't want to do – though sometimes I'm so tired I can't tell the difference. In short I have a normal life, the sort we all share. [...] For the most part, I am either in a hurry or in some state of psycho-fizz or obligation-overload and food has to be fitted in.

[...] In a way, then, this book has written itself. This is just as well, since I left myself barely enough time to write it.

[...] [I] have then given the method in a number of short, precise steps. This is to make sure you never have to turn a page to continue a recipe and to help every step read as clearly as it can.

(Lawson, 2007: Preface)

Perhaps the clearest indication given of increasing pace in 2007 is the contrast between the harassed tone of this introduction and the more languid tone of her signature publication six years earlier, which asks us to turn aside from a cooking style of 'briskness and little pleasure' to become a 'domestic goddess, trailing nutmeggy fumes of baking pie in our languorous wake' (Lawson, 2000: vii).

Despite her goddess status, the PR machine takes some trouble to present Nigella as one of us. *Nigella Express* insists that 'we all share' this busy, overloaded life, but asks the viewer/reader to accept this as normal, that life is disorganised, stressful and leaves us 'so tired' as more and more things must be accomplished in a shorter and shorter time that we 'can no longer tell the difference' between things we want, and do not want to do. This evident loss of control over properly evaluating one's activity cannot indicate anything other than the failure to direct one's life ethically. Recipe pages and chapter titles continue the hurried theme.[10] The personal impact of overstretch is acknowledged in the admission that 'desperate times call for desperate measures – and if an exhausted weeknight, after a six o'clock meeting, a row over homework and a reproachful list of unreturned calls and emails doesn't count as desperate times, I don't know what does' (Lawson, 2000: 139). Perhaps most astonishing is the effort made to ensure that 'you never have to turn a page to continue a recipe and [...] every step read[s] as clearly as it can' (Preface), which hints at Taylorist avoidance of unnecessary movements in which workplace time-and-motion efficiency is imported into the domestic domain. This is unashamed marketing aimed at purchasers desperate for a solution to their overburdened lives by implying the remedy is available within its pages of 'fabulous fast foods, ingenious short cuts, terrific time-saving ideas, [and] effortless entertaining' (inside front cover).

Analysing the target audience for this marketing tells a great deal about the 'us', those for whom an antidote to hurriedness is thought to have resonance. That audience is not the working mum whose baseline income comes from shift-work at the local supermarket. The appeal is made to the educated, middle-class, professional working woman familiar with up-market ingredients – Maldon salt, scallops, shitake mushrooms, chorizo, mirin (Japanese sweet rice wine), nam pla (fish sauce), Savoiardi (Italian lady's finger biscuits), wasabi – and earning enough to pay a cover price of £25.00 in addition to childcare costs. It is made to those who 'don't want to feel like a post-modern, post-feminist, overstretched woman but, rather, a domestic goddess, [...] no longer being entirely an office creature' (Lawson, 2000: vii) who, overdetermined by paid employment, are now mourning the loss of some aspects of both humanity and female domestic identity – giving, caring, sharing – caused by entering a (still) male-dominated workplace. Nigella's view that 'baking stands as a metaphor for the familial warmth of the kitchen we fondly imagine used to exist, and as a way of reclaiming our lost Eden' (vii) promotes rediscovery of the pleasures inherent in the selflessness of this domestic female role and in the values of an earlier, better and more spiritually aware era, even if their achievement is problematic.

The appeal of the past

Lawson's observation of 'how much easier things were in my grandmother's time[, s]he had a schedule, and an unchanging one. [...] a little of that Ordnung is desireable'[11] (2007: 3) acknowledges bygone structural order and stability, a time of predictability in which expectations and identity were socially defined. Today, 'liquid modernity' (Bauman, 2000) has broken down barriers, transgressed norms, dismantled typologies and refused classifications, producing social confusion that is problematic for the old middle-class. Viewers of the *Nigella Express* series are uncomfortable seeing the now time-poor goddess step down from her pedestal to eat on the hoof when standing at bus stops, riding in taxis and on the Tube. Not only is it unbelievable that she does so,[12] more importantly, eating in the street is an alarming sign of creeping social degradation. It seemingly gives the hurried middle-class female permission to transgress a social code but is, at the same time, evidence of 'falling' (Ehrenreich, 1989), a sign of the inexorable slide and dissolving boundaries that leave the old middle class vulnerable.

Undoubtedly, looking backwards is a way of handling this discomfort because 'lived or imagined experiences are intertwined with emotions that are a source of comfort in the present' (Hollows, 2003: 193) and as such, signal the attempt to recover a more secure identity:

> In a postfeminist landscape in which it is often manifest that contemporary femininity is multiple and complex, the desire to temporarily inhabit a figure of femininity which appears stable, which is of another time (literal or mythical) in which things seem simpler and less contradictory than the present, can also appear to offer a sense of escape from the pressures of managing and ordering both everyday life and feminine selves.
>
> (Hollows, 2003: 195)

However, the appeal of an earlier era signified by home-cooking and hand-baking is clearly not a desire to return to the social and gender limitations of that time. Rather the attraction is to something specific about the activities themselves and what they are still able to make relevant and desirable in the present day. Men are equally drawn by cookery, Hollows observes, and '[i]f the meaning of cooking is "in the process" rather than the end product, then these meanings *are not necessarily gender-specific*' (192 quoting Lawson, emphasis added). Thus the recent revival of older arts reaches for something beyond gender, beyond a specific time (though bound up with how time is experienced) to something universal.

Certainly, Jamie Oliver's example of cooking for friends and family challenges both the traditional feminine role and the 'skin-of-the-teeth efficiency' (Lawson, 2000: vii) associated with male chefs even as he trades also on 'a busy family life and a hectic working schedule' (Oliver, 2007: 9) and hides his upbringing in a genteel Essex village beneath a boy-of-the-streets, mockney accent. Other chefs across the spectrum of gender, age, sexual orientation, ethnicity, personality, skill level and cooking style fill our screens and bookshelves with niche-marketed material for any particular taste. However, publishers have also recognised a more widespread appetite for the value-laden associations of times now gone, which crosses all boundaries. This nostalgic turn can be seen in Lawson's *How To Be A Domestic Goddess: Baking and the Art of Comfort Cooking* (2000) and *Nigella Express* (2007) publications and Oliver's *Jamie at Home: Cook Your Way to the Good Life* (2007) where its presentation has produced the hybridity common to postmodernity. Nigella's speedy cooking recipes are countered with lithographic chapter illustrations reminiscent of 1950s cookbooks, while the duotone photographs of postwar domesticity hark back at least half a century. Jamie's book is offered in a printed textured cover that takes the imagination back even earlier to a time when books were clothbound. This retro presentation is bolstered by use of a nineteenth-century font (Clarendon) and lithographic illustrations entirely out of synchronicity with his modern, relaxed, full-colour cover photo and friendly lowercase 'jamie at home' title. These particular Janus-faced publications cleverly appeal on both levels: through lifestyle identification with a batch of current, niche-marketed, celebrity cooks catering for specific tastes and through a more widely shared and deeply felt acknowledgement that present-day misery can be mitigated by nostalgia evoking a Proustian remembrance of times past. This canny fusion of particularity and universality thus appeals to the widest possible market by capitalising on anomie (even while upholding the profits and values of the system producing the moral vacuum) and attempting to fill the void left by the retreat of religion (even while rejoicing in the abyss that provides a never-ending desire for comfort). The disenchanted, desperate for greater fulfillment and guidance toward a lifestyle that eschews the material accumulation, transience and superficiality of postmodernity, will be attracted by texts selling contentment through an engagement with activities attending to the fundamental and enduring need for food and the associated values of service and sharing that were part of the experience and values of earlier times, and yet are transportable to a predominantly secular context. Jamie recognises an essential contemporary truth when stating:

> we're all pretty spoilt now, as far as luxuries are concerned, but I reckon that the *best luxury in life comes from experience [...] and knowledge* and I think food and cooking are among the most important things out there for us to learn about.
>
> (Oliver, 2007: 9, emphasis added)

So, when he encourages the reader to buy from sources that respect nature, when Fearnley-Whittingstall (2001) says he has 'always found sharing food with friends to be among the highest of pleasures' (357), and when Lawson promises a 'thrill at the sheer pleasure you've conjured up' (2000: 185) and praises 'the sense of connectedness you get, with your cooking, your home, your food, [which] is the very opposite of constraint' (334), they are each celebrating the magical natural process and connectivity that turn seeds into plants, into ingredients, into food, into comfort and into friendship.

It is the engagement with humanity and the processes that serve humanity at the most basic level that create the wholesome identity of a person who is materially satisfied, psychologically happy and physically healthy. The nostalgic turn is a reaching back, not just for a less complicated time in which identities were less complex and contradictory, but for the wisdom of ages past, the accumulated knowledge that is in danger of being lost forever, that was passed down because it was considered valuable not only to an individual at a specific time but to all mankind forever. Recovery in this sense is not only about 'social and psychological sustenance' (Hollows, 2003: 193), it is about re-establishing the continuity between the past and the present, retrieving a sense of the self/ourselves as current-day inheritors of collective wisdom who, in turn, can bequeath something valuable and enduring to future generations. It is about ourselves as organic creatures whose bio-rhythms are tuned to the natural world in which life is experienced as a linear trajectory from origin to terminus as part of a regulated, never-ending cycle of death and renewal.

Labouring for heaven on earth

Nigella Express is just one of many products we temporarily think might hold the key to salvation only to find, after we have bought it, read it, and shopped for and cooked with wasabi, that conditions remain as stressful as ever. The one thing no product is able to achieve is altering the relationship of time to activity, for:

> perhaps it is the time famine that is the greatest blight of our age, [...] many of us are growing discontented with the questions that sustained us through the decades of greed: [...] Some of us are beginning to ask new questions: about how our quality of life might be improved by a more fulfilling relationship with the land around us.
> (Fearnley-Whittingstall, 2001: 357)

Here Fearnley-Whittingstall is telling us that the accumulation of personal wealth, the intensification of materialism, has led us to both the unhappiness and a way to seek its remedy. The required improvement to the quality of life is not to be had through hedonism, which is pleasure emptied of meaning, but by something closer to the Greek notion of *eudaemonia*, the contentment gained from purposeful activity. Cookery and gardening are intrinsically fulfilling and therapeutic because they are creative and purposeful. The food production process is ultimately linked to an end product that is vital to physical life, so in the search for meaning, by having a clear point, it impacts also on our spiritual welfare because of the way the human psyche tries to make sense of and find value in experience.

Nigel Slater indicates further reason for the current obsession with food. His writing indicates that a number of elements compromised by the lifestyles thrust upon us by the flexible economy – time, well-being, order, continuity, ethics – are intrinsically addressed by mindful attention to food production. Though presented with a personality differing from Nigella in gender and sexual orientation, he nevertheless is selling ideas of consolation for today's frantic lifestyles. He does so in *The Kitchen Diaries* (2005) by deliberately promoting seasonal produce as a means to re-establish connection, not just between food and the land, or food and kinship, but also between food and the regulated passing of time. In a book which took a year to write and photograph 'in "real time"', his mantra '[r]ight food, right place, right time' specifically honours the time-bound, organic process by 'rebuilding a cook's relationship with nature'. It is also enormously comforting, in an otherwise shaky world, to find that '[t]here is something deeply, unshakably right about eating food in season […] about going with the flow, cooking with the natural rhythms of the earth' (vii). It is no surprise that this 'rightness' also raises moral concerns for the impact of modern food production methods, with people like Nigel asking 'what effect will this [food] have on me, my well-being and that of the environment' (4), a question specifically linking one's actions with an ensuing identity, health and happiness, and with wider-world dynamics. More interesting is the claim that solace is found in '[f]ood *with a story you can follow* from seed packet to table' (viii, emphasis added) for in addition to the comfort, rhythm and ritual that is reinstated by organic, time-centred processes, this recognisable and coherent 'story' acknowledges the importance of narrative, continuity and connectivity that is missing in the absentminded eating habits encouraged by fast and fragmented lifestyles.

All the concerns aforementioned are picked up and played out in autobiographic escape narratives featuring food production. In these narratives the hero protagonist writes an identity in story that is secured through a 'good life' able to deliver material, psychological and physiological satisfactions rooted in recognition of the values of continuity, organic connectedness, accumulated knowledge and ordered slow time. Marketers may (and do) abuse and exploit these fundamental needs, but they cannot erase their essential meaning. So, even where TV cooks are recognised as media-hyped lackeys, or the domestic goddess dream is unmasked as a marketing sham selling enduring happiness, because 'food is how we mark the connections between us, how we celebrate life' (Lawson, 2004: vii), the value of activities associated with its production nevertheless remains to offset the unsatisfactory ethics and the lack of purpose, fulfillment, rootedness and community that is experienced in the competitive environment of paid employment. Unsurprisingly, where such deficiencies are felt by the time-pressured professional middle class, whose personal relationships are failing, whose identity is being eroded, and whose sanity and autonomy are threatened at work, one possibility is to make these activities not just a temporary diversion but the basis of a permanent new reality lived out in actual escape.

If the rise and popularity of autobiography indicates a need to (re)locate the self in the midst of the turmoil of post-structural multiplicity (Smith and Watson, 2001: 132–133), then it appears escapees are using that drive in an attempt to become creator, narrator and key protagonist in a life story over which they have seized full (godlike) authorial control as a means of resisting definition through hegemonic market discourse. However, the experience they have through the work they do is key to that new sense of self and their spiritual and psychological well-being. Robin Shelton (2006) makes this explicit, in *Allotted Time: Twelve Months, Two Blokes, One Shed, No Idea*, his account of the year of horticulture that rescues him from 'the deeper pits of futility and misery' (231) caused by the time-poverty of his teaching job (180). As he and his friend approach their overgrown allotment, it is with:

> the conviction that, somehow, the saviour of our sanity lies dormant under those grasses [...] we both feel an abstract desire to become more involved in and connected with the cyclic processes of nature, and in some senses 'play God' of our own vegetable world perhaps because we both feel a similar lack of control over the direction our respective real ones are going.
>
> (Shelton, 2006: 8)

Here Shelton links good mental health not only with regulated, time-dependent processes but, importantly, with work activity over which they can take control to satisfy the desire for God-like creativity that elsewhere is diminished. Recognising also the 'therapeutic nature of gardening' (36), and that he's 'changed since starting the allotment' (52), confirms how activity impacts character development. That Shelton also feels 'compelled to write' (52) adds a further creative dimension and marks the conscious effort to record the activity through which this character development and return to full mental health occurs. Thus the reflexive identity-formation process results from both the interface between the agent and the external world *and* the mindful activity that represents the interface between parts of the self, with writing a vehicle that concurrently enables and captures the development as it occurs. This simultaneous function of writing may explain why such memoirs do not take the form of situating the remedial episode in the more usual autobiographical birth-to-the-present-day trajectory (which necessarily has to project backwards into the deep recesses of memory and involves a deal of interpretation and editing from a distance). Instead the accounts use a diary format in which the understanding and response are taken from more immediate impressions (see Chapter 6).

Shelton's writing captures a transitional stage between books that view gardening or cookery as an activity scheduled alongside paid work (hobbies), and 'escape' texts recording a permanent geographical relocation and lifestyle change that symbolise a quest for alternative employment as one of many different and more fulfilling outcomes. Shelton is impoverished, remains in the UK and takes his year on the allotment as an interlude that returns him to sanity in a new understanding of what is involved in maintaining the spirit in good order. However, his title, *Allotted Time*, and the book's content confirm that temporality is a key issue of concern for full mental health while his exploration of the tripartite relationship between the natural cycles of life (birth, death and renewal), work (on the allotment) and the human agent (who is part of both processes) pinpoints an interconnected schematic that is used by many writers of escape narratives.[13] Certain other themes through which this primary relationship is explored – spirituality, fruitful activity (literally and metaphorically), education and knowledge, connectedness (to each other, the earth and to production) and mindful living – appear often enough in escape texts to be a noticeable counterbalance to the immediacy and flexibility that characterise contemporary business attitudes, behaviour and values.

Common to all is that each narrator has a view of paid work in a formal capitalist economy as a kind of hell. 'Unpleasant depression' had caused Shelton (2006: xvii) to be off work for a few months from a 'teaching job which gave [him] far too little time to kill […][and] was driving [him] literally insane' (180), while his friend 'had a job which was slowly driving him to the same place' (xvii). Shelton's opinion of formal employment as 'some kind of suit-encrusted endurance test' (122) ably describes the battling that takes place (sometimes vanquishing the weaker party) in the modern workplace. Similarly, Stewart in *Driving Over Lemons* (1999) sees 'besuited businessmen, waiting for the daily ride to the treadmill' and muses that 'whatever becomes of this decision [to move abroad] [...] it has to be better than that' (31–32). Mayle (2000) considers his visiting advertising executive, Tony, 'was welcome to every second' (75) of work described as 'tough business, bloody competitive' (66) that left him unable to relax, even though he 'had left the cares of office behind' (66). De Blasi (2004), at work, had 'always tripped' (253) on corporate ladders while her husband Fernando says of his new life there are 'times when I want things to be easier or clearer, but I had worse terrors sitting, day after day, in that office in the bank' (250).

Shipping out

If the decision is not to 'shape up' in the way that the corporate world requires, then 'shipping out' presents a reasonable alternative. The failure to thrive in paid employment could be why Passmore, the protagonist in David Lodge's *Therapy* (1995) quotes a Gallup poll that claims 'nearly half the people in the country would like to emigrate if they could' (85). If, as Passmore claims, we have 'become a nation of unhappy hopers' (103) waiting for 'some adventure, some encounter, some miraculous transformation of [our] ordinary lives' (214), it may be that the remedy lies in travel abroad, like the pilgrimage undertaken by his childhood sweetheart in order to achieve 'something quite challenging and clearly defined, something that would occupy your whole self body and soul, for two or three months' (302–303). Or, as McEwan's Perowne expresses it, one is urged to seek some 'colourful adventure, a drama of strong wills, inner resources, new qualities of character revealed under pressure' (McEwan, 2006: 266).

It is clear that some challenge is necessary in order to achieve a sense of reward and satisfaction. A life of complete ease is one of boredom as James Chatto (2005) recognises when he 'missed having a job to go to – a purpose in life beyond pleasure' (78). However, insurmountable challenge is no recipe for happiness. In the new economy this comes from unending pressure and lack of accomplishment brought on by demands to achieve a particular outcome without the necessary resources to do so, or to achieve a great number of things without the time to do so. Its audit culture measures and checks everything except the excesses of its own system, and workers failing inspection (a scrutiny built on lack of trust and designed to diminish it still further) are judged as unsuccessful.

By contrast, in the remote rural European cultures, where work and character are still valid measures of success, the valued attributes are of a different order. Stewart (1999) puts it starkly: 'watering is a measure of manhood in the Alpujarras' (119). Here are no violent or competitive man-to-man power games, sporting or otherwise. Where water is critical to livelihood, the man who regularly tends his *acequias*, and keeps the water flowing, ducting it this way and that as required by his crops, is king of a natural element. Battles in escape settings are pitched against natural powers and are about overcoming properly impersonal forces rather than those claiming to be impersonal as a means of avoiding responsibility (see Chapter 1). Resource management here is not the penny-pinching ways of the professional manager always having to do more with less by discounting the human consequences of the mathematics. Management in this guise sustains life; it does not destroy it.

Going backwards to go forward

In seeking escape from the workplace, migrants appear to take both a physical and spiritual journey in a move to recapture and espouse actions, values, attitudes and behaviours lost in the Anglo-American cultural model. The opportunity of creating synergy between lived experience and the expression of identity is sought in European communities that are not yet totally in thrall to the market, and which offer an older, more stable and structured time, in which life is lived slowly, communally and purposefully. If the 'shift towards reflexive individualization means that choice becomes central to people's existence as their identities are formed increasingly through lifestyle-oriented decision-making' (Lewis, 2006: 461), then the adoption of lifestyles chosen for their associated characteristics marks the deliberate attempt to make a particular kind of identity.[14]

Turning to the past for a lifestyle can appear merely as nostalgia, which is easily criticised as the inability of some to adapt in the changing environment. However, seeing these migrants as evolutionary laggards misses an important aspect of the action they take. There is no intention to colonise or fetishise the past; if anything, the market does that in order to sell retro products, such as celebrity chef-branded cookware, to the 'unhappy hopers' whose desire-led consumerism repeatedly glosses their materially full but spiritually empty lives. Neither is this nostalgia the kind of retreat of which Jameson (1984) speaks when he describes that 'we are condemned to seek History by way of our own pop images and simulacra of that history, which itself remains forever out of reach' (71). The cultures that the escapees join are not fake replicas of bygone societies; they are generally communities that, by virtue of their remoteness, enjoy a way of life that elsewhere has been erased by modern technologies; a way of life seen not merely as 'the good old days', but one in which certain non-economic values still have currency. The reasoning is summed up by the cook de Blasi (2004), living in Tuscany, echoing Stewart's appreciation of a life lived to different measure:

> We've come here to make a life scrubbed clean of clutter, a life that follows the rhythms and rituals of this rural culture. A life as they say here, that's made *a misura d'uomo*, to the measure of a man. We're hoping this is a place that still remembers real life, the once-upon-a-time life, the hard parts and the joyful ones. *Dolce e salata*, sweet and salty. Like fasting before a feast, each side of life dignifying the other. It may be that everywhere in this world there is the possibility to live with this balance, but it's here, right here, we've come to look for it. [...] We've come because we think it might be here where we can learn which way progress runs. Our suspicion is strong that there is a greater peace in going backward.
>
> (de Blasi, 2004: 36)

The fact that de Blasi and her husband hope to achieve balance indicates that the life they have left is out of kilter. Similarly, Shelton (2006) expresses the importance of historical continuity and balance to the human psyche:

> By being involved in, and in touch with, the rhythmic and cyclic nature of the processes of gardening, I am stepping in time with the feet of many millions of ancestors. Perhaps bipolar disorder is simply another name for what happens when we try to ignore this rhythm.
>
> (Shelton, 2006: 180)

A common notion of progress as unremittingly forward, such as that which underpins the ever-new of contemporary economics, is being challenged here as a failure properly to assess, honour and preserve certain learning that comes from not only personal but collective past experience.

The next chapter will demonstrate, through a more detailed analysis of escape narratives, how the writers' migration appears to be a deliberate attempt to disown the values and actions characteristic of the mainstream Western economic mode. Their engagement instead in a slower, more mindful existence recovers an older relationship of time and activity in which the continuity and connection to others and to the items of production, experienced through the rhythm, routines and rituals of horticulture and cookery, improve physiological and psychological health, and provide the spiritual satisfaction of a purposeful and meaningful (earthly) life. In turn, the characteristic values and actions of this slower life constitute a more wholesome identity of a kind that is achieved, owned and recorded in autobiographical narratives which bear witness to the agent's authorial control in the process of (self)creation while their formats also 'satisfy the desire for story killed by postmodern fiction' (Miller, 2002: 12).

Notes

1 Beck (2001: 2–4) is clear that although identity is a task, something to be worked for and achieved, there is not a free-floating freedom; rather, one is 'tied into a network of regulations, conditions and provisos' that are part of 'a densely woven institutional society'.
2 Atkins (2004) believes that a narrative 'provides the strategies for coherence and continuity' (350) by which one can carve out an actual story that one assumes responsibility for from the potential implied by all fields of action.
3 Flexible new capitalism also requires creativity and innovation, but merely to plug the gaps left when downsizing and delayering jettisons accumulated knowledge and experience. Likewise, whereas knowledge is enduring and reusable, information is mostly of-the-moment and throwaway.
4 Beck (2000) states: 'Just name any value in modernity and I will show that it assumes the very thing about which it is silent: participation in paid work.'
5 Jameson (1984: 87) draws attention to capitalism's reabsorption of 'even overtly political interventions like those of The Clash'.
6 Lawson (2005) tells of 'conjur[ing] up [a] chocolate heaven' that is 'divinely retro' (185). Rachel Allen (2007) describes one dish as 'heaven in a

casserole'(34), others as 'divine' (20). De Blasi (2005) has a chapter entitled 'Hell is where Nothing's Cooking' (245–268).

7 Office of National Statistics (2001): 'There is a trend for falling marriage rates and increased marital breakdown across Europe. […] In 2001 countries in northern and western Europe typically had the highest divorce rates … The rate in the United Kingdom, at 2.6 in 2000, was above the EU average of 1.9 per 1,000 people.' See also Eriksen (2001: 131–132, 150) and Parkins and Craig (2006: 43).

8 See Burchell (2007). Recent research shows the gender divide wider than ever (men in full-time employment work an average of 55 hours a week, including domestic duties, women 68 hours), with pay differentials favouring the male remaining employed and protecting promotion prospects.

9 The mobile phone is removed in the 2009 edition's cover photo.

10 Recipes in *Nigella Express* mention: being 'squeezed for time' (9), being 'really too exhausted' (19), 'life is spent on what feels like some sort of cakewalk treadmill' (139), 'I battle over homework or try to clear my desk or tackle whatever other doomed task I set myself' (117). Chapter titles include: Retro Rapido; Get Up and Go: Breakfast at Breakneck Speed; Quick, Quick Slow; Against the Clock: No Time? No Problem; Speedy Gonzales; On The Run; and Hey Presto.

11 This class-denying idealism discounts the real hardships for most in 'grandmother's time'.

12 *The Radio Times* (8–14 December 2007: 30) reports criticism from its ABC1 readership (www.nrs.co.uk) for Nigella's attempt to look ordinary – 'Like taking a bus to do her shopping!' – indicating they saw through a media image suppressing her economic status for the sake of imaginary presentation.

13 Shelton is an ex-public servant. Though other writers used as examples come from non-public service backgrounds, a clear verisimilitude to Shelton's position is demonstrated in the conditions which propelled their migration and in the temporality and qualities of working lives described in their new places of residence.

14 See also Atkins (2004), who confirms that 'through critical self-reflection, self-knowledge, and self-direction, one can emphasise an existing trait or replace it [and] the latter is achieved by placing oneself in situations that promote the acquisition of the desired trait' (363).

5
Recovery
Narratives of becoming: slow working towards a better life-story

Slow living – lifestyle politics

Where the fast pace of life is a key determining (but negatively experienced) feature of life in new-economy conditions, then slowing down appears an obvious means of counteracting its damaging effects. In addition to the growing (academic as well as general) interest in resistant modes of existence, recent decades have seen the evolution of whole social movements dedicated to slow life. One such movement, Slow Food, is examined by Wendy Parkins and Geoffrey Craig in *Slow Living* (2006); they conclude that 'the limits of capitalist consumption may be particularly exposed by the practices of so-called "alternative lifestyles", such as slow living [...] [which] focus on a politics of time and space' (139). For them also 'slowness can become a way of signalling an alternative set of values or a refusal to privilege the workplace over other domains of life' (1). Unsurprisingly therefore, slow living has become associated with downshifting; voluntarily opting for a lower income to pursue a less materialistic life at a pace in which it is possible to live a more considered and thoughtful existence than is possible in mainstream work/life patterns.[1]

In fact, 'slow living rejects a work culture that overwhelms everyday life and operates with such speed and fury that it denies the opportunity to consider mindfully the pleasures and purposes of each task' (Parkins and Craig, 2006: 67). More importantly,

> slow living is not a simple matter of 'slowing down' but rather is more fundamentally an issue of *agency* [original emphasis].

> It represents an attempt to exercise agency over the pace of everyday existence and the movements across and investments in, the respective domains of everyday life.
>
> (Parkins and Craig, 2006: 67)

By these definitions slowness rejects reflexivity – the conditioned response – in favour of reflectivity – the considered response. Slowness is about mindful agency, conscious and deliberate action by agents who both are in control and take responsibility for their action – the ethical action that Kim Atkins holds is part of a human's practical identity, i.e. one who must act in the world. What this means in practice, according to recent research by Breakspear and Hamilton (2004a), is that 'for most downshifters the dominant change in their lives involves taking control of their time and devoting it to more fulfilling activities' (17).[2] In the rejection of dominant market values and through a concern for physical and mental well-being, middle-class downshifters attracted to slow living show a determination to take control over their lives with the specific aim of reconnecting with other human beings and a different temporality.[3] Or, as Parkins and Craig conclude:

> In a climate of 'instantaneous time', 'frenzied families' and 'time-poor subjects' where the fragility of bodies and social relations may be all too apparent, the conscious cultivation of slowness may be a salutary reminder of how our rhythms and routines have the potential to either challenge or perpetuate the disaffection of everyday life.
>
> (Parkins and Craig, 2006: 140)

Narratives that establish the self as a being that is part of a natural order structured by biological and ecological rhythms sever allegiance to the mainstream economic order and substitute its value set with another. Not only is a calmer pace the antidote to the chaotic, unexamined and unhealthy fast culture lifestyle, fulfilment is achieved without a prestigious job title or the high wage it commands. The satisfactions of money are limited as the millionaire melon grower in Peter Mayle's *A Year in Provence* (1989) confirms: 'It was very agreeable to be rich but one needed something else' (179). The 'something else' Mayle finds is well-being. His watch 'stayed in a drawer' and he tells the time 'by the position of the shadows in the courtyard [...] The sun was a great tranquillizer, and time passed in a haze of well-being; long, slow, almost torpid days when it was so enjoyable to be alive that nothing else mattered (115–116).

By this he simultaneously rejects the materialist culture and its time-pressured living, and recognises the benefits to mental health in doing so. Where in his old life there is a reverence for the mechanical and scientific, in Provence rats are thought to be sharper than 'those complicated satellites', and the new moon more accurate in the matter of forecasting (23–24), which has nothing to do with the stock market and everything to do with the importance of weather patterns for a land-based life. Re-evaluation of materialism occurs in Chris Stewart's account of relocation to Andalucia (1999) in which 'the creature with the lowest priority on the road was the car' (4), which here obviously lacks the symbolism it has for Perowne in McEwan's *Saturday* (2005). Rejecting a selfhood that is annexed to *things*, Stewart and his wife view their 'ridiculous and embarrassing worldly goods' (65) as 'fripperies of [...] existence compared to the elemental earthiness' (58) of their neighbours. They recognise also consumerism's easy seduction when their excitement for some basic comforts for their new home – water, heater, cooker and a road – causes a feeling that they 'were fast becoming slaves again to all the things [they] had come to this benighted spot to flee' (70).

However, this perspective is possible because their new location is a 'benighted spot', the symbolic equivalent of a wilderness that allows mindful contemplation.[4] Remote communities partly insulated from the competitive striving on which a growing (world) economy relies also appear to demonstrate it is possible to survive in business with no excess profit and no desire to expand and to achieve happiness in doing so. Mayle's restaurant owner is one such example who seeks only 'enough business to allow him to stay in the valley with his horses' because, he says, 'it's good here. I have everything I want' (1989: 96–98), promoting a view that happiness lies in wanting what you have, rather than having what you want. The point is echoed by Marlena de Blasi's satisfied husband Fernando in *A Thousand Days in Tuscany* (2004) who considers 'I'm living the life I've always imagined. I want what I already have' (66).[5]

Where 'getting what you want' is promoted as a virtue in capitalist societies, 'being satisfied by having enough' is perfectly acceptable in more community-based societies. This attitude to the supply and use of goods is a result of how (natural) resources must be managed when survival is dependent on nature's inconsistent production. In communities operating to an agrarian logic, a life alternating plenty with impoverishment is the normal outcome of variable harvest. Sufficiency is created as an absolutely essential balance from the management of the two extremes of excess and lack, and is achieved by the avoidance of waste and a necessary withholding of desire in times of abundance in preparation for leaner times ahead. As Barlozzo (the unofficial village chieftain of de Blasi's Tuscan paradise, San Casciano dei Bagni) puts it, when the harvest was good 'we feasted [...] sucking in the sweet juices of plenty. But we saved some. We saved some for the other, less balmy time that always followed' (2004: 235). This feasting and fasting proceeds from an ideology and economic order very different from the deliberate overproduction and accumulation, and wastefulness characteristic of late-capitalism in which excessive consumption is normal and fasting is the sickness of the anorexic. Barlozzo again makes explicit that trade is moral and mutual:

> No one of us having anything of money to buy what we needed, or desired, it was by mutuality that we lived, everyone trading everyone else for what they didn't have. [...] But there was nothing casual about the trading. There were regulations, firm and constant, honored by everyone.
>
> (de Blasi, 2004: 235–236)

So different is the economic base on which this Tuscan village society operates that its inhabitants:

> don't understand this avid bent to accumulate things you can't eat, drink or wear or use to keep you warm [and] remember when accumulation still meant gathering three sacks of chestnuts rather than two.
>
> (de Blasi, 2004: 79)

It follows that agrarian-based communities would view the hoarding of an unequal share by the few as an immoral action that jeopardises the survival of the many. Certainly, such inequity seems manifest in the emerging dynamic of Anglo-American economies in which ultimately the greater proportion of created wealth accrues to a diminishing number of very rich at the expense of a growing underclass of citizens who have no stake in increasing affluence.[6] Moreover, if that affluence is neither equally shared nor creating satisfaction among the more affluent, questions arise about what affluence is and what else might contribute to human well-being.

Re-establishing balance seems 'timely' in more ways than one, particularly where a shift from the health and wealth of business, the market and the economy to the well-being of the mind, body and spirit implicates a temporal change from fast to slow and requires understanding our organic connection to the regulated rhythms and routines of the natural world in which resource management refers not to cost-cutting and wasteful overproduction, but to the effort to harmonise abundance and lack. Evidently, bias to either of these poles spells disaster (satiety, ennui, mental illness and dissatisfaction in the case of overabundance, and starvation, physical illness and death in the case of continued lack), so de Blasi (2004) urges balance, inferring the importance of the human organism's connection to nature's pulse and movements by advising: 'Our only task is to keep searching to understand the rhythm of things. Light, dark. The seasons. Live gracefully in plenty and live gracefully in need. Embrace them both or swindle yourself out of half a life' (79). Any regulated management should aim to counter dangerous extremes, to produce the equilibrium, which is instead a state of wider-spread sufficiency and survival.

If 'living gracefully' requires a commitment to sharing, this mutuality, prohibiting one from harming another depends largely on the extent to which kinship links can hold without breaking. Margaret Thatcher's declaration (1987) that there is 'no such thing as society' holds that mutuality is the result of voluntary individual effort to help our neighbour. (Ironically, David Cameron's later call for voluntary individual effort as part of a Big Society clearly challenges – or conveniently forgets – Thatcher's denial.) However, our mobile lifestyles decrease the likelihood of stable neighbourly connection (Sennett, 1998: 15–31) where it is clearly evident that this is not so in Loutses (Chatto, 2005). Indeed, when the whole village works together for the common good to construct a bridge, the essential connections on which community thrives are built literally and metaphorically (59). Similarly, though Stewart is the Andalucian community's newcomer, his neighbours freely give their time and labour to build the bridge he needs, proving that connections to 'place' are indeed also to people (1999: 38). In de Blasi's Tuscan village, the commitment to stay with old connections or to break them depends on one's attitude to 'moving on'. The wish for a new town flat captures the dilemma:

> The more clamorous of the two distinct San Cascianesi social sects, *i progressisti*, are chomping to leap into the future, pounding their fists and shrieking *bast*a, calling for progress like another round of gin. In voices more wistful, the other sect, *i tradizionalisti*, court the rituals, saying that the only true progress waits a few steps back into the past.
>
> (de Blasi, 2004: 77)

While the 'chomping', 'pounding' and 'shrieking' in this passage endow progression with the kind of noisy vigour 'change' usually trumpets for itself, the traditional voice, cast as thoughtful, regrets that history is overlooked by often unreflective marches into the future. For traditionalists, progress is to be viewed with caution because loosening bonds is, like business, full of risk and uncertain profit.

When societies get too big, and life gets too fast for us to know and care about others personally, mutuality disappears. The competitive environment underpinning the materially rich, developed world is built on a philosophy of self-responsible individualism, and, without God and an otherworldly heaven, self-interest fights against mutuality as a matter of personal moral choice. Where, in Britain, even the political left embraces the market, it is possible that the attraction of traditional, remote (even isolated) communities managing local production of essential commodities (food) lies in the ethical possibilities for mutuality and equitability, which appear not to be so easily demonstrable in a global, postmodern, transnational context.

This is not to suggest some absolute correlation exists in which the past or traditional communities are all good while the progress to modernity is all bad. Notwithstanding that happiness appears possible through slow life, and its associated values and temporality, this is not to romanticise past times or to propose reliance on natural or divine providence, nor is it a recommendation to jettison the technological or other developments on which Anglo-American advancement is built, but it is to suggest that greater judgement is called for in deciding what progress is for, and how to manage its fruits and mitigate its miseries.[7]

In summary, members of the remote community, by virtue of their geographical separation and 'slow' principles, are on the periphery of the dominant economic system and able still to live with mindful consideration of mankind's relationship to nature, time, history and each other. By not linking happiness to affluence, they are content to achieve sufficiency rather than excess. Their system of trade based on sharing and bartering avoids the greater inequities and indignities of capitalist organisation that cause a polarisation of power and wealth. It is worth remembering how disconnection from nature means severance also from *our* nature both as social beings able, in particular circumstances, to organise collaboratively, and as biological beings whose bio-rhythms are attuned to the earth's own.

However, an important watershed is reached when workers start to consider the loss in quality of life that is sustained as a result of the faster pace required for boosting production levels. For, at the point when speed is acknowledged as the problem, one naturally considers what it might entail to choose 'slow', and finds that the so-called slow movements based on organic principles appear to present not only the opportunity to step off the treadmill, but also a more ecologically and ethically sound, ideological framework on which a more fulfilling life can be built. The danger, of course, is that the new slow life may be as much an illusion as the fast one being escaped. Indeed, to a certain extent, migrants' impetus may have come from overly focusing on the negative elements of 'fast' (naturally enough if one is being adversely affected by them) while holding out hope on an equally skewed positive view of 'slow', when real experience, inevitably, will be composed of an inconvenient mix of both positive and negative aspects in either life (see Appendix 2). However, when considering why the negative impacts of a fast economy are being felt so disastrously, and to such an extreme degree, that they impel desire towards what may be seen as an equally excessive need for the attractive features of slowness, the answer may be that when the pendulum is pushed so far to one end, the most inevitable and immediate (though not necessarily measured) response is an equally violent swing, brought about by a natural dynamic, in the other direction. So even where visions of the 'good life' may be also partly false, the point they presage about naturally occurring balance is valid.

Structure, time, mortality and the individual

Migrants adjusting to living and working to the slower, organic time patterns recognise like Robin Shelton (2006) that 'nature is analogue, not digital' (153) and like Peter Mayle (1989) that the shift from hi-tech office to no-tech nature means 'learning to think in seasons instead of days or weeks' (209). Thus, Mayle's narrative, structured under chapter headings from January to December, reinforces a measured and sequential unfolding of events that is nevertheless related to an ongoing organic cycle. Likewise de Blasi's *A Thousand Days in Tuscany* begins in June, ends three complete years later in May and is organised under the section headings: Summer, Fall, Winter, Spring.[8] Within this cyclical movement there is nonetheless an emphasis on life as a series of beginnings and endings. Her husband Fernando's exit from Venice, over the aptly named Liberty Bridge, is '*his* escape, *his* new beginning [...] having resigned from his work and sold our home, he is tearing up the remains of his past life [...] his ending sealed, he says that *now* he can begin to be a beginner' (1–2, original emphasis). Her further comment that 'death is just moving house' (242) refers this linearity to a person's total allotted lifetime and one's final 'sealed' ending, death. There is thus a synergy between the structure and the content of the narratives and the predictable sequencing characteristic of the stability sought and found in the life that these tales emphasise.

In these stories, endings are as important as beginnings because of their metaphorical connection to mankind's greatest time-related fear – death. The relative ease or difficulty in considering mortality marks a key difference between the migrant's home and adopted cultures. In Western cultures, a great deal of effort and money goes into eradicating mortality's effects – cosmetic surgery, makeovers, gym attendance, vitamin taking, etc. – in an attempt to deny death altogether. While superficial solutions suit the postmodern sensibility, in which presentation has become not the surface of reality but reality itself, in traditional cultures death (mankind's ultimate limitation) is accepted in a way alien to the newcomer. Confronting death forces one to think about *the* fundamental philosophical question – the meaning of life – and posterity. In *A Thousand Days in Tuscany*, the sage Barlozzo puts it starkly:

> We are, every one of us, going to die.
> Rotting is the way of all things. A tree, a cheese, a heart, a whole human chassis. Now, knowing that, understanding that, living begins to seem less important than living the way you'd like to live. [...] All the energy we spend in trying to fix it, secure it, save it, protect it, leaves damn little time for living it. Pain or death or any other pestilence doesn't pass over us because we're careful or because we have insurance or, God forbid, because we have *enough* money. All right. So how does one come to understand exactly *how* one wants to live? How one wants to use up his time?
>
> (de Blasi, 2004: 129–130, original emphasis)[9]

Where mankind is reduced to common biology and the trappings of status become irrelevant, the elements that differentiate human beings from trees – consciousness, action and will – assume their proper importance. It is then that *how* one lives reflects *who* one is, so that one's practical identity, as Atkins says, becomes an ethical choice. By turn, the question of ethical living raises the further query concerning autonomy – the degree of agency involved in choosing one's lifestyle – so a migrant's 'flight' can seem as much avoidance of confronting ethical responsibility for the work life in which they were necessarily complicit as a choice that assumes it fully by the political decision to leave and start anew elsewhere.

Seen more positively, a new start in a village community, offering order and structure as a firm foundation, seems to hold the promise of a second chance, an opportunity to start again from the ground floor, to construct a life and a self that avoids the seductions and shallowness of materialism. This 'fresh page' has none of the negative connotations of newness for its own sake that is implied by the continuous renewal of people, ideas and processes used to boost turnover and financial profit. Instead, success, de Blasi says, depends on forethought, on knowing that having:

broken down the structure of one life [...] the immediate building up of another would only be a backlash. Especially before we've given ourselves a chance to determine what we truly desire from and believe we can accomplish by raising up a new structure.

(de Blasi, 2004: 36–37)

This call for reflection before action casts the process of individualisation as one that utilises personal history to inform one's present and future, and locates desire as self-determined rather than advertising-led. The individual striving for a better life carries the visionary implication that a personal philosophy can be a starting point for a political revolution that would make the spending of a life in this way particularly worthwhile.[10]

Self-determination of the type de Blasi describes seems to involve a point of stillness in the present, from which the past is reviewed and the future is assessed in order to plan and commit to a realistic goal (rather than to the pursuance of an illusory dream that is likely to prove equally unfulfilling). This present moment is, however, very different from the 'presentification' described by Leccardi (2005) from Beck as 'a form of contingency in which the self constantly adapts to what is required in changing conditions' (140–141). The latter is the market model's flexible approach, geared to the hallmark insistence on the ever-new, the fashionable, whose forward-projection is the immediate future and whose past merits consideration only where it denotes the still-current. De Blasi's 'present' acknowledges the prior experience and learning on which she presumes to build her new life. Similarly, for Chatto (2005), when work after the tourist season returns to 'its proper rhythm [...] the chores were many, but they were familiar and brought no stress, no problem that had not been solved two thousand years ago' (225); the circularities and repetitions constitute experience as a continuum whereas the market model dispenses with 'old' knowledge, failing to see that even changing contexts bring recurring problems.

These efforts to start anew in a society characterised by the order of the seasons and the cycles of birth and death bear out research that finds 'an increasing number of people seek reconnection with such seasonal patterns' (Parkins and Craig, 2006: 75). If the inevitability of death forces mindful attention to how one lives, there is compensation in the stability that order brings, in the organised structure to which de Blasi refers when Barlozzo says 'if you look carefully you'll see there are the pale tracings of a circle about us. Nothing much at all is accidental in a life' (2004: 268). Hundreds of miles away, and in a different country and culture, Shelton (2006) concurs. Feeling responsible for the continuation, rather than termination, of life cycles through horticulture he understands that 'not all burials are endings' (137) and that one can locate and orient oneself through such cycles because:

> the smooth succession and balanced opposition of our seasons mirrors so much else about the human condition and our environment – the waxing and waning of the moon and its associated tidal rise and fall, the ebb and flow of our moods – even our own cyclic existence of coming from, and returning to, nothing. This is simply the natural state of things.
>
> (Shelton, 2006: 37)

Connectedness and grounding

The move away from the 'natural state of things' is a consequence of industrialisation, mechanisation, automation and, lately, computer technology. This shift has been marked also by gravitation from the rural to the urban, and from the agricultural to the corporate. In the long process of cutting our ties to the land and embracing the free-floating flexibility and mobility required by the market, workers have become individual units of labour that can be endlessly assembled and dismantled in varying combinations or project teams as successive tasks require. In considering how these destabilised, uprooted conditions are harmful to health and personal relationships, it is interesting to find evidence that physical disconnection, occurring in the transition from the rural/agricultural to urban/corporate, signals a psychological detachment that reduces sympathy for others and affects moral conduct. Mayle (1989) finds rural connectivity carries certain obligations towards others:

> In the country [...] your neighbours are part of your life and you are part of theirs. [...] And if, in addition, you inherit a long-standing and delicate agricultural arrangement, you are quickly

made aware that your attitudes and decisions have a direct effect on another family's well-being.

(Mayle, 1989: 6)

A moral code is associated with this rural fraternity and is made explicit also by Stewart (1999): 'nothing [...] is as important as being honest and straightforward and treating people right'. However, there is suspicion for 'people of the town, they're rotten through and through – not to be trusted, screw you as soon as look at you' (28). Shelton (2006) confirms the topographically associated traits by noting his work on the allotment is accompanied by a change of character from 'a miserable, rude, good-for-nothing, unaccommodating and belligerent loser' to a person offering help to others 'on a purely altruistic basis with no expectation of any kind of reward' (47).

It is not difficult to extend this analogy when viewing how corporate practice seems also to have dispensed with 'treating people right'. Bakan (2004) explains that the flourishing organisation, by externalising the true (environmental and human) impact of its business, actually *depends* on its ability to dissociate itself from the ills it causes. Furthermore, this necessary disengagement from the 'routine and regular harms caused to *others*' is made innocuous through language, the term 'externalities' being part of a 'coolly technical jargon of economics' (56–60).[11] This jargon, together with a PR-driven concern for corporate social responsibility, forms the linguistically generated insulation deflecting the heated criticism drawn by corporate activities. Bakan quotes the judgement of (ex-Body Shop founder) Anita Roddick:

> The corporation [...] stops people from having a sense of empathy with the human condition; it separate[s] us from who we are ... The language of business is not the language of the soul or the language of humanity, [...] It's a language of indifference; it's a language of separation, of secrecy, of hierarchy. It is fashioning a schizophrenia in many of us.
>
> (Bakan, 2004: 55–56)[12]

This schizophrenia is evident in the compartmentalised thinking required to focus on destroying competitors in any way possible when at work while retaining a softer, more loving self at home.

While this strategy for individuals' psychological survival 'saves them from becoming psychopaths', it makes evident 'business's amorality, for forcing otherwise decent people to do indecent things' and the 'moral bifurcation' required for 'good' people to operate successfully in a corporate context (50–56, quoting psychologist Dr Robert Hare). Furthermore, switching between one mental state and the other is easier where work and home life occur in different spaces, but where the work/home divide dissolves, the effort to reconcile non-compatible worlds at the same time and within the same physical as well as mental space can lead to acute psychic discomfort and neurosis.

So the continuing quest for business efficiency involves a number of stresses on the human worker the more distance increases from their natural roots and time patterns. These include: accelerated timescales denying the present moment relates to the past and that we and our world are part of a continuum; the removal from land-dependent ways of life and 'place' that disturb the rootedness important to ethical identity; and lastly, the dehumanising technological processes that tend also towards forms of disengagement which facilitate the avoidance of moral responsibility to others. It is of little surprise, therefore, that workers riven between the hard-nosed competitive behaviour required by flexible individualism and the softer demeanour that is appropriate to a personal life hanker for a more wholesome, connected and ethical identity. In the migrants' narratives, reconnection or re-grounding carries with it a wider set of attitudinal implications. Living as a biological, ethical being in continuous, regulated time entails using the lessons of the past to take responsibility for the future, which includes accountability for the impact our present lifestyles are having on the earth by respecting that the resources of the world are also finite.

A number of statements in Shelton's narrative specifically confirm this connective, responsible philosophy and how his new activities are not only changing him but making him more content. He notes his horticultural work as 'the first real commitment, not only to a change of career, but also a shift in lifestyle and outlook' (100). For him, 'gardening is, at least in part, about a fuller appreciation of our place in the scheme of things, and leads to some kind of inner calm and generosity of spirit' (48), while neighbour Ken 'simply feels unbalanced without something to connect his hands to the ground'

(11). Shelton discovers for himself a 'new found pleasure that a combination of physical toil, almost literal connectedness with the earth, and easy trusted companionship bring' (16), and claims 'there is much to be said for putting down roots [as] not a great deal flowers without them' (101). He despairs that car users 'had not thought of walking or cycling' (135) and takes pleasure in reusing panelling from an old pavilion for a shelter because it is 'to do with the notion of continuation; the pavilion had seen the passing of three decades of history and passion, and by recycling its carcass into a shed [...] its story might continue' (185). Growing food gives him 'satisfaction – excitement even' (122); he is amazed at the 'kindness and altruism that [he and friend Steve] have encountered since working on the plot' (155); he feels 'brave, manly and purposeful' (213), is taught 'a little patience' (38) and is made 'happy and fulfilled' (231) by the 'therapeutic nature of gardening' (36). Shelton thus gives weight to Parkins and Craig's theoretical view that:

> Slow living generates an awareness of the specificity of place, and more particularly a material relationship to the land. This is not based upon a bourgeois, romantic valorisation of rural life [...] but is rather based upon a belief that in the contexts of our fast, deterritorialised, modern lives, we need to retain an ethical and political disposition that is grounded in an awareness of our fundamental relationships to the specificity of place, the land, its produce and each other.
>
> (Parkins and Craig, 2006: 85)

In a secular context, a broadly connective philosophy, which locates mankind as an integrated part of the world's structure and its energies, provides a palatable and workable alternative to a personalised God. This alternative spirituality, based on mindfulness, meditative practice and balance, seems to draw its impetus and guidance from Eastern transcendentalism as both a means of coping with the recognised 'profound uncertainties, insecurities and indeterminacies of postmodern living' and a route to (re)establish identity difference, because:

> where values are indissociable with lifestyles [...] self-consciously defined groupings [...] generate a strong sense of belonging that

takes over any larger civic or national incorporation. These communes share sets of identifications and values that separate them from those who are outside, defining them as distinctive.

(Ward, 2003: 133–138)

The interest in horticulture and cookery, enacted in both informal (dispersed) and formal (rooted) communities of likeminded individuals, is precisely the effort to deal with the identity problems of postmodern life in the secular context. The broad church of growing and cooking spans everything from the mystic polish and excess of the commodified 'divine' and femininely sexualised Nigella brand, through various versions of masculinity from the boorish Gordon Ramsay to Nigel Slater's open simplicity, via the careful attention of the wholesome Slow Food movement to the outright rejection of consumerism indicated by the wilderness experience based on much older, traditional philosophies.

Food and spirituality

The previous chapter discussed how food and food-related activity has become a key vehicle for a new spirituality based on slower and more mindful 'earthly' living. It proposed that 'real' food assumes greater symbolic importance as the nurturing and nourishing of the spirit becomes synonymous with its corporeal equivalent and, in this collapsing of distance between the literal and the metaphorical, food's rituals, mysteries and litanies of ingredients stand proxy for religious devotion and, through the sainted (media icon) practitioners, adopt its language.

Food plays a remedial role as part of a philosophy of slow life in bringing people together and challenging the ideological standpoint of the fast and change-hungry new economy by returning consumption to its literal meaning in which eating as a social practice takes on new significance. Parkins and Craig (2006) confirm that 'there is a positive potential in slowness as a means of critiquing or challenging dominant narratives or values that characterise contemporary modernity for so many' (ix), and that 'slowness can become a way of signalling an alternative set of values or a refusal to privilege the workplace over other domains of life' (1), which together indicate the aspect of modernity from which the dominant narrative and its associated values are thought to emanate. The Slow Food movement, founded in 1989 as part of a wider slow living ethos counteracting not only fast food but fast life also (www.slowfood.com), promotes food's central role in a new narrative. Slow Food is an:

> attempt to offer *an alternative story* about what makes a life good [...] [and] its insistence that fast life is not only bad for the planet or our health but robs us of the time and energy to live with attention and enjoyment, wonder and generosity, urges us to interrogate the consequences of the pace of our lives.
>
> (Parkins and Craig, 2006: 138, emphasis added)

The prime aim in slowing down is to achieve a necessary mindfulness about choice when living in a fast world often leaves one feeling somewhat dissatisfied, despite the vast number of opportunities on offer. Slow Food also places emphasis on more direct satisfactions, on 'understandings of pleasure and taste, conviviality, and the value of local products and cultures' (18), which it sees as countering globalisation's widespread, replicated homogeneity, and essential to recover the happiness, togetherness and quality that have fallen victim to modernity. Its philosophy also substantiates the argument that food has become a key carrier of wider meaning by using a concern for the taste and provenance of ingredients as a vehicle to advocate a fuller sense of our connections to history, other creatures and the environment, and to promote that our attitude to others is critical to ethical pleasure. The movement claims:

> that everyone has a fundamental right to pleasure and consequently the responsibility to protect the heritage of food, tradition and culture that make this pleasure possible [...] [through] a recognition of the strong connections between plate and planet [...] [that ensures production] does not harm the environment, animal welfare or our health; and that food producers should receive fair compensation for their work.
>
> (www.slowfood.com/about_us/eng/philosophy.lasso)

This holistic approach is above all connective. It acknowledges food's central role in providing both sensory pleasure and spiritual fulfilment consequent upon cultural and environmental guardianship and ethical action that refuses to accept 'the gap between production and consumption' (Parkins and Craig, 2006: 133).

On a human level food 'has a unique capacity to bring people together' (88). The spirituality implicit in food's communion is made explicit when Mayle (1989) informs us that in Provence 'the baking and eating of breads and pastries has been elevated to the status of a minor religion (171). Similarly, Parkins and Craig (2006) note food's association with pleasure and guilt and, through this, with sin (90), while for Shelton, food production is both mysterious and miraculous for:

> watching a tomato seed wake up and commence its remarkable but undeniable journey towards the Bolognese sauce is surely far more compelling than an apocryphal story about feeding 5,000 people with a fish and a few loaves.
>
> (Shelton, 2006: 171)

The notion of transformation from ingredient into dish is noteworthy as it forms the kernel of a profane equivalent of the sacred communion ritual. However, where the sacred rite closes down meaning (the bread and wine symbolically and invariably 'becoming' the body and blood of the Saviour), in cookery this is not so. As the source materials have infinite capability of being fashioned into various dishes, the conversion is open-ended, creative and inventive (ironically, much like the required ingredients for entrepreneurship).

It is in being both an essential of life and the basis of so much possibility that food operates specifically as an agent of connection, working both between individuals and between groups and cultures, at a time when other forces of dissociation impel separation and level difference to monoculture. De Blasi (2004) subscribes to this view. Her claim, that 'foodstuffs the world over are as connected as the humans who survive by them', emphasises the similarities between various cultures that turn grain into bread, find a use for grasses and herbs, distil fruit, vegetables or herbs into spirits, fashion dishes that combine bacon and cream, wrap one ingredient round another forming a range of dumplings or parcels, and soften cereals with liquid (215–216).

However, while such ingredients and practices mark cultural similarities they also, *at the same time*, by virtue of the particularity imparted by place (soil, climate and water) and process (recipes) indicate difference. By holding the contradictions of similarity *and* difference, stability *and* change, in a balanced tension, food demonstrates its own reconciliatory potential. Food thus operates on many planes as both a literal connector of actual persons at the table and as a symbolic marker of shared feelings, values and associated cultural histories in both local and wider contexts. Moreover, because the culinary arts are generated and practised in accordance with what is culturally customary, their performance is also ritualised. When de Blasi comments that 'lunch and supper here compose a twice-daily said mass' (209), it is clear that for those without formal religion, such practices may become in themselves a means of signalling continuity and belonging.

Customary practice is also a way of critiquing change and superficiality, not by simplistic opposition, but by being a mechanism through which one is led to pause and consider the value of development or amalgamation. In the traditional kitchen, de Blasi comments, 'there is the impulse for change, but, where the table is concerned, rituals die hard, die slowly or, one hopes, not at all' (212), so that in this case, continuity *contains* change, both in the sense of the contrary aspects co-existing and that change is held in check by continuity. This does not deny alteration but places a brake on it by questioning the root and purpose of change, and seeks to distinguish a more deliberate (and deliberated) development from the postmodern 'change for change's sake' that marks the fashionable. There is nothing wrong with innovation, but de Blasi unmasks this trend in the style of cooking whose presentation postures and counterfeits in being served on a 'primped and painterly plate, its elements so overworked and disguised that, try as [she] might, [she] could identify none of them' (214). This 'California cuisine', claiming originality, 'wasn't really new, of course, as much as it was a deft repackaging of history' (213). It is an example of the novel and exciting being no more than the superficial and sensational that is built on none of the heartiness or richness and fullness of flavour, or the piquancy, the authenticity even, that characterises slow food or traditional cooking. It is what Mayle means when he describes London's 'theme food and its grotesque prices' (1989: 97). The depthlessness and dazzle of California cuisine is the very opposite of what is signified by the ritual recurrence of the 'twice-daily said mass' to which de

Blasi refers, through which familiarity becomes the basis of group participation and anticipation.

While traditional and *nouvelle* modes of relating to food evidence an aesthetic difference, the labour and ingredients involved in each place them on the same plane with regard to their time/value ratio. It is in the opposition between slow and fast food that opposing cultural values surface and show a notable discrepancy in ways of valuing the self. Consumption (as a signifier of who one is) assumes a rather interesting literalness and far greater significance where it relates to food. Eating fast food – commercially reconstituted meats, cheaply made (lucrative) dishes, value-enhanced (profitable) ready meals and quick-cook convenience foods – is an act of devaluation of the self. By choosing these foods, one places a positive value on quick and easy, but because such foods are nutritionally poor, and are allowed passage through and affect the body, the act confers a negative value on the self. In circumstances where 'the quality of the food is more important than convenience' as Mayle finds in Provence, where people 'will happily travel for an hour or more, salivating en route, in order to eat well' (1989: 95), eating better, more expensive, more nutritional food transfers that food's inherent and signified value on the self by virtue of the care one is prepared to take of one's body.

It can certainly be argued that where consumption is a means of identity construction, 'slow food' is an attempt by the middle classes to reposition themselves firmly in some ground between the working class and an elite – to indicate by investment in different, specific values a retreat from both exclusive gastronomy and supermarket junk.[13]

Labour and the relationship of time to activity

The Slow Food manifesto (www.slowfood.com/about_us/eng/manifesto.lasso) states that 'Our century, which began and has developed under the insignia of industrial civilisation, first invented the machine and then took it as its life model'. In this blurring of boundaries between man and machine, certain aspects of humanity have ceased to have an outlet for their expression, and certain qualities and satisfactions associated with the hands-on labour of craftsmanship have been erased also. When Richard Sennett writes in *The Craftsman* (2008) that 'those in the grip of [...] competitive obsession easily lose sight of the value and purpose of what they are doing[,] they are not thinking in craftsman-time, the slow time that enables reflection' (251), we are made aware that it is not merely what we do but the lack of time for reflection about what we do, how quickly we do it and what little we achieve by it that characterises modern labour. With food already functioning in complex ways as a cultural barometer, its meaning is given a further dimension through the processes by which it is produced and prepared. Having dealt earlier with the nurturing involved in growing food and with its presentation and consumption, the element that is of the greatest import – the labour involved with bringing foodstuffs from the ground to the gastronome – requires more attention.

The roles of horticulturalist and cook, both their persons and processes, stand as critical connections between crop and consumer. When Shelton (2006) writes that his 'mood seemed buoyed by what [he] can only assume is the therapeutic nature of gardening' (36) or Graham Swift includes in his novel *The Light of Day* (2004) that 'In the careful and loving cooking of a meal there is [...] a sort of healing power' (218) and that cooking 'soothes the nerves' (220), we are pushed to reach for the cultural significance of the wide and continuing interest in gardening and cookery. Sennett (2008) can be our most useful guide in understanding the messages that labour of this type is speaking.

It is notable that for those alienated by (competitive) market principles that overwhelm and determine the non-work aspects of their lives and compromise the fulfilling (collaborative) relationships on which happiness depends, alternative values are found in lifestyles that are specifically task-led. From this we understand that work is an essential component of the satisfying life and that the requirement is for a set of values able to work across *all* aspects of existence, including labour. For Sennett, such an ethics exists in craftsmanship understood as an activity between amateur and virtuoso – neither the application of an unhoned or untutored skill of the former nor the demonstration of pure technical ability that dazzles of the latter, but something properly professional in the sense that it conveys the application of a learned and applied skill that may result from not just one flawed (but individual) attempt at production, but many such assays

– i.e. skill that in making, produces an article stamped from *within* by the identity of its maker, a product that embodies both the effort and result of that effort over time (Sennett, 2008: 115–117).

Sennett's analysis of craft labour identifies a number of features that offer the opportunity in a work context for kinds of fulfilment rarely possible in mainstream employment today. These satisfactions can predominantly (but not exclusively) be understood from the perspective of those who work with their hands, and flow from particular processes to do with problem solving, dynamic repair, inventiveness, spontaneity, absorption, repetition, rhythm and reflection. Together these operate, Sennett claims, to re-dignify the work of *animal laborans*, the lowest type of endeavour undertaken by humans in the classification Arendt uses in her lecture *Labour, Work, Action* (1967) on the human condition.[14] The continuous improvement of skill and outcome brought about by the repeated application of effort and intelligence to a task elevates such work above being merely routine, principally because it demonstrates an aptitude to discover and solve problems.[15] There is compelling evidence in autobiographical travelogues that this ethos and the satisfactions it provides are exactly what migrants find in engagement with work and workers in traditional communities.

As noted earlier, traditional communities are by no means blind to the seduction of progress and the apparent ease from toil it offers. However, a significant number of tasks are undertaken by those engaged in 'making' that seem guided by the particular philosophy about the process and outcome of work that Sennett describes. Firstly, there is a reverence for the work of the hand and an understanding of what is at stake when automation takes over. The following extract from *The Handmade Loaf* is pertinent:

> The handmade loaf is about making the most of what we have, about appreciating what grows in the soil. We have so much, too much, that we can buy yet the basic labour of doing the making with our own hands is what enlivens us and makes us feel human. Someone once asked me why I bother mixing and shaping bread by hand. I didn't have the words to answer them, nor could I understand why they just didn't know. I will not let my fingers be reduced to simple button-pressing, dial-twirling and switch-flicking. There is no instrument in my bag of baker's tools more

useful and adaptable than my two hands, and as long as I can use them to make and shape bread, I will.

(Leppard, 2004: 7)

Bread-making is an emotive subject as it involves 'the staff of life' and carries the symbolic weight of existence itself. For de Blasi's Barlozzo, the fact that 'no one bakes bread anymore[,] neither inside the house nor outside' (2004: 48) is a symptom of decline. For Mayle (1989), however, newly arrived from the UK, even village bakeries are a source of wonderment:

> Most of the bakeries had their own touches which distinguished their loaves from mass-produced supermarket bread; slight variations from conventional shapes, an extra whorl of crusty decoration, an elaborate pattern, the artist baker signing his work. It was as if the sliced, wrapped, machine-made loaf had never been invented.
>
> (Mayle, 1989: 171)

In the development of the bread-making process from its origins in the home to its destination in the factory, Mayle maps for us how the individuality of the artisan maker is encapsulated in the particularity of the product. A loaf distinguished – in both senses of the word – is marked out from all others by its difference and marked by its maker, thus identifying clearly by whom it was made. The signing is important, Sennett (2008) tells us. It denotes 'presence', one of the categories of material consciousness he elaborates (the others are metamorphosis and anthropomorphosis).[16] Though at its simplest the mark denotes 'I made this' or 'I exist', signing can also indicate the 'free agency' of the maker (119–146). It is perhaps in the specificity and wonderment at autonomy that Mayle and readers whose agency is compromised in their work appreciate such details of interest, while Leppard shows a reverence not just for the physicality of bread-making but for the hands that do the making. The 'simple button-pressing, dial-twirling and switch-flicking' that Leppard speaks about are the practices of automation which, in creating distance between producer and product, lose what Sennett describes as the dynamic intelligence that, through sight, touch, and smell, can assess and correct the variability of the organic process – the strength of yeast, the browning during cooking – by which it is possible to demonstrate one's *particular* skill (Sennett, 1998: 64–71).

Many undertaking manual work would agree that 'making with our own hands is what enlivens us and makes us feel human' (Leppard, 2004: 7), for where so much else can focus on inequality, 'our species' ability to make things shows more what we share' (Sennett, 2008: 268). Thus, Wendy and James Chatto in *The Greek for Love* (2005), find 'fantastically exhilarating […] the hands-on intensity of these kinds of experiences (193)', and Fernando through engaging with 'the first truly artisanal project of his life […] discovers his hands and how beautifully they can create' (de Blasi, 2004: 60). Likewise de Blasi comments that 'the world's food is a story of mirrors and reprises, just as music is a story of what genius, great or humble, can caress or liberate from those same eighty-eight keys' (215–216), indicating the high form of manual technique intimately linked to a transcendent inventiveness.

It is this inventive, productive, economically independent response that Shelton (2006) recognises and prizes in his two children happily playing with a stick in a sandpit, who, because 'times are financially laughable […] [are] imaginative, resourceful and easily pleased' (97). It is more clearly seen in Stewart's 'Spontaneous Architecture' where 'the height of the risers of the patio stairs […] was governed by the size of the stones [they] were using to build them, and almost everything else was likewise designed to fit the materials to hand' (1999: 141). This responsiveness is not the knee-jerk decision-making of the pressed executive. Rather, it is the ability to stop and think while working, to experiment and invent without fear, to correct and learn from mistakes, to design organically rather than mechanically – in short, to be guided by the materials and circumstances of production, not by predetermined expectations for output.

A critical difference between the working conditions of the new economy and those of craftwork concerns time and the attitude to failure. The continuous improvement and acquisition of skill associated with craftwork depends on attention to failure as a source of learning. In this case, even a first attempt at something is valuable. With repetition, the worker can develop the necessary techniques through experience that enable success, even given specific material difficulties or varying local conditions. In this formulation, time equals effort and quality. In the new economy, where time equals money and quantity, reflection on failure is neither possible nor desirable. It is not possible because the next task comes hot on the heels of the one just completed. This means there is often little material difference in quality between the outcome that an amateur or professional will produce because the just-in-time mentality pares down the period available for execution to an extent that even where professional skills are present that could improve quality, the time does not exist for their demonstration. It is not desirable because the poor-quality outcome of many tasks is tolerated as an acceptable by-product of budgetary concerns (or a necessary built-in obsolescence to drive future production) while staff turnover, or constant outsourcing to the lowest bidder, means that tasks are rarely looked at twice in succession by the same person or team so there is little point, and certainly no financial profit, in dwelling on error.[17]

However, profit of a different order is had when revisiting problems. Repeated attention to a challenging task is not to be thought of as dull or routine but rather a condition in which it is possible to become fully engaged or absorbed, through the coordination of one's brain, hand and eye, by the very process of that repetition. Sennett's description of this is as the opposite of mindless or boring:

> Doing something over and over is stimulating when organised as looking ahead. The substance of the routine may change, metamorphose, improve, but the emotional payoff is one's experience of doing it again. There's nothing strange about this experience. We all know it; it is rhythm. Built into the contractions of the human heart, the skilled craftsman has extended rhythm to the hand and the eye.
>
> (Sennett, 2008: 175)

Put like this the activity shows 'being as a thing' (174) where the join between person and thing, between subject and object, dissolves, just as happens in Perowne's ecstatic experience while operating (McEwan, 2005: 23) (see Chapter 3). It is marked by the transition that occurs in Shelton (2006) who first describes digging as 'four hours of doing the same thing over and over again, all the time feeling as if it is never, ever going to end' (83) but soon after realises that 'one of the things [he's] learned about digging is that success is predominantly to do with rhythm [...] the rhythm of digging can get kind of hypnotic and even meditative at times' (86).

In choosing food production over fund management, today's worker chooses a very different relationship of time to activity. Parkins and Craig (2006) recognise 'if gardening is consciously adopted as a practice of slow living it can be a different way of marking and inhabiting time, in which the temporality of the garden offers either respite or contradiction to the dominant temporality we experience' (40). In addition to off-setting the frenzy of modernity, slow work is also about insisting on the heft of humanity by which we are both designed and defined. When in de Blasi's tale, Fernando says, 'I have my two hands, which are older than I am' (2004: 25) or Shelton realises when digging that:

> to an outsider it probably didn't amount to much, but we sensed we had done something important – we had made the ground ready for growing. The sound of fifteen thousand years of agricultural evolution produces deep and resonant echoes
>
> (Shelton, 2006: 87)

they each acknowledge that legacy. We overlook our biology at our peril. Evolutionary development of *Homo sapiens*' bodies and brains has occurred over many millennia and fits us for particular types of activity to do with ensuring survival. For most of that time, for most of us, survival involved the strenuous physical activity and thought-processing skills required to ensure food, security and shelter. If the 100,000 years of that development is represented as a 24-hour cycle, says Hylland-Eriksen (2001), then 'television and commercial air travel have existed for a mere 30 seconds. And the Internet? Forget it' (32). Information technology has brought huge change to our working day over what is, by our evolutionary clock, a mere instant of time. Our mental processes will take a while to adapt and our now-sedentary bodies require hours of exercise outside of our working day to keep fit. So when Shelton (2006) considers that the 'best shelter [...] is that which you have fashioned yourself' (29), his satisfaction comes partly from a deeply rooted sense of fulfilling an essential biological need for self-protection, while his comment that 'despite our exhaustion, we [he and his friend Steve] bounced home full of the energy of achievement' (87) and Chatto's (2005) 'sheer pleasure of physical exertion' (247) say a great deal about the nature of healthy and unhealthy fatigue, and the matters that need attending to for the well-being of our current biological form.

A sense of achievement and control seem key elements for our well-being. Shelton (2006) finds satisfaction from his 'new found autonomy' (66) when working, while deeper fulfilment results also from improving a skill through practice. James Chatto and Peter Mayle appreciate this even in merely observing their tradesmen's work. Chatto, watching the stonemason cut and lay a marble floor, concludes, 'The man was an artist, smiling to himself at the pleasure of feeling his strong hands working. I stood […] marvelling at his skill […] Hours passed before he was satisfied' (198–199). Mayle is similarly impressed by his plasterer's expertise:

> He had a slow, rhythmical style, flicking the plaster on to the ceiling with his trowel and working it into a chunky smoothness with his wrist. […] He didn't believe in rollers, or sprayers, or instruments of any sort apart from his trowel and his eye for a line and a curve, which he said was infallible. […] I checked his surfaces with a spirit level. They were all true, and yet they were unmistakably work of a hand rather than a machine. The man was an artist.
>
> (Mayle, 1989: 43)

However, while the onlooker's reverence for artistry in the above extracts is clear, and dedication to a degree is necessary for the achievement of the highest quality, Sennett (2008) holds that a continuous obsessive striving for perfection aims for distinction which is against the virtue of social integration that attends good craftsmanship and makes craftsmanship appear as an uncommon ability (244–245, 252–254). For him, the value in the individuality of a craft item is as likely to result from the imperfection that eschews uniformity, for that imperfection signifies a problem encountered that makes possible virtuous improvement of both the article and the maker.

Reading imperfection in relation to the significance of food, we find here too that the literal and the symbolic are connected through the characteristic values of the thing that implies something also of the person. Hence, 'Ruskin believes that we are saying something about ourselves in preferring a vegetable whose appearance seems rough-hewn, irregular; the organic tomato mirrors the values of "home" for us' (Sennett, 2008: 138). Home in this context signifies self-recognition and, where imperfection is observed, self-acceptance and an opportunity for self-improvement; a state far from that of the modern neurotic for whom imperfection stands as a prompt for obsessive eradication and self-loathing.

Home conceived in Ruskin's sense is an altogether more comfortable and positive place: the key point of stability (as it is for McEwan's Perowne); the ground anchor that prevents exciting travel from becoming aimless, disorientating mobility; the connection that binds us one to another when separation means isolation; a refusal of artifice, marking truth equally in subject and object; the authenticity that unmasks the postmodern superficiality which aids self-delusion; the point denoting our inheritance from the past and our bequest to the future; and the synchronicity of doing and being that indicates a wholesome character. Where 'the archaic craftsmen occupied a social slice roughly equivalent to a middle class' (Sennett, 2008: 22), today's professionals are the inheritors of their social position. Thus, even for those away from their native land, the discovery of a more satisfying identity through different forms of work and in other kinds of community functions as a homecoming of sorts. De Blasi experiences this in a moment that finds her, among friends, instinctively fulfilled when sharing the labour (appropriately) of dough-making:

> It's this *connection* that I need and desire most from this life. Humble as it is, this is my legacy. I am a cook and a baker. Such an ancient metier is mine, descended from the loaf-givers, the keepers of the fire, the distributors of largesses. I've always known I was playacting whenever I'd tried to learn more about business, to 'ask for the order' or 'go in for the close'. I'd never fooled myself any more than I did other people. And it's so good to be home. This is what I've wanted to do and how I've wanted to be.
>
> (de Blasi, 2004: 289, original emphasis)

Notes

1 See also Hamilton (2003c: 9–10). Not all downshifters leave work altogether. Many change career, start their own business or cut down their hours of work.

2 See also 2003c, which links and compares downshifting in Australia and Britain to its historical beginnings in the US through Thoreau's 'voluntary simplicity'.
3 See also Schor (1998) who says, 'Downshifting often involves soul-searching and a coming to consciousness about a life that may well have been on automatic pilot.'
4 Stewart (26, 28, 74) also refers to his location by another Biblical term, Eden/Paradise.
5 See also Richard Schoch (2006). Epicurius defined happiness as the absence of desire.
6 See Toynbee (2008) *Unjust Rewards* and Ehrenreich (2008) *Going to Extremes: Notes from a Divided Nation*.
7 While applauding the collective ethos, de Blasi (2004) is not blind to the injustice of a feudal past – wealth difference, servitude and lack of education.
8 Stewart (1999) finds his new property 'in the warm January sunshine' of a New Year and starts his new life in August, and the tale also ends with August. Emma Tennant's *Corfu Banquet* (2004) is organised by Spring, Summer, Autumn, Winter. Robin Shelton's *Allotted Time* (2006) begins on 21 September one year and finishes on 20 September the following year.
9 See also Parkins and Craig (2006): 'the context of speed and global risk also highlights natural, human and social limits, prompting fundamental reassessments of the allocation of time and attention with regard to individual lifestyles and social relations' (134).
10 Parkins and Craig (2006) believe that small-scale attempts at slow living founded in the local context (even of one's native country) pave the way 'for broader cultural and political transformations' (133). David Harvey (2004) also sees the potential of approaching global political issues through local ones.
11 Bakan argues that the organisation's policies of 'corporate social responsibility' use the very real concerns about the damage done to people and our world by business practice as a cynical means to carry out its constitutional duty to shareholders to turn a profit.
12 Though Bakan appears to accept Roddick's business morality at face value, Thomas Frank (2000) does not. Frank believes Roddick's 'greenwashed branding' is a marketing ploy to attract the sensitive customer (213–216).
13 Though slow food seeks to avoid 'the elitism commonly associated with gastronomy' (Parkins and Craig, 2006: 36), a deeper look at the problematic interplay of economics *and* class might disclose how the higher price of 'quality' raw ingredients (e.g. those available at farmers' markets) still operates as an exclusionary factor.
14 See also Majid Yar (2001).
15 Sennett (2008: 24–27) cites open-source Linux programming and programmers as contemporary examples of work and workers engaged through an ethos of creative, collaborative, continuous improvement that results in freely available (shared) knowledge.

16 Metamorphosis denotes a change in procedure; anthropomorphosis, the imputing of human qualities to material.
17 Proofing errors seen frequently now in published books are evidence of the reduction in quality that occurs as a result of time-pressured process.

6
Autobiography
Writing the self

Autobiography and biographical certainty

The closing years of the twentieth century and early ones of the twenty-first were marked by two phenomena – the increasing production of, and interest in biography and autobiography, alongside an intense (re)engagement with traditional, creative, craft-based labours, particularly cookery and horticulture. This is not merely accidental where the two are self-evidently related (both told and connected) in autobiographical travelogues like those made popular by Peter Mayle *et al.* portraying lifestyles involving manual, creative labours. Neither does it seem purely coincidental that these stories of traditional cultures disclose an ideological message countering the fast, flexible, mobile, immediate and fragmented culture of the new capitalist workplace by proposing a replacement of the defining forces of pace, movement and separation by those of slowness, dwelling and connection.

Several closely connected reasons illuminate why reading and writing life-stories engages the human spirit at this particular time. Chief among these, I shall argue, is that autobiography holds possibilities for self-examination and self-expression, both of which are compromised by the pace and instantaneity of neoliberal productivity. Autobiography offers also a linguistically based means of healing the discourse-induced stress caused by corporate messages urging particular sanctioned identities that uphold economic growth in Western economies (see Chapter 1). It handles the process of self-making and the contradictions and resolutions facing the 'I' in general and the middle-class professional in particular by allowing the establishment and demonstration of character in conditions of biographical uncertainty. It satisfies a (now-secular) quest for posterity in a shifting and chaotic personal and social landscape. As literature proper, it presents the formal coherence and pleasing aesthetic unity missing from postmodern daily life. Where the travelogues are concerned, autobiography supports an imaginative leap prompting dreams of escape from the psychological gymnastics and moral compromise of new economy work by profiling the 'good life' as an endeavour involving alternative forms of labour and the values attending them.

At the very least, engagement with autobiography functions as displacement activity facilitating temporary withdrawal and respite for those troubled by the rapidly changing demands of the contemporary life-world. Finally, the production of autobiography is itself a creative labour, so the migrant's text, featuring a chosen lifestyle experience out of which they are able to (re)construct and narrate their self-story, mimics the aesthetic, reiterative processes and values of the craft activities on which they are based.

Narration and the self

The arrival on the booksellers' shelves since 1990 of a number of autobiographic 'escape' narratives is testimony both to the act of migration and the act of writing about it. Indeed, the autobiography theorist Nancy K Miller (2002) observes that 'the nineties [...] saw the spectacular rise of the memoir, which (along with biography) became the most popular (and symptomatic) literary genre of our contemporary culture' (1). Though Miller does not distinguish between writers and readers of memoirs, she agrees with Smith and Watson (2001) 'that the proliferation of autobiographic study since the 1970s (and its theorizing since 1990s) would suggest a preoccupation with selfhood that arises precisely in relation to notions of a decentred self' (132–133) and causes the 'growing audience demand for personal accounts of self-help' (147). Miller (2002) suggests that 'the memoir craze feeds the hunger for a different, or at least a more interesting, life through literature; [...] a desire to assert agency and subjectivity after several decades of insisting loudly on the fragmentation of identity' (12). This implies that the attraction of the coherent, narrated life proceeds from the destabilisation involved in forms of postmodern identity-making, the impotence of being denied true self-definition and the absence of worthy role models on which to base one's self-development.

More importantly, this suggests that autobiographical texts answer a very particular human need, for readers and writers alike, that relates to the psychological continuity necessary for the human individual to conduct itself as what the philosopher Kim Atkins (2004) terms 'a practical and ethical subject' through time; that is, a subject who must continually act in the world and whose reason for acting attests to the subject's essentially held values.[1] With this in mind it seems reasonable to propose that the emergence and popularity of these artefacts occurs precisely because they are able to recover and articulate a selfhood compromised by the flexible, fragmented culture of immediacy in which market-speak threatens autonomy and the ability to be author of one's own destiny, and owner of one's attitudes and behaviour. They represent a mode of speaking that holds to a self-recognisable truth about the self.

Atkins acknowledges this close relationship between identity and narrative because narrative, she argues, 'is oriented to the need for meaning in the lives of embodied, practical beings existing within the constraints of a temporal world'. We need this tool, she claims, because it can 'articulate a form of continuity in identity consistent with the importance a person attaches to being the same experiential subject over time' (2004: 341–342). Indeed, Atkins argues that only a narrative model is able to 'mediate and synthesise the diverse and heterogeneous aspects of life' and to 'coordinate different orders of time' (347) in which a self-reflective and future-oriented subject constructs itself, and understands and owns its actions.[2] She believes that 'as a practical being whose existence is structured by action, the meaning and continuity of my life and identity – who I am – is structured through the textual resources of narrative' (3). Most importantly, it is the first-person narrative perspective that not only ensures the subject's unity and continuity but ties responsibility for action, and for the character and story created by that action, firmly to the agent (349). In fact, action and character are mutually formative in that:

a person's actions are informed by her character and circumstances, while her character is informed by earlier actions and sufferings. The activity and passivity of character is simply expression of the ambiguities of an embodied and socially mediated subjectivity, which play out in a dialectic of the self as both a 'reader' and 'writer' of one's life story.

(Atkins, 2004: 351)

There is a sense in which market-defined subjects, denied the opportunity of becoming responsible active writers of their own lives, become passive readers of others' autobiographies precisely because such texts satisfy the human craving for coherent selfhood, and indicate the possibility of achieving a more autonomous existence than the conditions of late-capitalism allow. Given the curtailment of self-authorship under those conditions, the autobiographical response to problems of identity and ethical action makes perfect sense. When Chris Stewart in *Driving Over Lemons* (1999), an account of setting up life in Las Alpujarras, claims that he and his wife are 'numbed with surprise to find ourselves taking part in the script we had written' (56), he alludes to the making of the self as a co-creation formed by the adoption of a new lifestyle and the contemporaneous autobiographical recording of it, which is in turn a function of a simultaneous reading and writing of the circumstances of their existence.

The surprise for other middle-class couples may be because, having felt the loss of self-expressive power in one culture, they happily find it in another, but the fulfilment experienced by a renewed control over the self, which autobiography signifies, runs deeper. For as Atkins (2004) says, 'unless the reasons that direct our actions are grounded in core attributes of ourselves which we value […] our actions and beliefs will be arbitrary and pointless' (363), and pointless action is unrewarding. Thus when the values and attitudes that turn the corporate machine are misaligned with one's own character and ideals, there is a lack of satisfaction in work activity because the employee is unwilling to own responsibility for actions he or she is required to take. If Stewart (1999) recalls 'with a shudder the six months he'd once spent in an office' (31–32) and believes the 'exciting challenge [of his new life] beats being an insurance clerk' (56), it is because his personally chosen new life abroad offers both direction and purpose, and engages him in the kinds of deliberate and useful actions and attendant values for which he is willing to own and assume responsibility.

So, the autobiographical impulse is intimately connected to a kind of healthy psychological function associated with the self-direction and self-narration thought necessary for humankind to thrive. However, even if 'the narrative approach is one that is oriented to the need for meaning in the lives of embodied, practical beings existing within the constraints of a temporal world' (Atkins, 2004: 341), this alone does not explain the significance of linear 'escape' narratives that adhere specifically to the organic structure of cyclical time. After all, autobiography can be narrated just as well in a differently structured form – say, one moving freely backwards and forwards through episodes pulled from a memory cache that find logical connection with the benefit of the writer's and/or reader's subsequent interpretation. In seeking an answer to the linearity question, one must consider in greater detail the link between time and the self, or specifically the movement through time of the experiential human being.

Time and the self (and their relation to form)

If the self finds a comforting unity and continuity in narrative, it may find also that the linear form, in addition to such coherence, offers both stability and predictability. It is the linear form that most closely replicates quotidian (daily) time, or even, as Atkins says, 'cosmological time from birth to death' (347). This metonymic (sequential) rather than metaphoric connection provides two stable points, origin and terminus, for the construction of meaning. (By the term linearity I do not mean to imply a simple narrative in which the recounting parallels merely the sequential occurrence of events, as indeed seems to be the case with the business parables; rather, as Atkins claims from Ricoeur's work on Heidegger, even where a line connects beginning and end, or birth and death, 'that linear time-span is experienced in terms of an interplay of past-present-future orientations, or phenomenological time' (347).)

However, it is in understanding that 'the brain operates in cycles inherited from nature' (Bunting, 2005: (198–199) that we can appreciate the solace drawn from stories that run their linear trajectory within a cycle, for in this respect the literary form of 'escape' narratives replicates the organically established routine and rhythm of the natural world in which a line connecting birth and death (origin and terminus) occurs within the framework of cyclical time. These tales of creative selfhood typically recount the daily events of a new lifestyle and experience within a clearly seasonal or annual cycle just as McEwan's more sophisticated creative text, *Saturday*, narrates Perowne's beginning to end events framed within a 24-hour daily cycle. The pre-occupation with these specific structural properties at this particular time is not without significance.

This line-within-a-circle structural form clearly establishes a relationship between itself and a natural order of time and being in which events (or lifetimes) between birth and death occur within a larger ordering where seconds make minutes that make hours, days, months, seasons and years. It is a model that functions to situate the fragmentary and impermanent within a sense of the enduring and permanent (or at least functions to (re)establish some connection between them). This aesthetic replicates the 'conjoining of the ephemeral and the fleeting with the eternal and the immutable' that, according to David Harvey in *The Condition of Postmodernity* (1991), Baudelaire states as the opposing sides of a characteristic time-based tension in the creative work of art. Harvey also argues that 'the history of modernism as an aesthetic has wavered from one side to the other of this dual formation' (1991: 10). If this is so, new capitalism's economic discourse has now tilted the axis firmly toward the ephemeral and the fleeting, privileging the characteristics on one side of that formation as the defining aesthetic of the contemporary moment.

If a shift in bias towards impermanence upsets a critical artistic balance, then working from the correlation implied by Atkins between narrative creation and the creation of the self, it is possible to conclude that what destabilises the equilibrium of one will do likewise to the other. Just as the ever-new, fast-moving and always-changing superficiality of the contemporary time bias is reflected in discontinuous postmodern cultural forms, so the disturbance of the relationship between time and being similarly impacts the human psyche, with disastrous results. For those subject to narration through a market-defined late-capitalist discourse in which time is fragmented and behaviour and attitude are circumscribed by immediacy and flexibility, selfhood is similarly broken and incoherent. There is ample evidence that 'because a coherent identity is an achievement it can also fail' (Atkins, 2004: 347). It is failing with critical effect on mental health for an increasing number attempting identity-construction within the prevailing conditions of fragmentation and discontinuity. Hence, the attractions of a narrative form in which a discrete (but sensible) segment of time-experience occurs with reference to an endlessly renewing cycle of time. This particular form offers an aesthetic indispensable to the human psyche in terms of how it locates itself and makes sense of its experience of the phenomenological world. In other words, there is an essential three-way relationship between a self that uses narrative as a means to make its identity and understand its experience as a time-bound entity, the organic rhythms and routines of the earth, and a narrative form that reflects both. Considering this, the emergence and growing interest in other cultural forms and different lifestyles (especially those admitting autobiographical formation and other creative activities over which one can exert a measure of control, and which reject discontinuity and refuse fragmentation by recuperating the organic sense in which all time and all things are connected) are highly significant. They are evidence of political resistance to current circumstances *and* a bid to recover both agency and psychological health within a context of historical and narrative continuity which current employment denies.

Autobiography as genre – crossing boundaries

While the narrative structure of middle-class autobiographies is clearly an effort to create, order and control a life story, there is a particular aspect of these accounts that, at the same time, acknowledges the categorical breakdown that has made it so problematic for a social group trying to achieve coherence or maintain a sense of distinction (see Chapter 2). In those contemporary travelogues examined the form of autobiography itself undergoes a radical change, resulting from the postmodern challenge to genre writing, which once neatly packaged and defined the parameters of literary identity.

Autobiography, by definition, implies a story of the self from a first-person perspective and in that respect the label serves well. In other respects the classification is inadequate for the 'escape' narratives. The nature of the problem is found in reviews on the inside of *Under the Tuscan Sun* by Frances Mayes about which *The Mail on Sunday* says, 'this account of restoring a Tuscan farmhouse and its land is hard to classify', and which *The Guardian* describes as 'A memoir, a travelogue and a cookbook all rolled into one' (Mayes, 1996). Similarly, the book that began the British fascination with moving abroad, Peter Mayle's *A Year in Provence*, is classified as Travel/Autobiography, while Shelton's *Allotted Time* remains uncategorised but is an amalgamation of diary, crop management instruction, allotment history and bibliography. *A Thousand Days in Tuscany* is labelled Travel/Memoir but is also a cookbook complete with recipes; *Corfu Banquet* is Travel writing but is also an eclectic guide to recipes for food and alternative medicine, the history and cultivation of olives, the uses of herbs, local drinks and wines, a calendar of saints' days, festivals and holidays, and recommended walks.[3] The classification difficulty indicates that the boundaries once defining neat genre identities are collapsing like the social, gender, ethnic and class categories that once shaped human identity. So, while the accounts capture the creation of the author/protagonist's identity as shaped and made stable by narrative, simultaneously another moment of creation – one of formal hybridity – occurs. Both are responses to postmodern identity: one refusing fragmentation; the other a celebration of formal eclecticism.

Smith and Watson see the dissolution of categorical human identity as driving a new sense of community, saying in *Reading Autobiography* that:

> writers around the globe are proposing new concepts of subjectivity, as transcultural, diasporic, hybrid, and nomadic [and] such autobiographic acts move the 'I' toward the collective and shift the focus of narration toward an as-yet virtual space of community, across and beyond the old boundaries of identification.
> (Smith and Watson, 2001: 132)

However, the migrants' life-stories show the movement of the 'I' towards the collective is still firmly being sought through face-to-face connection in real, earthbound and contained communities rather than virtual unrestricted ones, and while migrants also confirm subjectivity as transcultural, diasporic and nomadic, the potential for hybridity seems displaced into the creative genre as a formal means of containing the further disruption or dilution that otherwise might be played out in multiple identity of the self. Thus, for the present, the kinds of mixing brought about by geographic spreading – one culture, nationality, religion, etc. coming into contact with another – seem tolerated better than changes acknowledging the formation of entirely new identities resulting from the wholesale interpenetration of earlier, now redundant local categories.

Rather than being simple accounts of lives, these autobiographic travelogues are multifaceted cultural artefacts that in form and content bear witness to the complexity of self-making at this historical moment and to the skills required for that task. They evidence the impulse to create and stabilise identity among postmodernity's fluidity by using authorial and editorial processes to create narrative, impose order, resolve contradiction, handle diversity and manage the dynamic tension between plot (place/situation/structural environment) and character (person/agency). There is no doubt about the appeal of these mixed content or hybrid publications – profit-conscious publishers do not produce books for which there is no demand and the commercial value of these hybrid genres, as in the cookbooks examined, is in their simultaneous appeal to particular and wider interests – so these narratives provide particular satisfactions for readers as much as for writers. While remembering the human psychological need for narration described by Atkins and how the instantaneity of modern work life compromises autonomy and reflective thinking, the appeal of these life-texts as vehicles of biographic certainty, political resistance and self-examination (in addition to the measured experience of linear and cyclical time denied by fast lifestyles as already discussed) relies on the peculiar characteristics and history of the genre.

According to LeJeune, two certainties are guaranteed by the 'autobiographical pact' that operates as a contract between narrator and reader. This contract verifies the work is fact not fiction and 'supposes that there is *identity of name* between the author (such as he figures, by his name on the cover), the narrator of the story, and the character that is being talked about' (Smith and Watson, 2001: 140, original emphasis). However, authorial reliability cannot be taken for granted. Autobiography typically results from an act of memory that reviews and interprets a life charted in development often from birth or a moment in the distant past to, in many cases, the moment of writing (even when not presented strictly chronologically) and memory is fallible. Thus the life text is the result of (often defective) recall, while the interpreting and editing of events introduces further uncertainty, and reader response imposes yet another hermeneutic level. Also the reader understands the possibility that where publication fixes a text, the subject may continue developing and may well review and reinterpret the story at a later date when its 'truth' will be affected by further revisions. Regardless of such potential for their meaning to mutate in transmission or change over time, at the moment they are written, the accounts must be recognised as attempts by the author to establish identity in an era of biographical uncertainty and, by implication, as also providing satisfyingly coherent life/person narratives for the reader.

The writers of the life-stories studied also draw on the form's history as a vehicle of moral examination and political resistance. Notwithstanding the formal hybridity now disturbing the genre, autobiography already presents itself in a variety of types – testimony, memoir, diary and confession – each having its distinct quality and usage. In seeking to establish not just character, but 'good' character, and in their spiritual and didactic content, the stories draw on early forms of personal testimonies of spiritual growth and thus they are linked historically to Puritan and Quaker accounts which 'represent an important stage in the identity and consciousness among an under-privileged minority' (Burnett, 1984: 9). While the authors' spiritual journeys also encompass personal, economic, social, cultural and historical dimensions, and in many senses they are not underprivileged, by holding out for principles undervalued by hegemony they do identify themselves through writing as a political minority.

In the light of this, the particular narrative form of the accounts under discussion takes on greater significance for a modern-day audience given that they focus on the experience of time, for by altering the temporal dimensions of autobiography, the texts under discussion draw attention to the temporal dimensions of contemporary life. They are less a whole life-story written from a more distant point than traditional autobiographies, and more a life-slice based on the almost simultaneous recording of events in diary form. Given that a diary's immediacy and structure lends itself to speedy capture and therefore near-instant *public*ation, one draws the conclusion that for the authors (and any group they represent), there is something particularly pressing about the specific moment of their personal development and its social significance. It is impossible to ignore that the longer-term linear and cyclical time frames affording both author and reader the comfort of stability and predictability are specifically drawn to the attention of a contemporary audience even while, ironically, capitalising on their immediacy and satisfying the market requirement for speed. And yet, though this form is a less mediated recording of events than the autobiography proper, and is less spiritual than a personal testimony, and not overly reflective like a memoir or confession that is an *apologia pro vita sua*, accounting for one's past lapses, for all their immediacy they are undoubtedly socially (if not self-) reflective and, in many cases, spiritual and philosophical. In this the accounts bring together quotidian time with thoughtfulness and remake an association that has been broken.

Principally, autobiographies are both written and read to assist knowing who one is. Through the process of writing the author captures an idea of the self in an external, concrete form that can be objectified, assessed and evaluated. Readers can identify with the autobiographic subject in whole, or in part, or not at all, and so locate their own identity in a relational context. In fact:

> reading the lives of other people with whom we do not identify has as much to tell us (if not more) about our lives as the lives with which we do. On the assumption that we read autobiographical writing in order to learn something about ourselves as well as about others, disidentification takes us as readers on a (sometimes circuitous, which is the whole point) journey back to ourselves.
> (Miller, 2002: xv)

In other words, the purpose of life-writing is that it enables authors and readers to self-examine in a way there is rarely time for in the daily busy-ness of the modern world. It also allows readers to evaluate another's life, adding authentication by means of the author/character identification and the piquancy that comes from contemplating the prospect of trying out that life experience for 'real', for these accounts function as 'good life' promotions.

Where first-person accounts signify a process of self-telling that is self-making, a diary makes that ongoing process explicit. When writing one's experience in diarised autobiographic form, the problems of identity are worked through on a double level, for the concrete product of the articulate process that records and expresses the author's self *as it is developing* is a work(item)-in-progress of a work(self)-in-progress. It is this potential for a mindful process of continuous judgement and improvement (rewriting) that is significant in terms of deciding the aesthetic value of the published-word-text and moral value of the created-life-text.

Finally, if autobiography is a means of locating *where one is*, we need to register also that these accounts are situated in geographically specific locations, so that our understanding is informed by the intersection of person and place that is marked by the overlap of autobiography with travel writing. For readers, the accounts' attractions clearly derive from the independence, veracity and authenticity of personal experience, to which, Peter Hulme and Tim Youngs (2002) suggest, the travel genre owes its power (1–10) too, notwithstanding debate on how memory can cloud the fact/fiction divide in this form also. Autobiography shares with travel writing, through the picaresque tradition that was a precursor to the novel, the important formal properties of linearity and a first-person perspective. Also, Hulme and Youngs confirm that 'travel writing and the novel, especially in its first person form, have often shared a focus on the centrality of the self, a concern with empirical details, and a movement through time and place which is simply sequential' (2002: 6), each of these elements being important when identity insecurity prompts a search for certainty and comfort in postmodernity. The last point of note is that the parallel between actual travel and the life journey evokes an even earlier antecedent which is traced to *The Canterbury Tales* since 'in many respects, pilgrims were ancestors of modern tourists' (Hulme and Youngs, 2002: 2), and this reminds us that these accounts are not merely the outward-looking observations of an independent traveller, they are also the reflective surface of the self-examiner. So, in addition to crossing the public/private divide, these migrant accounts are thoroughly implicated in many types of boundary-crossing – literal (national), cultural, political, metaphoric and generic.

The unitary subject? – stories of the 'I'

In theorising selfhood *Reading Autobiography* argues that:

> challenges to the concept of a unified sovereign subject and to belief in language's transparency have shattered the cultural authority of what Lyotard calls the 'master narratives' of the West, including the institution of canonical autobiography.
>
> (Smith and Watson, 2001: 132)

Taking this as true, we may then consider in what 'cultural authority' now resides and what has taken the place of 'master narratives' and 'canonical autobiography'. If grand lives (those of royalty, Nobel Laureates, pioneers, inventors, politicians, etc.) are produced within cultures sustained by master narratives, then the proliferation of lifestyle stories would seem to be the consequence of a culture divested of them. However, some alternative spiritualities provide a situational context for *petit reçus* every bit as overarching as the old-style grand narratives and the market narrative itself certainly appears to be grand in style. If one considers a dynamic of naturally occurring equilibrium (which preoccupies de Blasi's account in *A Thousand Days in Tuscany* (2005)), it would seem that *petit reçus*, far from emerging to replace grand narratives, arise precisely to counterbalance them.

The liberal humanist subject is now challenged by multiple cyber-identities and other modes of existence presented to us through electronic knowledge-sharing. That some of those modes apparently still honour the idea of a unitary self given public exposure through the autobiographic text warrants further investigation given that, in the texts scrutinised as part of this study, the 'I' seems to employ autobiography as a means of negotiating a problematic contemporary position. The examined texts show the quest for 'I' as a response to the problems of disconnection from the self, others, the land and the products of labour by focusing on 'I' as one connected in community to the rhythms, rituals and products of organic life. This basically frames the question of being as a political one negotiating the gap between liberal individualism and communitarianism (or between singularity and relationality). On the one (right) hand, the aim is for the singularity by which one is defined as specific or unique, (i.e. *me*);

on the other (left) hand, one is defined as like others (i.e. part of *we*). De Blasi appears exercised by this negotiation and plots three possible positions between *me* and *we*. One is willing submission to incorporation in the other, as when Barlozzo 'keeps stumbling over his use of *we*, changing it to *you* […] I wish he'd understand that *we* is most appropriate' (2005: 122). Another is neither resistant nor acquiescent as illustrated when de Blasi dons Barlozzo's (*il duca*'s) gloves. Though they feel good, she says, 'Maybe they'll enthral me and I'll become a duke. Or I'll enthrall the gloves and the duke will dance the tango' (144). A third position is a necessary resistance to incorporation when she claims:

> people who live in small clutches like we do, tend to be a chorus of sorts, everybody singing the same song, if in different keys. Everyone endorses the thoughts of everyone else here. And this, in most part, thwarts any hope man has of meeting up with himself, let alone with the peace it takes to nourish one or two of his particular hungers.
>
> (de Blasi, 2005: 166)

Human hungers (here endorsing the symbolic potency of food discussed at length in Chapter 4) sometimes require satisfying by the peace that is found in solitude – a solitude that is not isolation but gives one the space and time to get to know oneself and one's boundaries.

The autobiographic text synthesises positions one and three, being at once a (formal) vehicle by which the author draws attention to her or himself – separated from the common herd by the primacy achieved with having one's name on the book jacket – and a means by which an author locates her or himself as part of a common humanity through content that stresses her or his identification with others of the species *Homo sapiens*. This position holds *me* and *we* in tension, inviting either/neither identification or disidentification. It is the position elucidated in de Blasi's observation that her husband Fernando:

> remains equally unposed in company these days, this new life on dry land having somewhat loosened the despotic rule of his *bella figura*. He blooms, moves through his own quiet risorgimento. I

think even he is beginning to recognize his beauty – the beauty of who he is and not who he might contrive to be.

(de Blasi, 2005: 159–160)

This 'centred' self-confidence, this authenticity, comes, ironically, from having 'dissolved his professional history' (250), from relinquishing that part of his identity resting in a particular work skill, which Raymond Williams says 'is only an aspect of a man, and yet, at times, it can seem to comprehend his whole being' when greater ease lies in the ability to 'deepen the community which is even larger than the skills' (1985: 318–319). There is, of course, a sense in which it can never be known if the text, human or written, is 'unposed' when 'in company' precisely because there it shows the public face of a private life and because of the provisional nature of its truth. Also, that centre point can be occupied not as a place of comfort and perfect balance, but as one of neurosis where equal pull in both directions – towards or away from self-interest – presents the dilemma and responsibility of choice that will determine the agent as one character or another.

In fact, these texts embody an ironic stance concerning a tension of particular significance to middle-class existence. If the contradiction between hedonism and investment that plagues the professional middle class in the Anglo-American culture (Harvey, 1991: 19, quoting Bell) prompts escape, then these autobiographies provide an imaginative resolution to that contradiction. The migrant lifestyles are forms of indulgence that are the privilege of a moneyed class who can give up full-time salaried work, but they are also simplified and often hard-working lives based on a withdrawal from the excesses of hedonistic consumerism. However, another level of contradiction completes the circle. Those that publish lifestyle accounts about the simple life, in many cases, rely on their cultural capital and their personal (and virtual) network connections to contacts in the homeland to do so. Not only does this grant the author a new source of income, it produces a consumer product that, in some cases, sustains the very industries that were escaped from, while declaring a resistance to the work conditions and subjectivity experienced in them. Furthermore, one might ask if autobiography is not merely another form of conspicuous display, for migration may be not quite the drop-out it seems where writing recovers personal status by a new form of visibility. Even as Peter Mayle (2000) runs from his past life in the advertising industry and scoffs at the harassed ad-exec who visits him in Provence, he is, ironically, involved still in a form of self-promotion, an activity adopted by increasing numbers of individuals inhabiting a celebrity PR culture in which success is measured not in terms of good character, but in terms of being known. Escape lifestyle accounts involving publishing contracts or small business enterprises that by other means market their 'authentic' experience are thus thoroughly postmodern – the ironic product of a schizophrenic age – promoting withdrawal from the economic and, at the same time, a return to it.

The narrative self-making process, therefore, defines identity not as a settled state but a continuous process of negotiating selfhood against any number of variously opposed conditions and characteristics (public/private, individual/social, selfish/selfless, spender/saver, loyal/disloyal, fighter/quitter, optimistic/pessimistic, etc.). The outcome of narrative mediation defines at any moment in time, and from time to time, the identity story, a (fairly) consistent position, say, one mostly/always optimistic, social and miserly (enduring self) or one altered in degree from this character according to situation and circumstance (the various (performed) social roles) (e.g. I am mostly optimistic but there are certain social/public occasions when I present as a more/less optimistic or even a pessimistic character). This is identity theorised not as *either* constant (unchanging) *or* inconstant (always changing), but *developing* as a consequence of a degree (anything from 0 to 100%) of reflection on experience as one charts a course within the parameters of personal psychological comfort and social situations. If any deviation becomes extreme and/or persists in an uncomfortable zone for a length of time (dissonance), or one suffers a profound emotional or psychological disturbance (trauma or ecstasy), such movement will generally portend a more sudden development involving a change of character or urging correction. Escapes from the mainstream economic mode, and the autobiographies thereby produced, signify a multiple, corrective and stabilising identity effort by citizens resisting definition by hegemony that causes them to be in a conflicting, emotional and psychological state. Reflection is absolutely essential if one is to resist wholesale determination by another (person, institution or event), and for reflection, one requires time. Without the space and time to contemplate, to assess, judge and evaluate one's character as it is shown to the self through experience, the self either will not develop or will develop erratically. Given the time and space much is possible, as ever, with diligence and hard work. The mindful ways that can consciously maintain or alter the 'I', this study suggests, suppose a particular way of working.

The self as craftwork

Richard Sennett claims in *The Craftsman* (2008) 'that the craft of making physical things provides insight into the techniques of experience that can shape our dealings with others' (289). My argument metaphorically extends the mode of engagement he applies to the artefact and to 'our dealings with others' to the processes involved with the making the self. In fact, Parkins and Craig's notion of the 'slow arts of the self' (2006: 12) can be refined by more accurately and usefully referring to the slow *craft* of the self with this crafting made explicit through the autobiographical act.

The definitions of individuality and originality, so regularly applied when selfhood is seen as a work of art, are misleading. Clearly, the product – the self – is individual and thus original in one sense but no men or women make themselves alone. Where postmodern art may produce, suddenly, the avant-garde that seems to have no antecedents (Lyotard, 2001: 71–82), the human product, like the craft object, results from a social context in which it is developed and is shaped by a myriad of influences (social, cultural, political, etc.) as well as by experience and genetics. At every stage, and ongoing, there is multiple, influential input. The human character is not created in the sense that God creates from nothing, it is developed slowly and, in the best cases, constantly improved over time.

Similarly, autobiographies are social products. Though the genre is associated with the individual consciousness, it is a *human* consciousness subject to the influences described. Life-writing claims to be telling the truth, but not an objective truth, rather a declared subjective truth of experience. Where art may guard its truth, autobiography flings open its doors and invites everybody in, at least with the intention of getting them to see as the author sees. Writing, in this sense, though springing from an inward turn of the troubled person and energised by *retreat*, is a move towards the social and the communal. The recent growth of a genre that is thought to be a means for 'the author to give himself identity, to place himself in the context of history, geography and social change, and so make a kind of sense out of an existence which might otherwise seem meaningless' (Burnett, 1984: 10) invests the public-facing side of the product with great significance. For the writer, the outward turn expresses a desire for reconnection while the writing itself is the manifestation of a bid for sanity that comes with being able to narrate one's experience (Mukherjee, 2001: 49–62).

According to Sennett, the repeated actions, reworking, continuous assessment of progress and improvement involved in craftwork indicate an ability to stay with frustrating work (2008: 220). He tells us that 'the craftsman represents in all of us the desire to do something well, concretely, for its own sake' (144–145), but this requires application, time and an appreciation for 'the aspiration for quality' (9). Today's turnover rates hide the poor quality of consumer items. Quickly produced celebrity (auto)biographies are little more than hack journalism in which ghost-writers break LeJeune's contract by having little investment in, and no identification with, the subject. For such products immediacy is often the *only* issue – capturing and capitalising on a person's fifteen minutes of fame. Where self-making and self-development are concerned, quality is more critical. The ability to stay with the frustrating work on the self is existence that admits self-improvement but the diligence and persistence required for this is today neither practised nor valued as a character attribute in the time-pressured workplace, so is simply not available when needed. Self-making can be defined as a craft under Sennett's terms because it is an ongoing project, a work in progress, always flawed and individual, and requiring reworking. In the autobiography proper where there is total identification between author and subject, quality matters because capturing life-as-text openly displays what level of ability, persistence and diligence is represented both in the nature of the writing and in its representational truth.

A bid for posterity

A further matter concerns autobiography's relevance to posterity and heroes. A recent British Academy debate, *Posterity: Present concerns with the future* suggested that 'post-war social and economic debacles and looming ecological disaster have bred despair and anomie' and that 'without hope for posterity, life becomes bleak and society self-destructs' (2007). Without religion providing that hope, other means of transcending mortality are required. Burnett believes 'autobiographers seek to establish themselves in time and to leave behind a testimony that the significance of life does not end with death' (1984: 11). Thus life-writing supplies this need, immortalising the subject, overcoming the limitations of both humanity and time, and removing the anxiety and bleakness that attend thoughts of erasure.

Knowledge transfer is another means of serving posterity and it is a notable issue in each of the texts examined. Burnett, again, says 'a particular motivation behind such memoirs [of work was] most commonly the author's belief that he had some important message for others which it was his duty to communicate' (1977: 11). Each of the autobiographical accounts includes a revered master who teaches the uninitiated pupil. Stewart (1999) has Domingo, his 'mentor-neighbour' (133), Shelton (2006) adopts religious language to introduce three father figures – Ken, who has the 'aura of the Great One' (42), Ted, who 'has always known more about a subject than [Shelton] ever will' (292), and, lastly, a 'most trusted friend' introduced by the phrase 'there is a God and his name's Bob' (50–51). De Blasi (2004) has Barlozzo or '*il duca*' as she titles him while asking, 'has my husband found a hero?' (46–47). Understanding that 'old timers with long and varied experience do not have a high value in this new [economy] setting' (Eriksen, 2001: 125), migrants draw attention to where we might look for heroes in an irreligious world. At the same time a point is made that bequests for the future mostly depend on legacies from the past, emphasising that a historical time continuum is required for a concept of posterity to be workable at all.

In the shifting and chaotic lives of the mobile subject, the written text thus stands as a permanent record of continuity allowing a reader (or one's descendants) access to wisdom that for future generations might also prove valuable. At the very least, writing one's life and presenting it publicly proves an interest in the kind of self one is, or is able to be. In the texts studied, who 'I' am is important to the authors because their communitarian philosophy connects 'I' to 'we'. As Bauman (2001) reminds us:

> That our individuality is socially produced is by now a trivial truth; but the obverse of that truth still needs to be repeated more often: the shape of our sociality, and so of the society we share, depends in its turn on the way in which the task of 'individualization' is framed and responded to.
>
> (Bauman, 2001: 144)

The link from individual to community, to nation and to the world matters more than ever in an era of globalisation (Harvey, 2004). The concept of potential may have been hijacked in the workplace to urge workers to self-train for an undefinable future that remains always just out of reach, but it still has real currency with regard to the self-improvement of character for which an unattainable ideal can be more readily accepted. Potential in this regard expresses a wish for the best humanity can be. Last century saw it at its worst. In a post-Holocaust world, says Nancy Miller,

> the memoir boom [...] should not be understood as a proliferation of self-serving representations of individualistic memory but as an aid or spur to keep cultural memory alive [...] memoir is the record of an experience in search of a community, of a collective framework in which to protect the fragility of singularity in a postmodern world.
>
> (Miller, 2002: 14)

However, cultural memory is not only held in tragedy; something of this same impulse operates with regard to those wanting to preserve the likely-to-be-forgotten positive values of former eras. This is also a political act. If the middle class is overrepresented in autobiographies of 'slow life' and the supporting political movements, there is good reason. It indicates a class in trouble – one threatened by institutional and social developments that require them to vacate the ground of wealth and social conscience on which the foundations of their identities have, for so long, been built; one suffering from the pressures that beset us all in a fragmented, accelerated, competitive, market-driven culture; and one having many of its members employed in education, medicine, the social services and local and national government who find that business principles imported from the private sector undermine their professional integrity by denying them the opportunity to demonstrate the care of proper service for which they entered public service. These threats prompt personal acts of self-declaration that feed directly into the political acts of class preservation (see Chapter 2).

When identity fails and the instinct for doing a good job for its own sake is denied, people are forced to turn inward to understand their purpose and to find answers to the question 'who or what am I?' In this, the cultural heritage of the middle class fits it well for the kind of introspection that prompts the search for an alternative way of living that gives back meaning to life and re-secures identity. They appear to do this, in part, by putting the 'I' back on a firmer and better-connected footing with itself, with the products of its labour, and by respecting and reconnecting with the comforting biological rhythms and rituals of which the human being is part. The diarised accounts of a slow life are evidence of the everyday mindfulness and reflection that can be applied as much to the ongoing project of self-improvement as to the drafting and refining of the contemporaneous account for publication in which that character stars, and since both person and publication have the same aim, the one serves the other and the crafting skill serves them both.

The relevance and impact of Robinson Crusoe

The middle class has a long tradition of self-help, self-awareness, self-scrutiny and self-sufficiency born of the individualism that developed from Enlightenment thinking. A key text of the time, Defoe's *Robinson Crusoe*, draws attention to these characteristic aspects and relates them to labour and to ideas of investment and profit in a form that is not without significance for this study. In this context its relevance is threefold.

First, this account of lone survival by virtue of one's own effort and the propitious return (growth) from seed (stock) ties the economics and ideology of liberal individualism to identity through a newly emerging expressive form of singular character development (the novel) based on self-reflection. Ironically, the shipwrecked individual arriving battered and weary on an alien shore also narrates an agriculturally based existence similar to that chosen by migrants fleeing the very society that developed from the capitalist beginnings modelled in this early form of the novel – those for whom the original horticultural terms 'growth' and 'stock' are applied more usually today in a financial context. Thus another circle is completed.

Robinson Crusoe is a literary example of 'removal', but religious and psychoanalytic models also have relevance for employees adopting the flight response to work stress. One is the concept of wilderness, inhabiting a space in which the self is tested and can think apart from the influence and pressures of daily life and apply any learning on return. The other is the neurotic (often silent) state requiring reorientation of the self or a reordered understanding to progress. Both are withdrawal but the latter, involving the loss and recovery of speech, has most relevance for the argument of this book, which claims that corporate messaging effectively silences resistance and autobiography is that voice returned.

Second, the novel draws attention to the role of temporality in institutional development. Crusoe's account can be read as the Protestant position at a particular time, a point of negotiation between a changing ethics in which earlier pre-Reformation sacred values (denoted by his initials RC, which also stand for Roman Catholic) give way to those of progressive, independent, secular economic enterprise. With the name Crusoe, seemingly rooted in 'crux', denoting intersection, the cross he draws on the beach to mark the passing of time symbolises the transitional shift from the church-ordered, bell-marked time of religious devotion to mechanical clock-regulated commercial time which, related to production, ultimately links profit to pressure. A couple of centuries later, automation and mechanisation make that link explicit in Taylorism and further forward, digital age business drives our undifferentiated work/home lives with a deluge of communication tasks and the advertising-backed enticements of a twenty-four-seven selling culture in which all time is seen as potentially profitable.

Lastly, Defoe's first-person account, which is a formal and literary development from pilgrims' chronicles and confessional memoirs, through the picaresque tradition and *bildungsroman*, can be seen as forerunner of the autobiographical travelogues through which contemporary migrants record a personal journey by creating new self-narratives which mark both their flight from, and re-entanglement with, economic enterprise based, as in Crusoe's efforts, on food-related production.

In conclusion, it is of note that the establishment of the literary subject, by which character may be abstracted and held up for scrutiny, was made possible by the advent of the printing press (Wilson, 1991) and the consequent wider dissemination of the written form. This confirms how conceptions of selfhood are related to the developing methods and means of communication. So it is significant when communication technology takes a quantum leap again in the 1990s, facilitating the inventiveness and anonymity of the multiple, virtual forms characterising cyber-identity, that a parallel development occurs. For this movement towards instability and ephemerality is countered by a growing interest also in the identifiably authored, self-contained, concrete, coherent *and* creative form of autobiography – a genre responding *expressively* and through its formal eclecticism to the complexity of self-making in times of biographic uncertainty and categorical dissolution. Where every move contains, and may bring into being, its opposite, the autobiographic impulse presents itself as no mere cultural coincidence at the moment when working conditions exacerbate instability and voicelessness, and compromise autonomous identity formation. Rather, it is a reciprocal challenge to the intensive interpellation of employees through insistent methods of corporate communication towards flexible responsiveness, to a very specific entrepreneurial notion of 'success' in Western cultural identity that pitches many into a state of dissonance and identity fracture. It is a resistant response to existence predicated on continuous growth not of the self (despite HR empowerment rhetoric) but of production and profit. Crafting the self through different kinds of work, writing and thoughtful reflection is the attempt to achieve the meaning, coherence and stability missing from contemporary life. It is the bid for recovery from the psychological dis-ease brought upon those whose personal values run counter to hegemony. Above all, it is an indication that identity, work, time and well-being are inextricably linked in ways that may not yet be fully understood but are reflected in, and through, the narrative stories we endeavour to tell about ourselves.

Notes

1 The concept of being as a 'practical and ethical subject' through time is similar to Sennett's use of the French philosophic definition '*mantien a soi*' – maintenance of oneself over time, and '*constance a soi*' – fidelity to oneself (1998: 145).
2 See also Strawson (2004), who asserts that 'Diachronic' types see their lives in narrative terms but not so 'Episodic' types, who accept 'one has long-term continuity' (in terms of bodily existence through time) but whose psychology resists or is wary of employing the privileged position of the 'I' to determine meaning from the available facts of experience. This willingness to exist with uncertainty is, however, recognisable as a position taken in postmodern forms that narrate disruption, contingency and discontinuity by drawing attention to their own limitations in making meaning from a chaotic reality. I would assert that even Episodic types use narration that is internally coherent to relate discrete segments of experience, which still ties narration to meaning.
3 Listed here are the categorisations given by publishers to a number of 'escape' narratives: *A Thousand Days in Tuscany* – Travel/Memoir; *A Year in Provence* – Travel/Autobiography; *The Greek for Love* – Memoir; *Bonne Chance*, *Corfu Banquet*, *Extra Virgin*, *Snowball Oranges*, *A Castle in Spain* – Travel; *Driving over Lemons*, *A Parrot in the Pepper Tree*, *Almond Blossom*, *Under the Tuscan Sun*, *From Here You Can't See Paris*, *Allotted Time* – no category. Hugh Fearnley-Whittingstall, Jamie Oliver and Nigella Lawson have each published books having elements of hybridity.

Conclusion
The meaning and value of self-mastery

Heaven or hell on earth?

This study has given an account of the role played by literature (in its broadest sense) in human subjectivity and identity under the working conditions of late-capitalism as these affect the well-being of specialist, middle-class, public sector professionals. The argument claims that application of private business values to public service, backed by an increasing volume of organisational messaging, results in a number of performative contradictions and the loss of the inherent satisfaction of public service that, for some, is a key issue of identity. Chiefly, the corporate call to employees to align with organisational values and to adopt and internalise the behaviours and attitudes that serve the fast-producing, short-deadline, cost-conscious organisation is antithetical to many individuals' acculturated autonomy and to the satisfactions of a non-cost-dependent service ethic. In addition, the instability, uncertainty and disorientation caused by structural dissolution, plus the overstretch required in a lean organisation, produce the pressure and impotence that cause symptoms of mental ill-health recorded by many commentators through the 1990s with increasing incidence (i.e. Edwards, 2007: 8) – the overwhelming feeling of being out of control, an absence of a sense of achievement and progress, a confusion of identity and the lack of freedom and power to speak out or do anything about it.

While stress is recognised as increasing in the workplace, its cause is commonly attributed to job insecurity linked, more recently, to recessional conditions. However, work stress was already growing through the period of preceding growth, so the more vital investigation might concern the precise reasons regarding how and why job insecurity arises. It might ask how the experience of new economy work undermines personal identity, subsequently diminishing self-worth and affecting performance, which then contributes to the fear of job loss as the apparent immediate factor affecting mental health. In fact, though Layard states that *un*employment has negative psychic effects on self-esteem (2005: 172), this clearly implies that only when employment *delivers* self-esteem can it be said to contribute to happiness. Where it does not, it is just as likely that the nature and conditions for those in work are *causing* increasing numbers to become unwell, leave work and claim incapacity benefit. Though Cognitive Behaviour Therapy (182–183) helps sufferers learn psychological strategies for dealing with stress and depression, it does not tackle the uncomfortable truth of their cause. It is certainly legitimate to ask why a method of coping has become the appropriate attitude for dealing with the mental fallout from work. In addition, if well-being depends not on a high income but on feeling better off relative to one's peers (41–53), middle-class professionals losing their status, reputation and pension benefits (once the expected advantage of public duty) are likely to fall dramatically down the happiness scale and, given their potential for radicalism, may seek a change in circumstances that amounts to a political act.

Stress and declining mental health

Two of the many critics who have looked at the psychological effects of the instabilities of the new economy – Richard Layard and Madeleine Bunting – have commented on the relationship of professional status to motivation and well-being in the context of public reform. Layard considers 'the professional ethic is a precious motivation that should be cherished. If we do not cultivate it, we may well not even improve performance let alone produce workers who enjoy their work'. He believes 'universal human experience' has taught us that 'job satisfaction comes from work well done and not from "getting ahead" ' (159–160). However, lean organisations prizing quantity and cheapness above all else leave those aiming for quality always frustrated and this contradiction is not being fully acknowledged or investigated. Confirming this falling motivation, Bunting identifies the detrimental effects being suffered by public sector professionals who:

> find themselves caught up in rituals of accountability which often bear little or no relation to what motivates them to do their job in the first place – such as pride in the quality of service or the chance to make a difference to people's lives. [...] Central government intrusion [...] is also resented because it strikes at the heart of what it means to be a professional – the autonomy implicit in the expression 'professional judgement'.
>
> (Bunting, 2005: 128)

While Layard (2005) quotes the Eurobarometer survey (1996), in which 50% of respondents reported an increase in stress levels (158), and World Health Organization yearly figures for the US and Britain claiming 'about 20% of us have serious mental problems and 6% of us have severe depression' (181–182), Bunting's employment-specific statistics (2005) are even gloomier. She cites the 'blizzard of paperwork' generated by government processes as being the 'biggest cause of stress' in the workplace (121–130), with rising stress levels in all occupations 'now cited by 36 per cent of all professionals'. Public sector work increases the chances of stress, which are highest in the NHS (40%) (184–185, quoting AP Smith *et al.*).

With the pace, workload and accountability demands of employment adversely affecting workers' mental health and occurring mostly through a time of continuous economic growth and prosperity, the conclusion has to be that money is not, by itself, adequate compensation for some of the privations of new-economy conditions, particularly where impact occurs on identity-forming characteristics. Or, as Layard (2005) puts it, 'what madness it is if, as we become richer, we also become less secure and more stressed' (164). Bunting explains the cause and effect of such stress on public sector workers where:

> increasingly it is less about being a public servant and more about being a public entrepreneur. [...] The old public service ethos is challenged by a new rhetoric of 'social entrepreneurship', and the

stability of old bureaucratic structures is challenged by the constant invocation by politicians of the need for innovation, flexibility and continuous change. No wonder thousands of highly skilled public servants are voting with their feet.

(Bunting, 2005: 143)

With recession now biting hard at public jobs, the situation is already getting worse. Now, not even the promise of increasing affluence mitigates the misery. A CIPD press release dated 26 November 2010 reports respondents' falling standards of living over the previous six months and found a rise in job satisfaction was only due to the grin and bear it attitude of those fearing the worse fate of job loss. A massive '63% say stress has increased as a result of the economic downturn' and:

> [p]ublic sector workers are also most likely to report an increase in stress, conflict at work, bullying by line managers and an increase in people taking time off sick, as a result of the state of the economy. All these measures have increased when compared to the previous quarter.
>
> (CIPD press release, 26 November 2010)

Stress in the public sector worker is corroborated by Tarani Chandola's recent British Academy study (2010). Two of the key findings are that:

> the number of female employees suffering from job strain, an indicator of work stress, tripled from around 8% to almost 25% between 1992 and 2006 [and] since the 2008–09 recession, there has been a further steep increase in work stressors such as job insecurity, work intensity and inter-personal conflict at work, *particularly among public sector workers*.
>
> (Chandola, 2010: 15, emphasis added)

The 2011 CIPD/Simplyhealth Absence Management Survey 'has revealed, for the first time, that stress is the most common cause of long-term sickness absence' and that '[p]ublic sector respondents *identify organisational change and restructuring* [emphasis added] as the number one cause of stress at work'. The CIPD's Autumn

Outlook 2011 states that 'public worker job satisfaction has fallen even further this quarter to +24 from +30 last quarter' while '[p]ublic sector employees are significantly more likely to report they are under excessive pressure, with 52% saying they are under excessive pressure either everyday (19%) or once or twice a week (33%)'. Perhaps predictably, when it comes to the 'opportunity to feed views upwards' (to contribute to the organisational narrative, no less), scores for those working in the public sector are low at −8 compared with +13 elsewhere (2). This forewarns that over the coming years, employment-related mental ill-health will continue to rise. Public servants already struggling with the contradiction of trying to give proper quality-based service in an environment which prioritises speed and quantity of output in the name of efficiency will find their work satisfaction diminishes further.

Those trying to improve their lot may turn to the many self-help books that are produced by management gurus to aid those who may feel they are failing in the workplace. Readers of these publications will find further messaging placing the burden of responsibility for employee failure firmly in their own hands. In short, they are told it is not the system that is at fault, it is the worker who does not engender the right 'can do' attitude, which feeds into any self-esteem problems already being experienced. However, the self-help books communicate by employing certain narrative strategies. They use linear stories that move logically from beginning to end, that involve a hero or authority figure who is validated as a source of wisdom and admiration, and that invoke a sense of the mythic through magical secrets and otherworldly power. These are techniques familiar to a tradition of fairy tales and storytelling. They provide comfort in the form of structural coherence and the promise of rescue through the acquisition of new knowledge (known only to the chosen few). Their message, appealing to the reader's sense of self-responsibility, may prompt recognition among middle-class professionals acculturated to autonomy but the mode of address presumes an infantilised audience, one perhaps susceptible to persuasion that the blame lies with their own inability to handle the harsh realities of work in tough market conditions. However, in the case of many professionals required to alter radically their working approach following the importation of private sector values into public service, focusing on their transitional difficulties as personal failure simply misses the point, for it ignores both what is invested already in their occupational identities and the time-dependent psychological and neurological processes required for their alteration.

Subjectivity and identity

A wide-ranging debate producing a vast body of theoretical material has attempted to define the nature of the human self and the essence of human being as a mind/body entity with the capacity to think and act in relation to itself and others and to the influential circumstances in which it finds itself. This study argues that the primacy of the free market effectively makes us all subject to the over-determining forces of trade and institutional structure, which promote selfhood according to very specific competitive terms, thus compromising autonomy and any wish of the individual to choose alternative values. In addition, it proposes that subjectivity and agency are states of negotiation in which a rational thinking individual exists at a point of potential moral action. Individual identity is neither free floating and fragmented nor entirely unified and stable, neither wholly free nor wholly determined, neither all mind nor all body, neither an entire self-authority nor wholly in thrall to an external authority but situated at the point of convergence of all possible influence with a unique view that considers, reflects and implements action, in the light of previous experience and self-knowledge, a created and creating self, the self as an ethically acting individual.

Though such a view of identity might seem in line with the kind of postmodern, contingent identity-making such as that proposed by Ulrich Beck's 'reflexive individualization' (2001) in which one must be flexible and responsive to new possibilities for selfhood, it differs in three important regards. First is a belief that the cultural force of narrative and character indicates an essential role for continuity and coherence in the matter of purposive action. Second is an acknowledgment that some potential for agency exists regardless of the over-determining influence of a pervasive market discourse. Third is that mindful action is only possible by recognising a reflective space that can moderate reflexivity and make possible the placing of present action in the context of both the past and future on which successfully developing narrative and character depends. Pure reflexivity can lead to a loss of autonomy and meaning (and their associated mental health problems). By contrast, an agent using self-distancing as a means to objectify, scrutinise, consider and evaluate the self and the consequential impact of her or his proposed actions on the self and others, who brings into play patience, intelligence and negotiation before acting, retains autonomy and creates meaning through purposeful action regardless of unpredictable circumstances and unquantifiable social and cultural influence.

Self-distancing and reflection are absolutely necessary for plotting a self-development trajectory (whether that be through character, achievement, acquisition or however anyone personally defines 'development'). If control over one's circumstances is beyond possibility, we each still imagine (and are repeatedly led to believe in a liberal democracy) that we have control over our own selves: who we are or who we want to be. So when the scales tip too strongly in favour of institutional determination, the promise is shown to be false and hope is dashed. The recognition of story, agency and mindfulness means that individuals are responsible for deciding the direction of their own development, and in their aggregate, where society is heading.

The Promised Land?

Questions concerning the well-being of society have been prompted by the widespread disappointment that affluence has not delivered the promised rewards. The Western worker has been led to believe freedom is achievable through affluence, and that affluence attainable through work signifies virtue and worthiness. The Protestant ethic taught that self-reliance, hard work and becoming rich *are* being good, are proof of God's benevolence and one's assured place in heaven. In fact, where the satisfactions of work come predominantly as material rewards, there seems no need to wait for the afterlife – heaven can be achieved on earth. Products provide the transformation once the preserve of the religious. Eternal life, or at least youth, is promised with the latest rejuvenating cream or at the touch of a surgeon's knife, but while the forever-young cheat death, creeping atheism, agnosticism and materialism remove the anchor by which earthly actions take value, meaning and purpose.

In a secular market economy and consumerist culture where income equals buying power, purchased objects indicating personal taste, status and excellence come to symbolise the self; in short, the owner's literal worth has metaphorical value. You *are* how you spend. However, identity signified by the affordable 'signs of status, fashion or marks of individual eccentricity' is a 'sham individualism' that disguises conformity to market pressure (Harvey, 1990: 26, quoting Georg Simmel).[1] In reality, the satisfactions of goods are ephemeral and function not to end desire but to excite and extend it, not to enhance identity but to unsettle it. Capitalism and consumerism, for all the benefits they proclaim, tie the worker to an increasingly urgent and demanding cycle of salary-dependent buy-to-live and live-to-buy where keeping-up-to-the-minute is essential but changing fashion (driven by ever-faster rates of turnover) outruns anyone's ability to fund renewal at the required rate. The need for money is so pressing that the question of reaching to fulfil one's higher non-material needs is a moot one in the case of most individuals. One works and spends to achieve a higher standard of living and then must maintain that standard and increase it to remain happy (Layard, 2005: 41–53).[2] The virtuous circle of capitalism becomes the vicious circle of human entrapment that leaves a hollow in the individual who is always chasing the next retail fix or new business or personal relationship (now that these also are treated as commodities to be traded in when novelty and excitement wear thin) to placate unease, satisfy desire or indicate worth.[3] This perpetual feeling of lack, together with the loss of meaning and purpose and the absence of stability and autonomy, translates into rising occurrences of mental illness whose statistics testify that increasing numbers are finding no enduring sense of well-being despite increasing affluence, particularly where the work fuelling that affluence is itself unfulfilling.

The liberal idea of autonomy proceeded from a class not wholly defined by economic necessity, so when its members feel identity rests partly in one's buying-power, which is linked to earnings potential, which in turn relies on keeping a job in the unstable, fluid circumstances of new capitalism, the financial pressures and the contingency of selfhood are felt very strongly. It is then that the contradictions and political shortcomings are exposed of a system that promises independence and fulfilment through work and affluence, but instead delivers control, stress and dissatisfaction. For the middle class in particular, whose professional status is a key marker of identity, an economic system based on increasing consumption adds further pressure by subsequently valuing quantity of output above the quality required to maintain the occupational standards they have come to see as characteristic of their selves. This market determination of identity may leave individuals unwilling to take responsibility for and espouse the characteristic values of actions they are required to take in the labour context. The result is dissonance – a psychic tension resulting from the attempt to hold together opposing ideas/values that demands resolution – or a feeling of disempowerment.

In the effort to escape such determination, several factors predispose the members of the professional middle class to particular, rather than collective, acts of resistance in the effort to express a distinctive alternative identity through lifestyles involving different kinds of labour – especially the practice of writing which captures the coming-into-being (or rediscovery) of the more autonomous self. These factors include a class identity, once resting on educational, cultural and financial distinction, now weakened by encroachment into their ranks by those from other classes; an attack on their professional skills by the move away from specialism; the predisposition of public sector professionals to be more radicalised than those in the private sector; their consequent, more regular involvement in new social movements; and, uncannily, their apparent affinity with an old persistent category of farmers and artisans (to whom horticulture, cookery and writing might appeal). So when the demand to develop in a particular way to achieve success in the modern workplace threatens their characteristic autonomy, the urge to realign their actions to a personal code of ethics becomes strong, while the prospect of positive action restores a sense of efficacy to those no longer able to claim pre-eminence as a right merely by accident of being born into a privileged class.

The novel and 'I'

Ian McEwan's novel *Saturday* (2005) is a mainstream creative text that includes a reflection of contemporary cultural issues concerning the experience of the professional at work. Like other novels and biographies it provides an example of another's life against which we may measure our own. Through the perspective of the main protagonist, Henry Perowne, we are made aware of story as the means by which we understand ourselves and our world. However, all narrative is comprised of the arrangement of common elements in variation, with the created story being affected also by acts of imagination and interpretation, so that even when we believe we are dealing only with facts, we are dealing with fiction also. The alteration in what Henry first believes when he sees the burning plane and what he believes subsequently when the third person/party view is brought into play specifically alerts us to the role that this (mis)interpretation plays in determining and displaying any apparent truth. The intertwining of fact and fiction in the novel makes it clear that though story is a cognitive instrument, it is a fallible one even when used by living persons in real life. Nevertheless story is indispensable to self-telling, and according to Atkins (2004), this method of constructing ourselves in and through language using narrative is a psychologically comfortable, even necessary, way of coordinating our identity through time. Though Henry claims to the contrary, it is evident that he maintains his coherent selfhood by using the processes of a creative imagination to author, interpret and edit the material from which his self-story is made. The ubiquity of these processes is why narratologists and authors believe we cannot live without story. In fact:

> If selves and identities are constituted in discourse, they are necessarily constructed in stories. Through storytelling, narrators can produce 'edited' descriptions and evaluations of themselves and others, making identity aspects more salient at certain points in the story than others.
> (Benwell and Stokoe, 2006, quoting Georgakopoulou, 2002)

McEwan draws attention to the authorial role by having the intimate narrative of Henry's consciousness told by a third person, making the reader aware that there are apparent truths about our own stories that are deduced from another's hermeneutic perspective of which we may be unaware.

In Henry's case he is cognisant of a creeping unease affecting his daily life that is something to do with a lack of freedom, which he recognises his son Theo demonstrates in musical performance. He is less aware that the emotional sensibility possessed by his daughter, Daisy, needs developing in him in order for him to see that, in addition to the unrest caused by 9/11, and the fearfulness brought on by Baxter's attack on his person, the professional life through which he achieves status important to his identity is also under threat. The demand to deal with the mounting paperwork and emails of an IT-led audit culture creates a performative contradiction, as the value system of Henry-surgeon is misaligned with the actions he is required to take as Henry-administrator. Principally, this work-related contradiction is affecting his ability to narrate coherently and the long, relentless days of overstretch are tiring Henry bodily and mentally; through this we understand the mysterious connection between the physiological and the psychological that interests Henry and McEwan.

However, there are occasions on which Henry achieves an almost ecstatic alignment of self and other, subject and object. This is when he is thoroughly absorbed in other-directed action that also serves his self-interest. The instances described are when he is operating in theatre, using the skills he is proud of to good effect, and when he is cooking a meal as an act of giving to his family. These moments give us a glimpse into the release from pressure that occurs when values and action align (while highlighting the existential difficulties that result when they do not) and an indication of the circumstances under which work can truly be said to contribute to well-being. The presentation of work-related stress in a mainstream novel prompts two additional observations: first, and worryingly, its appearance indicates that work stress is now formally and culturally embedded; second, to some extent, this normalises the adverse conditions making it less likely, despite how widespread they are, that resistance will arise as it has done to express the macro-political concerns of the nation.

Alternative labour

In the latter part of this argument, the employment-generated contribution to ill-health at the turn of the twenty-first century is examined in the context of coincidental and rapidly growing interest in particular manual creative activities such as horticulture and cookery, and in biography and autobiography. By analysing various forms of literature, the attempt has been made to understand how other types of labour counter the experiential difficulties caused by modern work conditions. The findings suggest that the negative subjectivity of new-economy work is redressed through an alternative discourse based on a narrative means of speaking coherence and self-definition, and a story with which the agent is 'actively' willing to identify. In fact, the investigation of the dialectic of stress and recovery is made more compelling from a literary angle by the fact that autobiographical writing plays a key role in the representation of a return to well-being, particularly as the psychological effects of identity disruption can be reversed by an act of intelligible narration. In this way the rising interest in creative pursuits is not merely accidental. For the middle class, it seems to owe something to the powerful cultural precedent, linking writing to character development, which is found in the coincidental rise of individualism and the novel which, in the particular early example of Defoe's *Robinson Crusoe*, is tied also to production.

It is evident that where work no longer satisfies, and affluence is found to be hollow, and religion is in retreat, a void is left in which we cast around for meaningful and enduring values and role models to provide valid examples of how to live the good life. It is clear also that the market is willing to serve the unsatisfied desires of the ungodly by attempting to provide heaven on earth in whatever way the public has indicated their need might be met. The huge uptake of allotment horticulture and equally steep rise in vegetable seed sales together with a proliferation of programmes and books on cookery over the last twenty years is testament to an interest in activities, based on alternative activities and the identities they support, that are able to satisfy where formal employment does not.[4] While modern, mobile life disrupts the times we connect with our nearest and dearest at mealtimes or at other moments, the cookery writers' uptake of a redundant religious lexicon indicates that a secular communion has now taken the place of a once-sacred ritual[5] and that the production and preparation of food are a means of political assertion. There is ample evidence in lifestyle biographies organised around 'slow' activities that their appeal is through values that are difficult, if not impossible, to espouse in the fast, flexible and responsive conditions that characterise modern life. These accounts not only evidence the restorative possibilities of the alternative lifestyle, they also recover a vocabulary that has been devalued and marginalised and which is evidently now being used to restore personal control over narrating the self as a means of challenging a persuasive, market-supporting, hegemonic discourse.

Importantly, the writers of the travel autobiographies examined in this study are not looking for a life with plenty of money, ease and leisure. It is how they occupy themselves that is critical to their sense of self, because it is through the circumstances of their employment that their dissatisfaction and identity difficulties initially arise. When mortality makes clear each person's time is finite, and fewer and fewer believe an afterlife will be recompense for earthly ordeal, how one chooses to use one's time becomes all the more important. If fulfilment comes from producing work that speaks of care and quality, in circumstances admitting that today is connected to yesterday and tomorrow, then the accounts produced as 'escape' texts are the attempt to articulate those needs and a selfhood seeking a remedy for the powerlessness, fear, instability and ephemerality experienced in the chaotic conditions of flexible employment whose corporate messaging makes unsustainable demands for quantity and speed to service efficiency and profit.

Into the future

It is concerning, therefore, that downsizing government departments will intensify the market imperative and severance programmes will be aimed at so-called poor performers while those remaining employed will get bigger jobs. The idea (though never specifically admitted) is occupational Darwinism along the lines of the business survivor manuals' dictum – shape up or ship out. The neoliberal cry that competition will drive up standards begs the question, 'Whose standards?' or 'What standards?' There are few nurses and doctors in a repeatedly reshaped NHS that will find the professional standards of which they are proud (and which they would like to practise fully) being protected by such competition where calls for efficiency are being met. 'More for less' are the regularly spoken watchwords where spending cuts are to be implemented, but if this is to push the public sector further toward the ultra-lean flexible organisation, then the quality of the services provided for the vulnerable will be compromised further and the detrimental psychological impact on public servants (indeed is the word 'servant' now of any relevance?) will be heightened both by the onslaught to their service identities and the financial instabilities of contract employment. Indeed, 'even more for even less' is the mantra now chanted in government bodies without anyone having the slightest idea of how to judge when the limit has been reached and the individual is at (or past) breaking point. The question of what mechanisms are in place to ensure limits are not breached is met with skilful evasion.

There *are* inefficiencies that need improving and there *are* employees whose daily commitment to work needs to be better. That is the case in any system. Today, inefficiency happens when twenty people read the same email but only one needs to know and act; duplication of effort occurs when three managers attend separately to a problem because there is no clear hierarchy of responsibility and they are not talking to each other even when sitting at adjacent desks; overspending occurs when untrained and inexperienced people procure specialist services without a full understanding of what constitutes good or poor value for money, and are kept in post because it keeps the administration bill down as the cost is deferred to the project side of the business; poor management flourishes when older, knowledgeable staff who would be intelligent buyers are 'let go' to keep salary costs low, when one competent decision by that professional would recover their salary in a single transaction. Where staff commitment is concerned, senior managers seem perplexed that overburdened staff in chaotic organisations who are unable to use their expertise to full and good effect do not seem fully engaged at work. Is it so surprising professionals are unfulfilled in such circumstances, or that parents juggling their full-time employment and curtailed social lives with a long commute, punishing hours and responsibilities to their children lose concentration at work, or that sickness absence is increasing despite the draconian measures being taken by some companies to turn this quickly into a disciplinary matter?

In an economic upturn, when there are more jobs than employees, organisations benefit from having each worker covering a little more than a full-time post thus achieving the Holy Grail of lean efficiency, regardless of the impact on workers. In a downturn, when posts are removed rather than filled, the overstretch effect is intensified by the belief that there is a *surplus* of staff (when in many cases there is already a *deficit* and an overload of work). In either circumstance employees shoulder the burden and management care for welfare does not appear to match the corporate rhetoric. In this ever-intensifying demand for cost-cutting, management anxiety is palpable and is being translated into bullying, harassment and disciplinary action dressed up as firm management and validated by the standards of tough private sector CEOs. Those about to be put out of work will suffer low self-esteem, which makes their re-entry into the job market more difficult. Those freely choosing exit as a positive way forward may fare better psychologically if they can survive financially. Those remaining employed can expect their working conditions to become harsher and their capacity for reflection and mindful decision-making to be further diminished and yet, they will be expected to be accountable for the outcome of even forcibly ill-considered action.

If we continue towards fast flexibility, we need to consider where responsiveness is leading us, not only in work, but in our private lives also. The 'can do' attitude, valued in the workplace as a means of approaching the tough business problem (and perhaps so prized because it is getting harder to find) is a characteristic developed through persistence acquired in earlier problem-solving situations when (hopefully) one was tested to reasonable limits, guided and supported by those with the requisite knowledge and experience to handle challenge and difficult emotions. However, in flexible circumstances, structural dissolution and staff mobility remove the stable connections on which collaboration and cooperation depend. The creativity needed for new ideas and true entrepreneurship cannot gestate and surface until some quiet stillness and space is injected into the system and yet, ironically, such creativity is constantly called for.

In a competitive system that generates circumstances of overstretch and speed and urges us to 'move on' too quickly from failure, there is little opportunity to learn anything much, particularly how to handle the real disappointment one feels when losing after long preparation for a particular outcome. In the workplace, to beat off the competition and 'go in for the kill', to close a deal at the unconcerned expense of some other loser – in short, to be more ruthless – may win the immediate prize but, while these attitudes are pursued to raise (unspecified) standards, some thought must be given to the costs and implications for society at large and just how much else is lost in the process. Put simply, the values supporting profit do little to profit the person. Quick thinking, flexibility, mobility and responsiveness can mean bad decisions, weakness, rootlessness and disconnection. Certainly, it seems both hopeless and delusional to wish to devolve responsibility for some public services to communities increasingly comprised of individuals who, exhausted by work and short of time, are more self- than other-serving, whose acculturation to the profit motive makes volunteering less likely, and whose seduction by the market into an ever-growing pursuit of competitive 'having' makes 'giving' seem weak and self-defeating.

Proper concern for our future must demonstrate that our society, including the workplace, values personal qualities other than competition and winning. The diligence, patience, continuous assessment and evaluation needed to overcome frustration when facing a problem marks the kind of steady persistence and judgement required to create something of good quality *and* a good self. Spending the majority of our time in a work environment where the skills required for improving quality are not used or valued will mean we lose them or, for the young, never develop them. Neglecting the principles on which the self-improvement of character depends (or being careless about their disappearance) means abrogating responsibility not only for our own particular self-development but in turn for the developmental direction of our society that relies on the aggregate of all acts of personal growth or failure.

The shorter-term effects of failing to help human characters handle frustration, anger, boredom, envy, jealousy, impatience, betrayal, etc. can be readily seen on our streets. The breakdown of relationships, whether demonstrated by an increasingly unhappy workforce, in antisocial behaviour or in a growing failure to sustain family life, is a manifest result of the inability to manage the emotions generated by challenging life events except by seeking sensation, emulating scenes from TV soaps, taking instant gratification through violence and hooliganism, or avoidance of such challenging feelings through escape in the form of drink or drugs and often both. Turning an individual's energies away from destruction (increasingly self-destruction) and towards constructive creativity means recognising when escape is being sought to assert agency, prevent further self-harm and find the space and time for the psychological recovery necessary for good decision-making.

The slower and more mindful, more grounded life, centred on the values required for mastery of a practical skill, can aid the development of the personal qualities needed to cope with the more difficult parts of life, transferable qualities (to steal a business phrase) that can aid self-mastery and develop the attitudes and behaviours of a strong personal character that is self-responsible and other-regarding, one able to cope with the pitfalls, not just the pleasures, of life. Those about to lose their jobs will need such strength; those carrying on in ultra-lean organisations will need it more. Ultimately, *successful* life – intimate, business and social – is about managing relationships and building trust, and that requires time. No good society – 'Big' or otherwise – can flourish without this foundation. The flexibility, mobility and responsiveness of late-capitalist work makes acquiring the skills for relating – at home or at work – all the more necessary and the likelihood of learning or demonstrating them as rare as a bonus-refusing banker.

The different investment required for encouraging the qualities and skills described above brings valuable returns, though it may not be possible to put a figure in any balance sheet for it, or indeed for the similarly unquantifiable longer-term learning, experience and knowledge embodied in professionals which is every bit as valuable (and perhaps more so) as the knowledge of how to increase profit by speeding production and cutting staff. In fact, business is self-sabotaging by failing to allow professionals to apply that knowledge fully in practice or to spend their time according to their own judgement and the result will be to our own social cost both morally and economically. When a doctor stays for an uncompetitive few minutes at a patient's bedside or a teacher devotes a non-profit-making half hour to a struggling but willing student, it is in these moments of compassionate judgement that the best of our humanity is demonstrated. The *truly* nurturing workplace would see value in that and would ensure that the senior people earn their high salaries by making the *really tough* decisions on priorities to ensure fewer things are done, but are done to a satisfying standard, rather than demanding a whole raft of tasks be completed, in one way or another, to enable the issuing of a press release or a paragraph in an annual report claiming more has been accomplished. Where ethical identity is reflected through action and speech, those wishing to account for their time by telling a life story through labour, in which they feel truly empowered and have achieved progressively increasing *quality* of production and a developing self, will find the language of current business, which typifies our market age, neither useful nor humane nor heroic.

Notes

1 The contemporary situation differs in one key respect from what Veblen describes in *The Theory of Leisure* (Chapter 4). Veblen's conspicuous consumption signified distinction based on an underlying leisure and wealth; its contemporary equivalent is baseless, speaking only the homogenisation and debt that results from widespread market advertising.
2 Layard explains how happiness through affluence is achieved only by a higher relative income than one's peers. Such 'social comparison propels towards ever-greater acquisition'.
3 I do not suggest all personal relationships should endure whatever the circumstances.
4 In the US, some suppliers reported up to 80% growth of vegetable seed sales in 2009 (www.mnn.com/your-home/organic-farming-gardening/blogs/vegetable-seed-sales-soar) while one UK supplier of vegetable seeds reported a sales growth of 60% in 2008. Of the many reasons given for the shift to vegetable growing, many are to do with political and environmental concerns about how food is produced today by those choosing to act against the hegemony, but one allotment holder definitively states that horticulture is 'the best way to relax, the nearest thing to personal and political freedom' (www.guardian.co.uk/lifeandstyle/2008/apr/22/foodanddrink.food). Similarly, sales of cookery books peaked in the late 1990s and, though the total value of the market fell between 2000 and 2002, nine of the top 100 best selling titles recorded between 1998 and 2010 were cookery titles (www.guardian.co.uk/news/datablog/2011/jan/01/top-100-books-of-all-time#data).
5 An Amazon search for 'cookery bible' (autumn 2011) found 396 titles.

Appendix 1

Defra Departmental Report covers

1   Departmental Report cover 2002

Appendix 1 217

2 Departmental Report cover 2003

3 Departmental Report cover 2004

Appendix 2
Table showing the positive and negative meanings of descriptors commonly associated with 'fast' and 'slow' conditions

The words in bold (columns 2 and 5) show descriptors of the 'fast' and 'slow' conditions respectively. Either side of these columns, the positive and negative associations of those descriptors are listed. From this it can be seen that the judgement of potential migrants, those dissatisfied with the work and social conditions, would rest on seeing that the negatives of their 'fast' experience could be traded for the positives of the 'slow' existence (columns 3 and 4). Conversely, it is possible also that those content in 'fast' conditions would focus on the positive meanings of each new economy descriptor and consider these preferable to the negatives that can be associated with an alternative slower life (columns 1 and 6).

Appendix 2

New economy characteristics		Remedial characteristics	
Positive associations	Negative associations	Positive associations	Negative associations
accelerated	fast	manic	paced, still	slow	emmui
variable/buoyant	free floating	unregulated	regulated	time-rooted	entrenched
instant	immediate	easy	invested/valuable	deferred	postponed
agile	mobile	rootless	rooted	grounded	static
unrestricted	global	dissipated	distilled	local	restricted
eclectic	fragmented	incoherent	coherent	wholeness	totalising
bite-sized	episodic/discontinuous	no narrative line	narrative line	diachronic/continuous	predictable
ever-fresh	disposable	throwaway	endurable	reusable	tired
intelligence	information	data	learning	knowledge	reiterative
responsive	flexible	malleable	firm	stable	rigid/unbending
exciting	new	unknown	known	old	dull
avant-garde/forward	cutting-edge	untried	reliable	traditional	backward
open to possibility	pointless	lacking meaning	meaningful	purposeful	decided
efficient	automatic	mindless	mindful	considered	pedestrian/ponderous
lightweight	superficial	presentation/facade	substantial	deep	buried
excellence	competitive	dog-eat-dog	cooperative	collaborative	collusive
managed	inorganic	disconnected	natural	organic	uncontrolled
unbound	ahistorical	dislocated	located	traditional	bound
opportunistic	chaotic	disorientated	structured	ordered	imprisoned
independent	individual	aloof, isolated	connected	collective	dependent/herded

Bibliography

Abbott, H Porter. 2002. *The Cambridge Introduction to Narrative* (Cambridge: Cambridge University Press).
Abrams, M H. 1971. *The Mirror and the Lamp: Romantic Theory and the Critical Tradition* (London: Oxford University Press).
Adorno, Theodor W. 2006. *The Culture Industry*, Ed. J M Bernstein (London: Routledge).
Allen, Rachel. 2007. *Food for Living* (London: Collins).
Alvesson, Mats and Hugh Willmott. 2002. 'Identity Regulation as Organizational Control: Producing the Appropriate Individual' in *Journal of Management Studies* 39:5, 619–644.
Amernic, Joel and Russell Craig. 2006. *CEO-Speak: The Language of Corporate Leadership* (McGill Queen's University Press: Montreal & Kingston, London, Ithaca).
Atkins, Kim. 2004. 'Narrative Identity, Practical Identity and Ethical Subjectivity' in *Continental Philosophy Review* 37, 341–366.
Attwood, Feona. 2005. 'Inside Out: Men on the Home Front' in *Journal of Consumer Culture* 5, 87–107.
Bailey, Roy. 1995. *How to Empower People at Work: A Guide to Becoming a Green-fingered Manager* (Didcot, Oxon: Management Books).
Bakan, Joel. 2004. *The Corporation: The Pathological Pursuit of Profit and Power* (London: Constable).
Bal, M. 1997. *Narratology – Introduction to the Theory of Narrative*, second edition (Toronto, Buffalo, London: University of Toronto Press).
Barker, Francis. 1984. *The Tremulous Private Body: Essays on Subjection* (London; New York: Methuen).
Bauman, Zygmunt. 2000. *Liquid Modernity* (Cambridge: Polity).
——. 2001. *The Individualized Society* (Cambridge: Polity).

Beck, Ulrich. 2000. *The Brave New World of Work* (Frankfurt/New York: Polity Press).
Beck, Ulrich and Elisabeth Beck-Gernsheim. 2001. *Individualization: Institutionalized Individualism and its Social and Political Consequences* (London: Thousand Oaks, New Delhi).
Beck, Ulrich, Wolfgang Bonss and Christoph Lau. 2003. 'The Theory of Reflexive Modernization: Problematic, Hypotheses and Research Programme' in *Theory Culture Society* 20: 1, 1–33.
Bell, Daniel. 1973. *The Coming of Post-Industrial Society: A Venture in Social Forecasting* (USA: Harper Collins).
Benwell, Bethan and Elizabeth Stokoe. 2006. *Discourse and Identity* (Edinburgh: Edinburgh University Press).
Berger, Arthur Asa. 1997. *Narratives in Popular Culture, Media and Everyday Life* (Thousand Oaks, London, New Delhi: Sage).
Blanchard, Kenneth and Robert Lorber. 1994. *Putting the One Minute Manager to Work* (London: HarperCollins).
Blanchard, Kenneth, Patricia Zigarmi and Drea Zigarmi. 1994. *Leadership and the One Minute Manager* (London: Harper Collins).
de Blasi, Marlena. 2005. *A Thousand Days in Tuscany* (London: Virago (Workman)).
Bliss, Edwin C. 1993. *Getting Things Done* (London: Warner Books).
Boje, David M. 2001. 'Corporate Writing in the Web of Postmodern Culture and Postindustrial Capitalism' in *Management Communication Quarterly*, 14:3, 507–516.
Boje, David M, Cliff Oswick, Jeffrey D Ford. 2004. 'Language and Organisation: The Doing of Discourse' in *Academy of Management Review*, 29:4, 571–577.
Braverman, Harry. 1998. *Labor and Monopoly Capital: The Degradation of Work in the Twentieth Century* (New York: Monthly Review Press).
Breakspear, Christie and Clive Hamilton. 2004. *Getting a Life: Understanding the downshifting phenomenon in Australia*, Discussion Paper No.62 (Canberra: The Australia Institute).
Bourdieu, P. 1984. *Distinction: A Social Critique of the Judgement of Taste*. London, Routledge.
Bunting, Madeleine. 2005. *Willing Slaves: How the Overwork Culture is Ruining Our Lives* (London: Harper Perennial).
Burchell, Brendan, *et al.* 2001. *Job Insecurity and Work Intensification* (London: Routledge).
Burkitt, Ian. 2004. 'The Time and Space of Everyday Life' in *Cultural Studies*, 18:2, 211–227.
Burnett, John. 1984. *Destiny Obscure* (Middlesex, New York: Penguin).
———. 1997. *Useful Toil* (Middlesex, New York: Penguin).

Burns, David D. 1990. *The Feeling Good Handbook* (New York: Penguin).
Butler, Judith. 1997. *The Psychic Life of Power: Theories in Subjection* (Stanford, California: Stanford University Press).
Carlone, David. 2001. 'Enablement, Constraint and the 7 Habits of Highly Effective People' in *Management Communication Quarterly*, 14:3, 491–497.
Chandola, Tarani (2010) *Stress at Work* (London: British Academy).
Chatto, James. 2005. *The Greek for Love: Life, Love and Loss in Corfu* (London: John Murray).
Childs, Peter (ed.). 2006. *The Fiction of Ian McEwan* (Basingstoke: Palgrave MacMillan).
Clarke, John *et al*. 2007. *Creating Citizen Consumers: Changing Publics and Changing Public Services* (London, Sage).
Collinson, Charlene and Alexander MacKenzie. 1999. 'The Power of Story in Organisations' in *The Journal of Workplace Learning* 11:1, 3–40.
Collinson, David. L. 2003. 'Identities and Insecurities: Selves at Work' in *Organization* 10:3, 527–547.
Czarniawska, Barbara. 1997. *Narrating the Organisation: Dramas of Institutional Identity* (Chicago: University of Chicago Press).
Deane, Alexander. 2005. *The Great Abdication: Why Britain's Decline is the Fault of the Middle Class* (Charlotttesville, USA, Exeter UK: Imprint-Academic).
De Cock, C. and C. Land. 2006. 'Organization/Literature: Exploring the Seam' in *Organization Studies*, 27:4, 517–535.
Department for Environment, Food and Rural Affairs, 2002. *Departmental Report* http://webarchive.nationalarchives.gov.uk/20031220221853/ http://www.defra.gov.uk/corporate/deprep/default.htm#2002 (accessed 08 November 2011).
——. 2003. *Departmental Report* http://webarchive.nationalarchives.gov.uk/20031220221853/http://www.defra.gov.uk/corporate/deprep/2003/deprep2003.pdf (accessed 08 November 2011).
——. 2004. *Departmental Report* http://webarchive.nationalarchives.gov.uk/20070101084356/http://www.defra.gov.uk/corporate/deprep/2004/2004report.pdf (accessed 08 November 2011).
——. 2005. *Departmental Report* http://webarchive.nationalarchives.gov.uk/20071204125941/http://www.defra.gov.uk/corporate/deprep/2005/2005report.pdf (accessed 08 November 2011).
——. 2006(a). *Departmental Report* http://webarchive.nationalarchives.gov.uk/20071204125941/http://www.defra.gov.uk/corporate/deprep/2006/2006deptreport.pdf (accessed 08 November 2011).
——. 2006(b). *My Priorities for Defra*, Open letter from Secretary of State, David Milliband to Prime Minister Tony Blair, 11 July, http://

webarchive.nationalarchives.gov.uk/20061209022624/http://www.defra.gov.uk/corporate/what-do-we-do/strategy-documents.htm (accessed 08 November 2011).

———. 2006(c). *Personal Minute to Secretary of State David Milliband from Prime Minster Tony Blair*, May, http://webarchive.nationalarchives.gov.uk/20061209022624/http://www.defra.gov.uk/corporate/what-do-we-do/strategy-documents.htm (accessed 08 November 2011).

———. Undated(a). *Delivering the Essentials of Life: Defra's Five Year Strategy* http://archive.defra.gov.uk/corporate/about/reports/documents/5year-strategy.pdf (accessed 08 November 2011).

———. Undated(b). *Working for the Essentials of Life* http://webarchive.nationalarchives.gov.uk/20050301192907/http://www.defra.gov.uk/corporate/prospectus/defrawork.pdf (accessed 08 November 2011).

———. 2003–2006. *Our Strategy: Defra Corporate Strategy* http://webarchive.nationalarchives.gov.uk/20071204125941/http://www.defra.gov.uk/corporate/strategy0306/defra_strategy.pdf (accessed 08 November 2011).

———. *Staff Handbook* (Defra intranet).

———. *Stress at Work: Policy and Guidance* (Defra intranet, accessed 3 March 2007).

———. 2007(a). *Renew Defra Programme Developments: A Vision for the Future of Defra*, Address to staff by Helen Ghosh, Permanent Secretary, 12 March.

———. 2007(b). *New Voluntary Early Retirement/Voluntary Early Severance Scheme Launched*, Address to staff by Helen Ghosh, Permanent Secretary, 27 July.

———. *Advisory Committee on Novel Foods and Processes* (ACNFP) Annual Report 1997, PB 3694, 1998, www.food.gov.uk/multimedia/pdfs/97annrep.pdf (accessed 18 Oct 2010).

———. *How Do We Work* http://webarchive.nationalarchives.gov.uk/20061209022624/ http://www.defra.gov.uk/corporate/how-do-we-work/index.htm [Accessed 29 Feb 2012].

Dodd, Philip, 1986. *Modern Selves: Essays on Modern British and American Autobiography* (London, Totowa N.J.: Frank Cass).

Dorling, Danny and Charles Patti. 2004. 'Commentary: Smile, Be Happy' in *Environment and Planning A* 36, 761–762).

Dorling, Danny and Neil Ward. 2003. 'Commentary: Social Science, Public Policy, and the Search for Happiness' Editorial, in *Environment and Planning A* 35(6), 954–957.

Dunbar, R.I.M. (2006). 'From Lucy to Language: The archaeology of the social brain' in *British Academy Review* 9: 13–18.

Eagleton, Terry. 1985. *Literary Theory: An Introduction* (Oxford: Basil Blackwell).

———. 1985. 'Capitalism, Modernism and Postmodernism' in *New Left Review*, I/152 (July–August).
Edwards, Paul. 2007. *Justice in the workplace: Why it is important and why a new public policy initiative is needed*, Provocation Series 2: 3 (London: The Work Foundation).
Edwards, Richard. 1979. *Contested Terrain: The Transformation of the Workplace in the Twentieth Century* (New York: Basic Books).
Ehrenreich, Barbara. 1983. *The Hearts of Men: American Dreams and the Flight From Commitment* (New York: London: Pluto).
———. 1989. *Fear of Falling: The Inner Life of the Middle Class* (New York: Pantheon Books).
———. 2008. *Going to Extremes, Notes from a Divided Nation* (London: Granta Publications).
Elgaard, Torben and Ann Westenholz, eds. 2004. *Identity in the Age of the New Economy* (Cheltenham, UK: Edward Elgar).
Eriksen, Thomas Hylland. 2001. *Tyranny of the Moment: Fast and Slow Time in the Information Age* (London: Pluto Press, 2001).
Fearnley-Whittingstall, Hugh. 2001. *The River Cottage Cookbook* (London, HarperCollins).
Ferris, Joshua. 2007. *Then We Came to the End* (London, New York: Penguin).
Foucault, Michel. 1979. *Discipline and Punish* (Harmondsworth: Penguin).
Frank, Thomas. 2000. *One Market Under God: Extreme Capitalism, Market Populism and the End of Economic Democracy* (New York, London: Doubleday).
Freud, Sigmund. 1987. *Art and Literature*, The Pelican Freud Library, Angela Richards and Albert Dickson (eds) (Middlesex: Penguin).
Friedman, Lawrence M. 1999. *The Horizontal Society* (New Haven: Yale University Press).
Gabriel, Yiannis. 2000. *Storytelling in Organisations: Facts, Fictions, and Fantasies* (Oxford, New York: Oxford University Press).
Gagnier, Regenia. 1991. *Subjectivities: A History of Self-Representation in Britain, 1832–1920* (Oxford: Oxford University Press).
du Gay, Paul. 2007. ' "Without Affection or Enthusiasm": problems of attachment and involvement in "responsive" public management' in Centre for Research on Socio-Cultural Change (CRESC) *Working Paper Series*, Working Paper No.33.
Goffman, Erving. 1986. *Frame Analysis: An Essay on the Organisation of Experience* (Boston, Mass, Northeastern University Press Edition).
———. 1990. *The Presentation of the Self in Everyday Life* (Harmondsworth, Middlesex: Penguin).

Griffin, Joe and Ivan Tyrell. 2006. *How to Lift Depression ...Fast* (Chalvington, E. Sussex: HG Publishing).

Gunn, Simon. 2005. 'Translating Bourdieu: Cultural Capital and the English Middle Class in Historical Perspective' in *The British Journal of Sociology*, 56:1, 49–64.

Hall, Donald E. 2004. *Subjectivity*, New Critical Idiom series (London, New York: Routledge).

Halperin, John, ed. 1974. *The Theory of the Novel: New Essays* (London, New York: Oxford University Press).

Hamilton, Clive. 2002. *Overconsumption in Australia: The rise of the middle-class battler*, Discussion Paper no. 49. Canberra: The Australia Institute.

——. 2003b. *Overconsumption in Britain: A culture of middle-class complaint?*, Discussion Paper no. 57. Canberra: The Australia Institute.

——. 2003c. *Downshifting in Britain: A sea-change in the pursuit of happiness*, Discussion Paper no. 58. Canberra: The Australia Institute.

——. 2004b. *Carpe Diem?: The deferred happiness syndrome*, Web Paper. Canberra: The Australia Institute.

—— and Christian Downie and Yi-Hua Lu. 2007. *The State of the Australian Middle Class*, Discussion Paper no. 98. Canberra: The Australia Institute.

—— and Christie Breakspear. 2004a. *Getting a Life: Understanding the Downshifting Phenomenon in Australia*, Discussion Paper no. 62. Canberra: The Australia Institute.

—— and Elizabeth Mail. 2003a. *Downshifting in Australia: A sea-change in the pursuit of happiness*, Discussion Paper no. 50. Canberra: The Australia Institute.

Harvey, David. 1990. *The Condition of Postmodernity: An Enquiry Into the Origins of Cultural Change* (Cambridge MA, Oxford UK: Blackwell).

——. 1990(b). 'Flexible Accumulation through Urbanization Reflections on "Post-Modernism" in the American City', *Perspecta*, 26, Theater, Theatricality, and Architecture, 251–272.

——. (For 2004 see Net and other references.)

Haslett, Moyra. 2000. *Marxist Literary and Cultural Theories*, Transitions series (London: Macmillan).

Herman, David, Manfred Jahn, Marie-Laure Ryan, eds. 2005. *Routledge Encyclopedia of Narrative Theory* (New York, Abingdon: Routledge).

Hochschild, Arlie Russell. 2001. *The Time Bind: When Work Becomes Home and Home Becomes Work* (New York: Henry Holt).

Hollows, Joanne. 2002. 'The Bachelor Dinner: Masculinity, Class and Cooking in Playboy, 1953–1961', in *Continuum: Journal of Media & Cultural Studies*, 16: 2, 143–155.

———. 2003. 'Feeling Like a Domestic Goddess: Postfeminism and Cooking' in *European Journal of Cultural Studies*, 6:2 (2003) 179–202.

Hulme, Peter, ed. 2002. *The Cambridge Companion to Travel Writing* (Cambridge: Cambridge University Press).

Humphreys, Michael and Andrew D. Brown. 2002. 'Narratives of Organizational Identity and Identification: A Case Study of Hegemony and Resistance' in *Organization Studies*, 23:3, 421–447.

Jackson, Bradley G. 2001. 'Art for Management's Sake' in *Management Communication Quarterly*, 14:3, 484–490.

Jameson, Fredric. 1984. 'Postmodernism, or The Cultural Logic of Late Capitalism' in *New Left Review*, I/146 (July–August), 53–92.

———. 2005 [1991]. *Postmodernism, or The Cultural Logic of Late Capitalism* (Durham: Duke University Press).

———. 1981 [2002]. *The Political Unconscious: Narrative as a Socially Symbolic Act* (London: Routledge).

Jones, Campbell. 2007. *Literature, Reading, Organization*, paper presented at 'The Novel and Organization' conference, 10–12 May, Department of Accounting, Finance and Management, University of Essex.

Joyce, Patrick, ed. 1995. *Class*, Oxford Readers Series (Oxford, New York: Oxford University Press).

Kerr, Peter. 2000. *Snowball Oranges: One Mallorcan Winter* (Chichester, W. Sussex: Summersdale).

Kidd, Alan and David Nicholls, eds. 1998. *The Making of the British Middle Class? Studies of regional and cultural diversity since the eighteenth century* (Stroud: Sutton).

King, Roger and Neill Nugent. 1979. *Respectable Rebels: Middle Class Campaigns in Britain in the 1970s* (New York: Holmes and Meier).

Kranzberg, Melvin and Joseph Gies. 1979. *By The Sweat Of Thy Brow* (New York: G.P. Putnam and Sons).

Kuhn, Annette. 1995. *Family Secrets: Acts of Memory and Imagination* (London, New York: Verso).

Lakoff, George and Mark Johnson. 1999. *Philosophy in the Flesh* (New York: Perseus Books).

Land, Christopher. 2005. 'Apomorphine Silence: Cutting-up Burroughs' Theory of Language and Control' in *Ephemera*, 5:3, 450–471.

Lane, Robert E. 2000. *The Loss of Happiness in Market Democracies* (New Haven and London: Yale University Press).

Lawson, Nigella. 2000. *How To Be A Domestic Goddess: Baking and the Art of Comfort Cooking* (London: Chatto & Windus).

———. 2001. *Nigella Bites* (London: Chatto & Windus).

———. 2004. *Feast: Food that Celebrates Life* (London: Chatto & Windus).

———. 2007. *Nigella Express: Good Food Fast* (London: Chatto & Windus).

——. 2010. *Nigella Kitchen* BBC2 TV series.
——. 2010(b). *Nigella Kitchen: Recipes from the Heart of the Home* (London: Chatto & Windus).
Layard, Richard. 2005. *Happiness: Lessons from A New Science* (New York, London: Penguin).
Leccardi, Carmen. 2005. 'Facing uncertainty: Temporality and biographies in the new century' in *Young*, 13, 123–146.
Legge, Karen. 2005. *Human Resource Management: Rhetorics and Realities* (Basingstoke: Palgrave MacMillan).
Leppard, Dan, 2004. *The Handmade Loaf* (London: Mitchell Beazley).
Lewis, Tania. 2006. 'DIY selves?: Reflexivity and habitus in young people's use of the internet for health information' in *European Journal of Cultural Studies*, 9, 461–479.
Lodge, David. 1995. *Therapy* (London: Martin, Secker, Warburg).
Lyotard, Jean-François. 2001. 'Answering the Question: What is Postmodernism?' in *The Postmodern Condition: A Report on Knowledge*, trans. by Régis Durand (Manchester: Manchester University Press).
Margerison, Charles J. 1991. *Making Management Development Work: Achieving Success in the Nineties* (London: McGraw-Hill).
Mayle, Peter. 2000. *A Year in Provence* (London: Penguin).
McEwan, Ian. 2005. *Saturday* (London: Jonathan Cape) (hardback).
——. 2006. *Saturday* (London, Vintage) (paperback).
——. 2005. 'In Conversation with Melvyn Bragg', *South Bank Show*, ITV 20 February.
——. 2001. *Atonement* (London, Jonathan Cape).
McGonigal, Jane. 2011. *Reality is Broken: Why Games Make Us Better and How They Can Change the World* (London: Jonathan Cape).
Mercurio, Jed. 2004. *Bodies* (London: Vintage).
Miller, Nancy K. 2002. *But Enough About Me – Why We Read Other People's Lives* (New York: Columbia University Press).
Muir, Rick and Wetherell, Margaret. 2010. *Identity, Politics and Public Policy*, IPPR, April.
Mukherjee, Ankhi. 2001. 'Stammering to Story: Neurosis and Narration in Pat Barker's 'Regeneration'' in *Critique*, 43:1, 49–62.
Musson, Gill and Joanne Duberley. 2007. 'Change, Change or Be Exchanged: The Discourse of Participation and the Manufacture of Identity' in *Journal of Management Studies*, 44:1, 143–164.
Nace, Ted. 2003. *Gangs of America: The Rise of Corporate Power and the Disabling of Democracy* (San Franscisco: Berrett-Koehler Publishers Inc.).
Nussbaum, Felicity, A. 1989. *The Autobiographical Subject: Gender and Ideology in Eighteenth Century England* (Baltimore: Johns Hopkins University Press).

O'Neill, Onora, 2002. *A Question of Trust*, the Reith Lectures 2002 (Cambridge: Cambridge University Press). www.bbc.co.uk/radio4/reith2002/lecture5.shtml (accessed 24 September 2006).

O'Neill, Patrick. 1994. *Fictions of Discourse: Reading Narrative Theory* (Toronto, Buffalo, London: University of Toronto Press).

Olins, Wolff. 1995. *The New Guide to Identity: How to Create and Sustain Change Through Managing Identity*, the Design Council (Aldershot, Hants: Gower).

Oliver, Jamie. 2007. *Jamie at Home: Cook Your Way to the Good Life* (London: Penguin).

Oswick, Cliff, Tom Kennoy. 1997. 'Managerial Discourses: Words Speak Louder Than Actions?' *Journal of Applied Management Studies*, 6:1 (June) 5–12.

Parkins, Wendy and Geoffrey Craig. 2006). *Slow Living* (Oxford UK, New York: Berg).

Peters, Tom. 1999. *The Brand You* (New York, London: Random House).

Porter-Abbott, H. 2002. 'Character and Self in Narrative' in *The Cambridge Introduction to Narrative* (Cambridge: Cambridge University Press).

Pritchett, Price. 1997. *The Employee Handbook of New Work Habits for a Radically Changing World: 13 Ground Rules for Job Success in the Information Age* (Tyne and Wear: Pritchett and Associates Inc.).

Pugh, Derek S. 1997. 'E. Mayo, Hawthorne and the Western Electric Company' in *Organization Theory: Selected Readings*, fourth edition (London: Penguin).

Reich, Robert B. 2002. *The Future of Success: Work and Life in the New Economy* (London: Vintage).

Rimmon-Kenan, Shlomith. 1993. *Narrative Fiction: Contemporary Poetics*, New Accents Series (London, New York: Routledge).

Robbins, Ruth, 2006. *Subjectivity*, Transitions Series (Basingstoke: Palgrave MacMillan).

Ross, Andrew. 2003. *No Collar: The Humane Workplace and its Hidden Costs* (New York: Basic Books).

Rowe, Dorothy. 1991. *Depression: The Way Out of Your Prison* (London and New York: Routledge).

Sanders, Michael. 2004. *From Here You Can't See Paris* (London, New York: Bantam).

Savage, Michael, James Barlow, Peter Dickens and Tony Fielding. 1992. *Property, Bureaucracy and Culture: Middle Class Formation in Contemporary Britain* (New York, London: Routledge).

Schoch, Richard. 2006. *The Secrets of Happiness: Three Thousand Years of Searching for the Good Life* (New York, London, Toronto, Sydney: Scribner).

Selden, Raman and Peter Widdowson. 1993. 'Marxist Theories' in *A Reader's Guide to Contemporary Literary Theory* (London: Harvester Wheatsheaf).

Sennett, Richard. 1998. *The Corrosion of Character* (New York: W.W. Norton & Co.).

——. 2006. *The Culture of the New Capitalism: The Personal Consequences of Work in the New Capitalism* (New Haven, London: Yale University Press).

——. 2008. *The Craftsman* (London, New York: Allen Lane).

Shelton, Robin. 2006. *Allotted Time: Twelve Months, Two Blokes, One Shed, No Idea* (London: Sidgwick & Jackson).

Slater, Nigel, 2005. *The Kitchen Diaries* (London: Fourth Estate).

Smith, Sidonie, c1993. *Subjectivity, Identity, and the Body: Women's Autobiographical Practices in the Twentieth Century* (Bloomington: Indiana University Press).

—— and Julia Watson, eds. 1998. *Women, Autobiography, Theory: A Reader* (Madison: University of Wisconsin Press).

—— and Julia Watson. 2001. *Reading Autobiography: A Guide for Interpreting Life Narratives* (Minneapolis: University of Minnesota Press).

Stein, Rick. 2002. *Food Heroes: Recipes Inspired by the Champions of Good Food* (London: BBC Books, BBC Worldwide).

Stewart, Chris. 1999. *Driving Over Lemons* (London: Sort Of Books).

Strawson, Galen. 2004. 'A Fallacy of Our Age: Not Every Life is a Narrative' in *Times Literary Supplement*, 15 October, 13–15.

Swift, Graham. 2004. *The Light of Day* (London, New York: Penguin).

Tennant, Emma. 2004. *Corfu Banquet* (Chichester: Summersdale).

Toynbee, Polly. 2008. *Unjust Rewards* (London: Granta Publications).

Walker, J. 1982. *British Economic and Social History 1700–1982*, fourth edition, rev. C.W. Munn (Plymouth: MacDonald and Evans).

Ward, Graham. 2003. *True Religion*, Blackwell Manifestos (Malden MA, Oxford: Blackwell).

Watson, Tony J, 1995. *Sociology, Work and Industry* (London: Routledge).

Watt, Ian. 1974. *The Rise of the Novel* (London: Chatto & Windus).

White, Nicholas. 2006. *A Brief History of Happiness* (Malden MA, Oxford, Victoria: Blackwell).

Williams, Raymond. 1977. 'Introduction', 'Determination', 'Hegemony' and 'Genre' in *Marxism and Literature* (Oxford, Oxford University Press).

——. 1985. *Culture and Society* (Middlesex: Penguin).

Willmott, H. 1997. 'Rethinking Management and Managerial Work: Capitalism, Control, and Subjectivity,' in *Human Relations*, 50:11 (1997) 1329–1359.

Wilson, David. 1991. 'The Death of Orality and the Rise of the Literate Subject' in *Subjectivity and Literature from the Romantics to the Present Day*, Philip Shaw and Peter Stockwell (eds) (London: Pinter).

Net and other references

Arendt, Hannah. 1967. *Labor, Work, Action: A Lecture*, The Hannah Arendt Papers at The Library of Congress, http://memory.loc.gov/cgi-bin/query/P?mharendt:4:./temp/~ammem_8WVu:: (accessed 14 March 2007). http://memory.loc.gov/cgi-bin/ampage?collId=mharendt&fileName=05/051810/051810page.db&recNum=0 (accessed 28 January 2010).

Blaug, Ricardo, Amy Kenyon and Rohit Lekhi. 2007. *Stress at Work*, The Work Foundation (London, The Work Foundation), www.theworkfoundation.com/assets/docs/publications/69_stress_at_work.pdf (accessed 27 November 2008).

Brookes, Martin. 2004. *Watching Alone: Social Capital and Public Service Broadcasting*, www.theworkfoundation.com/Reports/148/Watching-alone-Social-capital-and-public-service-broadcasting (accessed 5 March 2012).

Burchell, Brendan, Collette Fagan, Catherine O'Brien, Mark Smith. 2007. *Working Conditions in the European Union: The Gender Perspective*, www.eurofound.europa.eu/publications/byauthor/list_author180.htm (accessed 2 June 2008).

Chartered Institute of Personnel and Development, *Personnel Management: A Short History*, www.cipd.co.uk/subjects/hrpract/hrtrends/pmhist.htm (accessed 15 May 2007).

——. 2010. 'Rise in job satisfaction against backdrop of government spending cuts suggests 'fixed grin' has returned to workplace, particularly in public sector', www.cipd.co.uk/pressoffice/_articles/Employeeoutlook 291110.htm (accessed 8 December 2010).

——. 2011. Absence Management Survey, www.cipd.co.uk/research/ _absence-management/?wa_src=email&wa_pub=cipd&wa_crt= 121011_na_textlink_editorial.link1&wa_cmp=cipdupdate (accessed 19 October 2011).

——. 2011. Employee Outlook: Autumn 2011, www.cipd.co.uk/hr-resources/ survey-reports/employee-outlook-autumn-2011.aspx?wa_src=email &wa_pub=cipd&wa_crt=261011_na_textlink_editorial.link2&wa_cm p=cipdupdate (accessed 26 October 2011).

Cowling, Marc. 2005. *Still At Work? An Empirical Test of Competing Theories of the Long Hours Culture*, http://theworkfoundation.com/

assets/docs/publications/51_Still%20At%20Work.pdf The Work Foundation, March (accessed 2 March 2008).

Cummings, Dolan. Undated. *The Trouble With Being Human These Days*, Overview of Zygmunt Bauman's 'Identity', www.culturewars.org.uk/2004-02/identity.htm (accessed 23 November 2007).

Demographics classifications, www.businessballs.com/demographicsclassifications.htm (accessed 20 December 2007).

Diaz-Serrano, Luis and Jose A. Cabral Vieira. 2005. 'Low Pay, Higher Pay and Job Satisfaction within the European Union: Empirical Evidence from Fourteen Countries,' IZA Discussion Paper No. 1558, Institute for the Study of Labor (IZA), April, http://ideas.repec.org/p/iza/izadps/dp1558.html (accessed 4 October 2007).

Donovan, Nick, David Halpern. 2002. *Life Satisfaction: The State of Knowledge and Implications for Government*, Cabinet Office, Prime Minister's Strategy Unit, www.cabinetoffice.gov.uk/strategy/seminars/life_satisfaction/index.asp (accessed 8 October 2006).

Dorling, Danny and Neil Ward. 2003. *Social Science, Public Policy and the Search for Happiness*, www.sasi.group.shef.ac.uk/publications/2003/dorling_and_ward_happiness.pdf (accessed 8 October 2006).

Dorling, Danny and Phil Rees, *A Nation Ever More Divided*, sasi.group.shef.ac.uk/publications/danny_papers.htm (accessed 8 October 2006).

Edwards, Prof. Paul. 2007. *Justice in the Workplace: Why it is Important and Why a New Public Policy Initiative is Needed* (London: The Work Foundation), www.theworkfoundation.com/assets/docs/publications/67_justice%20in%20the%20workplace.pdf (accessed 5 March 2012).

van Gelder, Sarah. 1998. *The Overspent American*, Interview with Juliet Schor, Senior Lecturer, Harvard University, www.yesmagazine.org/article.asp?ID=836 (accessed 28 January 2008).

Gutmann, Peter. 2002. www.classicalnotes.net/classics/goldberg.html (accessed 31 August 2006).

Harvey, David interviewed by Harry Kriesler. 2004. 'Conversations with History' series at The Institute of International Studies, UC Berkeley, 2 March, http://globetrotter.berkeley.edu/people4/Harvey/harveycon0.html (accessed 17 January 2007).

HM Treasury, Sustainable Development Commission. 2004. *Redefining Prosperity: Delivering Well-Being*, www.sd-commission.org.uk/publications.php?id=189 (accessed 12 September 2006).

Hollows, Joanne 2000. *The Bachelor Dinner: Masculinity, Domesticity and Food Practices in Playboy, 1953–63*, http://food.oregonstate.edu/ref/culture/hollows.html (accessed 14 December 2006).

Kaulingfreks, Ruud, Geoff Lightfoot and Simon Lilley. 2007. *Labour in Literature: Reading the Myth of Work*, paper for the Novel and Organisation Conference. 10–12 May. www.essex.ac.uk/AFM/emc/novelconference/kaulingfreks_paper.pdf (accessed 23 April 2008).

Layard, Richard. 2006. *Mental Health Group Programme Overview*, http://cep.lse.ac.uk/research/mentalhealth (accessed 20 October 2006).

Lazar, Sara *et al.*, 'Meditation Experience is Associated with Increased Cortical Thickness' in Lippincott Williams & Wilkins, *NeuroReport*, 16:17 (28 November 2005), 1893–1897.

Lazzarato, Maurizio, Critical Management Studies Conference, Naples 11–13 July 2011, Plenary Address and www.senselab.ca/inflexions/volume_4/n3_lazzaratohtml.html (accessed 23 August 2011).

Margaret Thatcher Foundation. 1987. Interview for Woman's Own, Douglas Keay, *No Such Thing as Society*, 23 September, www.margaretthatcher.org/speeches/displaydocument.asp?docid=106689 (accessed 7 June 2008).

Newton, Leonard E., Biosci Rep. 2007. 27: 185–187, *What Makes Us Human?* Symposium Report, Pub 27 June, www.springerlink.com/content/e03v77285j366443/fulltext.pdf (accessed 3 December 2007).

Noon, Paul. 2007. 'Loyalty and Commitment have been pushed too far' in *Profile*, 2, 2.

Nunn, Alex, Steve Johnson, Surya Monro, Tim Bickerstaffe. 2007. *Factors Influencing Social Mobility*, Department of Work and Pensions, Report No. 450, http://research.dwp.gov.uk/asd/asd5/summ2007-2008/450summ.pdf (accessed 5 March 2012).

Office of National Statistics. 2001. *Marriage and Divorce Rates: EU comparison, 2001: Social Trends 33*, www.statistics.gov.uk/StatBase/ssdataset.asp?vlnk=6354&Pos=3&ColRank=1&Rank=272 (accessed 2 October 2007).

Schor, Juliet B. 1998. *The Overspent American*, Chapter 1, www.nytimes.com/books/first/s/schor-overspent.html (accessed 28 January 2010).

Slow Food. www.slowfood.com (accessed 16 January 2008).

Tryham, Chris. 2008. 'New Labour-style rebuttal unit for ITV,' *The Guardian*, Thursday, 28 February, www.guardian.co.uk/media/2008/Feb/28/itv.marketingandPR (accessed 19 May 2008).

Woodhuysen, James. 2005. *Cybersalon: The Future of Creativity and Innovation*, Royal Institution Christmas Lecture, 15 December, www.danacentre.org.uk/events/webcasts (accessed 13 November 2006).

Work Foundation, The, *Public Sector Work-life Balance is More Rhetoric than Reality* http://www.theworkfoundation.com/assets/docs/publications/155_unison.pdf (accessed 5 March 2012).

Wylie, Ian. 2006. *Downshifting: Swapping PR for Petals Rekindled One Woman's Creative Spark*, The Guardian, Saturday 21 January, www.guardian.co.uk/money/2006/jan/21/careers.work4 (accessed 16 January 2008).

Yar, Majid. 2001. Lancaster University, *Hannah Arendt: The Human Condition*, www.iep.utm.edu/a/arendt.htm (accessed 28 January 2010). Review of book by Robin Dunbar. 2004. *The Human Story: A New History of Mankind's Evolution* (Faber and Faber), www.uboeschenstein.ch/texte/dunbar_cit.html (accessed 21 February 2007).

Index

ability xii, 38, 49, 53, 58, 63, 82, 111, 121, 130, 164, 167, 170, 176, 188, 191, 208
  see also inability
abundance 148–9
acceleration 1, 24, 53, 56, 59–60, 64–5, 95, 119, 125, 127–8, 157, 194
accountability 23, 35, 101, 108–10, 157, 200
action(s) 4, 26, 35–6, 39, 44, 50–7, 60–7, 71–2, 74–5, 82–5, 89, 92, 94, 96–7, 100, 111, 116, 121, 123, 126, 128, 137, 141, 143, 146, 148, 153–4, 161, 177–8, 191, 203–4, 208, 212, 214
  collective 103, 206
  political/resistant 54, 65, 73–4, 78, 119, 121, 143, 153–4, 199
    see also dissent; political resistance
  recursive 30, 55, 64
  reflexive 64–5, 107
adaptability 114
  see also versatility
administration 30, 68, 74, 101, 115, 211
administrative load 11, 101, 103, 124
adolescence 57
Adorno, Theodor W. 61
affluence 70, 77, 149, 151, 201, 204–5, 209, 215n.2

agency 21, 50–1, 82, 92–3, 110, 116, 122, 145–6, 153, 166, 175, 180, 182, 203–4, 213
agency staff xii, 68
Althusser, Louis 50
Alvesson Mats 72
  and Hugh Willmott 29
Amernic, Joel and Russell Craig 5, 10, 14–15, 29, 40, 46n.1, 71
animal laborans 165
anxiety 54–5, 58–9, 102, 105, 114, 212
Arendt, Hannah 165
Arnold, Matthew 111–12, 127
artist 92, 166, 170
  quick change 25, 33
Atkins, Kim xi, 25, 33, 51–2, 57, 62, 83–4, 116n.3, 121, 143n.2, 144n.14, 146, 153, 176–82, 207
authorial control *see* narrative control
authority 3, 16, 18, 20–1, 33, 36–8, 40, 42, 61, 66, 82, 97, 101–4, 109, 113, 122, 186, 202–3
autobiographical act *see* autobiography
autobiographical pact *see* LeJeune
autobiography 8, 32, 64, 83–5, 92, 123, 126, 138–9, 174–97, 208
  uses of 174–5
automation 2, 61, 101, 155, 165–6, 195
autonomy 3, 12, 15, 29, 33–4, 45, 46n.1, 61, 67–8, 70–1, 73, 81,

Index

102, 115, 121–2, 137, 153, 166, 170, 176, 182, 198, 200, 202–6

Bach, Johann Sebastian 94
Bailey, Roy 35–7, 39–41, 43
Bakan, Joel 14, 18, 26, 46, 156, 172
balance 7, 111, 116n.10, 142, 148–9, 152, 155, 157–8, 162, 179, 188
  counterbalance 125, 139, 186
  see also rebalance
  work/life 53, 76, 107
Bauman, Zygmunt 23, 38, 49–50, 53–4, 57, 59, 119, 121, 127, 133, 193
Beck, Ulrich 51, 53–4, 56, 59, 65, 119–21, 124, 143, 154, 203
Bell, Daniel 24–5, 47, 127, 188
Bernays, Edward 18
Bettleheim, Bruno 92
biology 7, 123, 153, 169–70, 179
  biological rhythm 146, 151, 194
Blair, Tony 10, 17, 23
Blanchard, Kenneth and Robert Lorber 38–40, 42–3
  and Patricia Zigarmi and Drea Zigarmi 38
Bliss, Edwin C. 38
Boje, David M. 6
Braverman, Harry 6
bread 125, 161, 165–6
Breakspear, Christie and Clive Hamilton 75–6, 146
Bourdieu, Pierre 50, 62, 79n.4
Bunting, Madeleine 24, 119–20, 122, 178, 190–200
bureaucracy 104
Burnett, John 183, 191–2
Butler, Judith 50

Cameron, David 149
capacity 18, 27–8, 30, 50, 52, 57, 59, 62, 81, 83, 87, 95, 107, 161, 203, 212
capitalism 1, 6, 31, 44, 46, 82, 113, 179, 205
  see also late-capitalism; new capitalism

challenge 41, 113, 140, 177, 212
  see also resistance
Chandola, Tarani 201
change 1, 7, 15–19, 24–6, 28–35, 44, 46n.7, 50, 53–4, 56–9, 94, 100–1, 103, 109, 118, 150, 162, 201
  lifestyle 76, 124, 139, 157
  organisational 5, 73, 82, 119, 128, 201
  personal 138, 156–7, 189
chaos 26, 33, 62, 89, 100, 108
character 6, 8–9, 12–13, 18, 25, 27–8, 33, 40, 44, 53, 55, 57–61, 65, 72, 81–2, 84–9, 91–7, 99, 105, 108, 114, 119, 122, 138, 140–1, 171, 175–7, 182–4, 188–91, 193–6, 203–4, 209, 213–14
Chatto, James 140, 149, 154, 167, 169–70
Childs, Peter 85
Chrysler 36
civil servant(s) x, 3, 6, 74, 116n.11
  see also public servant
civil service 37, 104
  see also public service; service
Clarke, John 32
clinical detachment 102
coherence 20, 33, 83, 90, 95, 129, 175, 178, 180, 196, 202–3
  identity 5, 91, 94
  narrative 16–17, 143n.2, 209
  see also unity
communication(s) x, xii, 2–3, 5–6, 11–16, 23, 28, 41, 45, 46n.3, 71, 78, 79n.2, 81, 95, 106–8, 195–6
community 110, 123, 137, 148–51, 153, 171, 181, 186, 188, 193
competence xi, 113, 211
connectedness 7, 98–9, 119, 122, 135, 137–9, 155–9
connection(s) 4–5, 9, 44, 60, 85, 93–4, 98–9, 106, 114–15, 129, 136–7, 143, 149–52, 154–5, 157–8, 160–2, 164, 171, 174, 178–81, 186, 188, 191, 193–4, 208, 209–11, 212

consumer 31, 54, 56, 58, 77, 127, 164, 188, 191
consumerism 66, 75, 77–8, 113, 121, 142, 147, 159, 188, 205
consumption 51, 62, 67, 69, 74, 77, 145, 148, 161, 163–4, 206, 215
continuity 7, 25, 27, 52, 55–7, 60, 64–5, 135–7, 142–3, 143n.2, 162, 176, 178, 180, 192, 197n.2, 203
control 2, 6, 12, 14–15, 26, 28–9, 34–6, 44, 54, 60–2, 67–8, 71, 76, 82, 84, 89–90, 96, 101, 109, 113–15, 116n.12, 124, 138, 146, 170, 177, 180, 204–5
 brand 13
 loss/lack of xii, 81, 101–2, 131, 138, 198
 narrative/authorial 14, 44, 84–5, 87–8, 116n.3, 118, 121–3, 138, 143
cookery xii, 4, 7, 112, 122–3, 126, 133, 136, 139, 143, 159, 161, 164, 174, 206, 209, 215n.4, n.5
corporate (CEO) speak *see* speak
cost-efficiency 2
craft *and* craftwork 7–8, 111, 115, 165, 167–8, 174–5, 190–1, 194, 196
craftsmanship 163, 170
Craig, Geoffrey *see* Parkins, Wendy

death 108, 112–13, 135, 139, 149, 152–4, 178–9, 192, 204
De Blasi, Marlena 77, 127, 140, 142, 143n.6, 147–50, 152–5, 161–3, 166–7, 169, 171, 172n.7, 186–8, 192
De Cock, Christian 4
Defoe, Daniel 194–5, 209
defra *see* Department for Environment, Food and Rural Affairs
Department for Environment, Food and Rural Affairs 6, 12, 15–23, 28, 30, 46n.5, n.6, 104, 216–18
De Tocqueville, Alexis 2
diary 139, 181, 183–5
discontinuity 56, 180, 197n.2

discourse 8, 11, 18, 26–32, 50, 54, 64, 66, 71–2, 84, 87–8, 99, 105, 118, 121, 138, 174, 179, 203, 207, 209–10
dissatisfaction 99–103, 110, 113, 122, 149, 205, 210
 see also unhappiness
dissent 13–14, 27–8, 31
 see also political action; resistance
dissociation 113, 156, 161
dissonance 3, 12–13, 72–3, 189, 196, 206
doctor and patient relationship 97
Dover Beach *see* Arnold, Matthew
downsizing *see* downshifting
downshifting 1, 47, 75–6, 78, 79n.8, 143n.3, 145–6, 171,172n.2, n.3, 210
Duberley, Joanne *see* Musson, Gill

ecstasy 112, 114, 189
Edwards, Paul 198
Edwards, Richard 28, 46n.4, 67–8
efficiency 9, 11, 16, 18–19, 24, 26–7, 30, 37, 70, 132, 134,157, 202, 210–11
Ehrenreich, Barbara 43, 45, 67, 69–70, 73, 119, 133, 172n.6
email 11, 70, 106, 132, 208, 211
empowerment xii, 3, 11, 15–16, 20, 26, 34, 37–9, 54, 84, 121–2, 196, 206, 215
entrepreneur 10, 31, 33, 40, 46n.1, 48, 55, 67, 161, 196, 200, 212
Eriksen, Thomas Hylland 4, 11, 24, 47n.8, 50, 53, 57–8, 79n.1, 119, 127, 144n.7, 169, 192, 224
Erikson, Erik H. 57
error *see* failure
escape x, 7, 23, 59, 66, 78–9, 82–3, 85–6, 92–3, 95, 99, 115, 118–43, 151–3, 175, 178–9, 188–9, 195–6, 197n.3, 206, 210, 213
eudaemonia 136
exhaustion 50, 100, 103, 115, 129, 131, 144n.10, 169, 213
 see also tiredness

experience xi, 2–3, 7, 30, 53, 57, 62–5, 81–6, 97, 101, 112, 135–6, 138, 143, 143n.3, 151, 154, 167–8, 180, 189–90, 199, 203
see also knowledge and experience

fact and fiction *see* fiction
failure 21, 25, 35, 38, 42, 58, 69, 82, 108, 112, 116n.14, 128, 131, 167–8, 202, 212–13
see also imperfection
fast 1, 30–1, 44–5, 52–4, 65, 78, 114, 119, 121, 123–4, 127–8, 130, 132, 137, 146, 149–51, 158–60, 163, 174, 179, 182, 198, 205, 209, 212
fatigue *see* exhaustion; tiredness
Fearnley-Whittingstall, Hugh 5, 122–4, 127, 135–6, 197n.3
fiction 4, 30, 80, 85–7, 91–2, 94, 115, 182, 185, 207
flexibility 1, 6, 12, 15–16, 25, 28, 30–1, 33, 43, 50, 62, 68, 73, 99, 109, 115, 119, 123, 127, 139, 155, 180, 212–14
flexible accumulation 1, 24, 118
flight *see* escape
food 5, 8, 26, 53, 123, 125–6, 129–32, 135–7, 150, 158–64, 167, 169–70, 187, 196, 209, 215n.4
and religion 124–7, 161–2
Ford, Henry 36
Fordist, Fordism 8, 19, 24, 38, 46n.7, 47, 50, 69, 75
forecasting 147
Foucault, Michel 29, 50
fragmentation 16, 23–4, 46n.7, 50, 56, 65, 119–20, 129, 176, 180–1
Frank, Thomas 10, 14–15, 34, 43, 54, 58, 119, 172n.12
freedom 3, 11, 15, 38, 49, 53–5, 61, 65, 77, 101, 107, 110, 143n.1, 198, 204, 207, 215n.4
fulfillment 1, 5, 15, 73, 76–7, 115, 119, 124, 146, 161, 165, 170, 177, 205, 210

Gagnier, Regenia 49–50, 64
gardening *see* horticulture
gastronomy 163–4, 172n.13
globalisation 34, 123, 193
Goffman, Erving 72
Goldberg Variations see Bach, Johann Sebastian
good life 79n.8, 123, 134, 137, 152, 160, 175, 184, 209
grand narrative 186
growth 15, 35, 73, 183, 194–6, 215
economic 12, 81, 174, 195, 199–200
personal 11, 30, 62, 213

Hall, Donald 49
Hamilton, Clive 47n.10, 75–8, 79n.7, 146, 171n.1
see also Breakspear, Christie
hands 108, 157, 165–7, 169–70
happiness xi, 37–8, 59, 61, 77, 79n.9, 101, 112–13, 115, 117n.19, 119, 137, 140, 147, 150–1, 160, 164, 172n.5, 199, 215n.2
see also satisfaction
Harvey, David 1, 17, 24, 46n.7, 47n.8, 119, 123, 127, 172n.10, 179, 188, 193, 205
Hawthorne Experiment *see* Mayo, Elton
heaven 7, 62, 66, 118, 125, 127, 136, 143n.6, 150, 198, 204, 209
hedonism 40, 61, 70, 121, 136, 188
hegemony 5, 9, 30, 49, 59–60, 66, 118, 125, 183, 189, 196, 210, 215n.4
hero 6, 7, 36–7, 44, 118, 124, 126–7, 137, 192, 202
heroes *see* hero
heroism 41–2, 122, 215
Herzberg, Frederick 2, 36
Hobsbawm, Eric J 4, 81
Hochschild, Arlie Russell 24, 119
Hollows, Joanne 127, 129–30, 133, 135
home 5, 38, 72, 93–4, 98, 106, 115, 116n.8, 125, 135, 147, 152, 156–7, 166, 171
work and 61–2, 72, 107, 128–9, 157, 195, 214

Home Secretary 104
horticulture xii, 4–5, 7–8, 74, 76, 112, 118, 122–3, 125–6, 136, 138–9, 142–3, 155, 157–9, 164, 169, 174, 206, 208–9, 215n.4
Hulme, Peter and Tim Youngs 185
hybridity 87, 134, 181–3, 197n.3

identity crisis 1, 45, 57, 65–6, 69, 85, 110, 118
identity-formation
  reflexive 138
  see also reflexive individualisation
illusion 54, 86, 90–1, 127, 151
immediacy 15, 24–5, 44, 65, 111, 122–3, 127, 139, 176, 180, 184, 191
imperfection 108, 170–1
  see also failure
inability 25, 29, 44, 57, 83, 100, 141, 202, 213
  see also ability
incoherence *see* coherence
individualism 11, 44, 46n.1, 56, 59–61, 74, 81, 124, 150, 157, 186, 194, 205, 209
Industrial Revolution 61
insanity 47, 139
insecurity 7–8, 46n.7, 48, 54, 62, 66, 79n.5, 80, 86, 97–8, 105, 109, 114, 185, 198–9
instability 1, 7 24, 44, 46n.7, 84–5, 196, 198, 210
  see also stability
isolation 171, 187

Jameson, Fredric 23, 25, 47n.8, n.9, 129, 142, 143n.5
jargon 103, 136
judgement xi, xii, 59, 63–4, 151, 185, 200, 213–14

King, Roger and Neill Nugent 67, 69, 74–5
knowledge 30, 42, 93, 102, 108, 172n.15, 202, 214
  accumulated 135, 137, 143n.3
  specialist 68–9
knowledge and experience xii, 30–1, 81–2, 97, 102, 109, 112–14, 143n.3, 212, 214
  see also experience
knowledge transfer 15, 123, 192, 214
Kranzberg, Melvin and Joseph Gies 61, 81

Lacan, Jacques 49
Land, Christopher *see* De Cock, Christian
late-capitalism 118, 127–8, 148, 177, 198
  see also new capitalism; new economy
Lawson, Nigella 124, 126, 130–5, 137, 143n.6, 197n.3
Layard, Richard 37, 70, 79n.9, 101–2, 116n.8, 117n.15, n.19, 119, 199–200, 205, 215n.2
legacy 169, 171
  see also posterity
LeJeune, Philippe 182, 191
Lewis, Tania 121, 141
lifestyle 57, 59, 69, 73–6, 78, 83, 110, 114, 119, 121–2, 124, 127, 134, 136–7, 139, 141, 145–6, 149, 153, 157–8, 164, 172n.9, 174–5, 177, 179–80, 182, 186, 188–9, 206, 209
linearity 6, 33, 43, 52, 56, 79, 123, 135, 152, 178–9, 182, 184–5, 202
literary and life world 85–7, 91–2
local 123, 150, 160, 162, 167, 172n.10, 182
Lodge, David 140
Lorber, Robert *see* Blanchard, Kenneth
loser(s) 33, 35, 42, 69, 100, 107, 156, 212
Lyotard, Jean-François 186, 190

McEwan, Ian 7, 80, 83, 85–6, 88–94, 96, 99, 101–7, 110–11, 113–14, 116n.2, n.10, 140, 147, 168, 171, 179, 206–8

marketing 7, 42–4, 56, 129, 132, 137, 172n.12
Marx, Karl 2, 69, 73, 81
Maslow, Abraham 2, 120
materialism 77, 136, 147, 153, 204
Mayle, Peter 4, 127, 140, 146–7, 152, 155–6, 161–3, 166, 170, 174, 181, 189
Mayo, Elton 2, 24, 26–8, 72
mental health xii, 7, 21, 37, 57, 65, 70, 83–4, 89, 100, 115, 138–9, 146–7, 180, 198–200, 202, 204
see also mental illness; neurosis; psychological health
mental illness 103, 149, 205
see also mental health; neurosis; psychological health
meta-fiction 85
middle class 6–9, 11, 44–5, 48, 55–78, 79n.4, 81–2, 118, 121, 126, 129, 132–3, 137, 146, 163, 171, 175, 177, 180, 188, 193–4, 198–9, 202, 205–6, 209
Miller, Nancy 92, 124, 143, 175, 184, 193
mobility 1, 26, 28, 31, 44, 53, 81, 109, 115, 123–4, 155, 171, 212–14
modernism 24, 46n.7, 179
morality 75, 157, 172n.12
mortality *see* death
Mukherjee, Ankhi 63, 83, 191
music 74, 112–13, 116n.10, 167, 207
musician; musicianship 90, 110
Musson, Gill and Joanne Duberley 4, 29–30, 32, 71–3
mutuality 105, 148–50

neurosis 57, 64–6, 157, 188
see also mental health; mental illness; psychological health
new capitalism 143, 179
see also late-capitalism; new economy
new economy 1, 4, 6–7, 10, 12, 15, 32–4, 43–5, 52, 55–6, 58, 67–8, 71, 73, 80–1, 100–1, 119, 145, 159, 167, 175, 192, 199, 200, 209, 218–19

see also new capitalism; late-capitalism
New Labour 10, 46n.3, 232
Noon, Paul 37
nostalgia 7, 100, 115, 129, 134, 141–2

Oliver, Jamie 5, 123, 127, 134–5, 197n.3
O'Neill, Onora 23, 32, 101–2, 104, 109–10

Parkins, Wendy and Geoffrey Craig 79n.6, 119, 121, 127, 144n.7, 145–6, 154, 158–61, 169, 172n.9, n.10, n.13, 190
Pavlovian 39, 57, 107
perfection 125, 170
political action *see* action(s)
posterity 153, 175, 192
see also legacy
post-industrial 25, 47n.8, n.9, 122
postmodernism 46n.7, 47, 119
potential 15, 25, 30, 120, 159, 193
potentiality 50, 89
practical identity 116n.3, 153
Pritchett, Price 25, 33–5, 37, 42–3, 127
professional identity 7, 78, 81, 95–6, 114–15
professional insecurity *see* insecurity
professionalism 11–12, 97, 114, 164
professional(s) xi-xiii, 21, 23, 30, 33, 68, 76, 79n.4, 80, 82, 99, 100–3, 121, 141, 168, 171, 211, 214
and middle class 3, 6, 8–9, 45, 48, 66–7, 69, 71, 73, 77, 121, 132, 137, 175, 188, 198–9, 202
and middle ground 69–70, 171
pride 105, 109
and private sector 74, 194
and public sector/service 3, 8, 31–2, 44, 55, 74–5, 81, 109, 198, 200, 206
standards 11, 102, 109, 206, 210, 214

profit 12, 18, 24, 31, 46n.1, 120, 127–8, 134, 147, 150, 153, 168, 172n.11, 182, 194–6, 210, 213–14
profitable 62, 114, 129, 163
profit-hungry 48
profit-making 26, 46n.1
psychological distress 32
psychological health 57, 60, 84, 135, 138, 143, 178, 180
  see also mental health; mental illness; neurosis
public relations 72
public sector x, 1, 3, 6, 8, 11–12, 18–23, 29–30, 32, 37, 44, 48, 55–6, 60, 67–8, 71, 74–5, 78, 79–82, 102–4, 194, 198, 200–2, 206, 210
  see also civil service; civil servant; public servant; public service
public servant 11, 67, 109, 119, 144n.13, 200–2, 211
  see also civil servant
public service 3, 5, 9, 12, 31, 67, 70–1, 144, 194, 198, 200, 202, 213
  see also civil service; service
Pugh, Derek S. 24, 27

quality 45, 54, 68, 109, 112, 160, 163, 167–8, 170, 172n.13, 183, 191, 200, 202, 206, 213, 215
  of life 59, 136, 151
  of service 31, 109, 200, 202, 210, 213
  reduction in 173n.17
quantity 168, 199, 202, 206, 210

Ramsay, Gordon 126, 159
rebalance 114, 119
recovery 27, 66, 83, 135, 145–73, 195–6, 209, 213
recursivity 30, 55, 64
reflection 6, 8, 52, 57, 64–6, 82, 85, 103, 108, 110–11, 120, 154, 164, 168, 189, 194–6, 204, 239
reflexive individualisation 51, 121, 141, 203
  see also identity formation

reflexivity 57, 146, 203–4
relationship(s) 7, 12, 19, 20, 53–4, 58, 77, 79n.9, 83, 95–9, 105–7, 109–10, 114, 116n.3, 117n.19, 128–30, 136–7, 139, 151, 155, 158, 164, 179–80, 205, 213–14, 215n.3
religion 7, 15, 66, 124, 127, 134, 161–2, 182, 192, 209
repetition 64, 101, 165, 167–8
replacing professionals 68
reputation 14, 41, 105, 108, 199
resistance 13, 29, 31–2, 40, 46n.4, 51, 56, 60, 64, 66, 71, 73–6, 78, 82–3, 100, 103, 113, 119–20, 122–4, 143, 146, 180, 182–3, 187–8, 195–6, 206, 208
  see also dissent; political action
resource(s) 3, 21–2, 36, 55, 90, 121, 140
  management 2, 19, 141, 148–9, 157
responsiveness 6, 8, 11, 16–17, 24–6, 30, 33, 44, 58, 70, 80, 82, 100, 109, 115, 167, 196, 203, 212–14
rhythm 7, 40, 78, 83, 107, 111, 118, 123, 135, 137, 142–3, 146, 149, 151, 154, 165, 168–70, 179–80, 186, 194
Rimmon-Keenan, Shlomith 91
ritual 40, 118, 120, 124, 126, 137, 143, 150, 159, 161–2, 186, 194, 200, 209
Robbins, Ruth 49
Robinson Crusoe see Daniel Defoe
rooted 43, 73, 123, 159, 169
rootedness 137, 157
  see also connectedness
Ross, Andrew 24, 34, 119, 127
Ruskin, John 2, 170–1

sacred 61, 124, 161, 195, 209
satisfaction xi, xii, 3, 5, 7, 27, 36, 71, 112, 115, 128, 137, 140, 143, 146, 149, 158, 160, 163, 165, 169–70, 177, 198–9, 201–2, 204–5

see also happiness
narrative 43, 182
Savage, Michael et al. 67–8, 74–5, 79n.4
schizophrenia 156
scrutiny 102, 141
  see also surveillance
seasons 123, 136, 149, 152, 154–5, 179
secular 41, 61–2, 66, 112, 124–5, 135, 158–9, 175, 195, 205, 209
self-esteem 30, 37, 70, 109, 128–9, 199, 202, 212
Sennett, Richard xiii, 2, 26, 30, 53, 82, 100, 105, 116n.11, 119, 127, 149, 164–6, 167–71, 172n.15, 190–1, 197
service x, 2–3, 5, 9, 11–12, 16, 20, 24–5, 31, 33, 35, 37, 70–1, 135, 194, 198, 200, 202, 235
  see also civil service; public service
Shelton, Robin 126–7, 138–9, 142, 144n.13, 152, 155–8, 161, 164, 167–70, 172n.8, 181, 192
skill 30, 34, 68, 74, 78, 89, 97, 100, 102, 105, 108, 111–15, 134, 164–5, 167–70, 182, 188, 194, 201, 206, 208, 213–14
Slater, Nigel 136, 159
slow; slowness 7, 11, 38, 44, 48, 59, 75, 78, 110–11, 115, 120–3, 125, 137, 139, 143, 145–71, 172n.10, n.13, 174, 190, 193–4, 209, 214
Smith, Sidonie and Julia Watson 138, 175, 181–2, 186
speak 23, 27, 87, 198
  corporate (CEO) 11, 15, 21, 28–9, 44, 65, 124
  inability to 103
  market 43, 176
stability 6, 16, 24, 46n.7, 94, 100, 119, 125, 128, 133, 152, 154, 162, 171, 178, 184, 196, 201, 205
  see also instability

status 13, 29, 41, 43, 45, 54–5, 62, 66–71, 73, 79n.5, 81, 95–7, 99, 105, 109, 116n.12, 118, 131, 144, 153, 188, 199, 205–6, 208
Stein, Rick 149
Stewart, Chris 127, 139, 141–2, 147, 150, 156, 167, 172n.4, n.8, 177, 192
story x–xi, 3–5, 7–8, 27, 37–8, 40–5, 58, 63, 66, 80, 83–95, 116n.5, n.6, n.10, 122–3, 137, 143, 143n.2, 158, 160–1, 167, 175–83, 189, 202, 204, 207, 209, 214
  corporate 12–13, 27, 29
stress x, xii, 2–3, 5, 12, 20–2, 30, 32, 34, 37, 47, 70, 75–6, 78, 98, 102, 104, 116n.12, 119, 123, 131, 136, 154, 157, 174, 195, 198–201, 205, 208–9
structure 6, 24, 45, 50, 61, 64–6, 71, 81, 84–5, 101, 114, 118, 141, 146, 152–4, 158, 176, 178, 201
  narrative 63, 87, 93–5, 152, 180, 184
  organisational 2–3, 5, 11, 24, 46n.7, 82, 103–4, 203
subjectivity 4–6, 49–50, 64–5, 82, 85, 175, 177, 182, 188, 198, 203–4, 209
surveillance 29–30, 36, 70
  see also scrutiny
survival 12, 26, 29, 32, 44, 51, 55, 60, 80, 95, 100, 105, 148–9, 157, 169, 194

Taylor, Frederick 2, 26–7, 69, 132, 195
teacher and student relationship 38, 214
teamwork 103–5
technology 2, 5–6, 11, 15, 24–5, 32, 61, 78, 82, 93, 95, 101, 106, 109, 123–4, 126–7, 142, 151, 155, 157, 169, 196

Thatcher, Margaret 10, 67, 75, 119, 149
time 5, 7, 12, 42, 51–2, 56–65, 73, 76–8, 79n.2, 83, 93, 95, 98, 100–15, 118, 120, 123–4, 128–44, 145–7, 149–53, 157, 160, 163–5, 167–9, 172n.9, 176, 178–80, 182–5, 187, 189–92, 195, 203, 210, 213–14
  and activity 136, 143, 163, 169
  and motion 2, 25, 27, 132
  pressure xi, 6, 21, 38, 44, 57, 80, 106, 110, 129–30, 173n.17, 191
tiredness 99, 131
  see also exhaustion
training 31, 33, 39, 99, 106
transformation 6, 15–16, 18, 30, 50, 89, 140, 161, 172n.10, 204
travel writing 4, 181, 185, 196
trust 20, 53, 58, 101, 108–9, 113, 117n.19, 141, 156, 158, 192, 214
turnover 1, 12, 24, 33, 52, 58, 128, 153, 168, 191, 205

uncertainty 25, 33, 183, 196, 197n.2, 198
  biographical 7, 54, 128, 175, 183
unhappiness 37, 70, 101, 136
unity 6, 16, 20, 95, 114, 175–6, 178
  see also coherence

value(s) xi, 1, 6–8, 11–12, 14, 20, 29–30, 40, 44–5, 46n.1, 48, 51, 55–6, 60–3, 65, 67, 70–8, 81, 84, 92–4, 98, 100, 116n.6, n.11, 119–27, 132, 134–7, 139, 141–3, 143n.4, 145–6, 150, 158–64, 170–1, 175–8, 193, 195–6, 198, 202–3, 206, 208–9, 213–14
Veblen, Thorstein 2, 215n.1
versatility, 30–1, 114
  see also adaptability

waste 113, 123, 148–9
Watson, Julia *see* Smith, Sidonie
Weber, Max 3, 101
well-being x, xii, 2, 6–7, 16–17, 48, 59, 77, 83, 119, 125, 136–8, 146–7, 149, 156, 170, 196, 198–9, 204, 208–9
wilderness 147, 159, 195
Williams, Raymond 50, 81, 188
Willmott, Hugh *see* Alvesson, Mats
winners 33, 41–2, 69–70
work/life balance *see* balance
writing 4–8, 20, 44, 64, 74–5, 78, 86–7, 111, 116n.5, 121, 138, 174–5, 177, 183–5, 188, 190–2, 196, 206, 209
  see also travel writing